THEORIES OF COUNSELLING AND PS

THEORIES OF POVERTY AND ANTI-POVERTY PROGRAMS

Theories of Counselling and Psychotherapy

An Introduction to the Different Approaches

Stephen Joseph

First published as *Psychopathology and Therapeutic Approaches* 2001
Reprinted four times

This edition published 2010 by
PALGRAVE MACMILLAN

Palgrave Macmillan in the UK is an imprint of Macmillan Publishers Limited,
registered in England, company number 785998, of Houndmills, Basingstoke,
Hampshire RG21 6XS.

Palgrave Macmillan in the US is a division of St Martin's Press LLC,
175 Fifth Avenue, New York, NY 10010.

Palgrave Macmillan is the global academic imprint of the above companies
and has companies and representatives throughout the world.

Palgrave® and Macmillan® are registered trademark in the United States,
the United Kingdom, Europe and other countries.
and other countries.

ISBN 978-0-230-57637-7

This book is printed on paper suitable for recycling and made from fully
managed and sustained forest sources. Logging, pulping and manufacturing
processes are expected to conform to the environmental regulations of the
country of origin.

A catalogue record for this book is available from the British Library.

A catalog record for this book is available from the Library of Congress.

10 9 8 7 6 5 4 3 2 1
19 18 17 16 15 14 13 12 11 10

Printed in China

To Victoria and Isabelle

Contents

List of Figures and Tables

Figures

Tables

Preface

People come to counselling and psychotherapy training from a variety of backgrounds in life. One of the surprising things is finding out that there are so many approaches to therapy. There are so many different ideas! Which of the ideas is right for me? The first aim of writing this book is to provide a brief and easy-to-read introduction to the different theories of therapy. For those new to therapy this book will be a road map.

I hope that trainees in counselling and psychotherapy on certificate and diploma level courses will find this book useful. Although I have aimed the book at new trainees in counselling and psychotherapy, students in the social and behavioural sciences, social work, and mental health nursing will also find the book useful in its overview of therapeutic approaches.

This is a book that looks at some of the main ideas behind the practice of therapy. My aim is to introduce the trainee counsellor and psychotherapist to the essential ideas that inform the different schools of therapy. All of the various therapeutic approaches employed by counsellors and psychotherapists are based on particular models which attempt to explain why it is that some people and not others come to develop psychological problems. Explanations might focus on, for example, unconscious conflicts and repressed desires, irrational thinking and maladaptive learning, conditional regard and thwarted personal growth. These are the main explanations that are usually put forward by therapists in their attempts to understand why psychological problems come about.

I also want to introduce the biomedical approach, the transpersonal approach, and the sociocultural approach, which are often overlooked or marginalized in books on therapeutic techniques. We are not only psychological beings, but we are also biological beings who live in a social world and who have spiritual needs. It is no longer appropriate to ask which of these is the correct way to understand human beings; each of these aspects of human experience is worthy of study. It is only through understanding the combination of these aspects that we are able to appreciate the richness of what it means to be human.

Following an introduction to counselling and psychotherapy in Chapter 1, Chapter 2 describes biomedical and medical approaches, Chapter 3 psychoanalytical and psychodynamic approaches, Chapter 4 behavioural and cognitive approaches, Chapter 5 humanistic and transpersonal approaches, Chapter 6 sociological approaches. Finally in Chapter 7, new developments are discussed. The book is not intended to be comprehensive in scope but simply to provide an accessible introduction to therapeutic approaches. The main theorists to be discussed are: Freud representing the psychodynamic approach; Ellis and Beck representing the cognitive-behavioural approach; and Rogers representing the humanistic approach, as it is their work that is most often the focus of introductory counselling and psychotherapy classes.

STEPHEN JOSEPH

Acknowledgements

Many people have contributed in different ways to this book and to its first edition. I would like to thank the anonymous reviewers for their comments and feedback on an early draft of the book, and the friends, colleagues, and students over the years for their discussions around many of the issues and topics in this book. Thanks in particular to Lindsay Cooper, Delia Cushway, Belinda Harris, Maureen Haynes, Rob Hooper, Jerome Marshall, Richard Mauger, Hugh Middleton, David Murphy, Steve Regel, Cindy Salmon, Pete Sanders, Jeremy Tudway, Alex Wood, Richard Worsley, and Gill Wyatt. Grateful thanks go to Catherine Gray at Palgrave Macmillan for her encouragement and support for the project; and to Ann Edmondson for her editorial services.

STEPHEN JOSEPH

The author and publishers wish to thank the following for permission to use copyright material:

Alcoholics Anonymous World Services, Inc. ('AAWS') for permission to reprint the Twelve Steps in Table 1.2. Permission to reprint the Twelve Steps does not mean that AAWS has reviewed or approved the contents of this publication, or that AAWS necessarily agrees with the views expressed herein. AA is a programme of recovery from alcoholism only – use of the Twelve Steps in connection with programmes and activities which are patterned after AA, but which address other problems, or in any other non-AA context, does not imply otherwise.

American Psychiatric Association for Tables 2.2 and 2.3 from the *Diagnostic and Statistical Manual of Mental Disorders*, text revision, fourth edition (2000).

American Psychological Association for Table 5.2 from C. Rogers (1957) The necessary and sufficient conditions of therapeutic personality change, *Journal of Consulting Psychology* 21: 95–103.

Every effort has been made to trace all copyright-holders, but if any have been inadvertently overlooked the publishers will be pleased to make the necessary arrangements at the first opportunity.

Chapter 1

Introduction

Helen walks into the therapist's office. The therapist smiles and offers her a seat. Helen sits down and within seconds she bursts into floods of tears. The therapist hands Helen a tissue which Helen uses to wipe away her tears. Slowly, Helen begins to tell her story, and the therapist begins to build up a picture of how Helen feels so tired all of the time, finds it difficult to get out of bed in the morning, is unable to take an interest in things, has lost interest in her appearance, constantly feels like crying, wonders what is the point of it all and has thoughts of taking her own life. Socially, Helen has withdrawn from her family and friends, rarely accepting invitations to go out, behaviour which seems so out of character for Helen. Her friends have always thought of Helen as outgoing and gregarious and are now worried about her, wondering what has caused Helen to behave so differently to the way she usually is with them. Helen's employers have also warned her about persistent lateness and she is now at risk of losing her job. How should we, as therapists, go about helping Helen with her problems?

Alex tells the therapist of how he finds himself exploding in a rage at the slightest provocation. His behaviour, he says, has cost him his marriage and several friendships. In the latest episode he had been out drinking with his work colleagues to celebrate a birthday, but as the evening wore on he became increasingly irritable and towards the end of the night attacked one of his colleagues, beating him to the ground and kicking him until he was pulled away by the others. Now even his job is at risk as a result of his temper. How can the therapist help Alex to understand his rage and help him find ways to deal with his feelings more effectively?

Tom was driving home one winter evening with his fiancée Sharon. They had been out Christmas shopping in the nearby town. Tom reached down, only for a second, to change the CD that was playing. He looked up just in time to see that the traffic in front of him had slowed. He slammed on the brakes and swerved to avoid the car in front. He

1

remembers thinking how slow everything seemed to be happening. His car rolled over several times, before slamming into a barrier. Other cars behind Tom skidded to a halt, some of them crashing into the back of the cars in front. This was a horrific accident in which Sharon died. That was one year ago. As the anniversary looms, Tom is in a state of high distress. As he tells the story of what happened that night he begins to talk more slowly. His memories and feelings come flooding back. Tom feels like his life has been turned upside down. Every time he hears the music that was playing in the car he is catapulted back to that night. He wakes up in the morning with thoughts of Sharon and he describes himself as crippled by the feelings of guilt that he killed her. How can we help Tom?

Matt is a young man who has worked since leaving school and has several close friends whom he sees regularly. All of Matt's friends would agree that he has always been someone who seems happy with life, content with himself, and who has a bright career ahead of him. However, in the last few months, Matt's friends have noticed that he is acting very strangely compared to the way he used to be with them. Matt has taken to spending more time by himself, refusing invitations, and saying that he has important work to do for the benefit of the world. His parents too have noticed that they often hear voices coming from Matt's room as if he is talking with someone but they know that he is alone in his room. They are becoming increasingly concerned about him. Matt's parents have suggested that he visits the doctor but Matt refuses to go along, saying that nothing is the matter with him.

Sarah has been working for fifteen years in her job as an estate agent. Although she has enjoyed her work over the years, she has recently turned forty and has begun to long for a more restful and fulfilling way of life. At school Sarah loved art, and always wanted to go to art school. She looks back on her life and wonders where it has gone. She longs to do something different and more personally fulfilling with her life now. She would love to just be able to paint and be more creative but she feels trapped in her job. Sarah desperately wants to find a way to live a life in which she feels free to pursue her creative passions. She is dissatisfied with her life, feels trapped in her job and hates the commute to work every day. She daydreams about just walking away from it all and not going back.

Different therapists will give different answers to the question of how they might help Helen, Alex, Tom, Matt, and Sarah. In this first chapter, the nature of counselling and psychotherapy will be discussed. What is it that counsellors and psychotherapists do that is different from the support we get from family and friends? What is the definition of counselling and of psychotherapy? What are the different approaches to therapy?

The nature of counselling and psychotherapy

Helen, Tom, Alex, Matt, and Sarah are all people whose difficulties in living might lead them to seek help. Of course, the types of problems seen by counsellors and psychotherapists will vary depending on a number of factors, such as whether they are in private practice, work in a hospital, or in a general health practice. Some counsellors and psychotherapists will specialize in seeing clients with particular difficulties. Some will specialize in people who have experienced trauma, others with clients who have problems with eating, or young people in a university setting, for example. In recent years the range of client difficulties seen by counsellors has greatly diversified as the profession has developed. Compared to the late 1990s, more counsellors and psychotherapists now work in psychiatric settings, primary care settings such as General Practitioners' surgeries, workplaces, schools, and agencies specializing in crisis counselling (Barnes et al., 2008). Also, it is becoming increasingly common for counsellors and psychotherapists to work with clients with more extreme difficulties who would traditionally have been seen by psychiatrists and psychologists.

Of course, often when we are troubled in some way our first port of call will actually be friends or family and not a professional therapist. Friends and family can provide very important resources for us in times of need. Before going on to look at the roles of counsellors and psychotherapists, I'd like to say a little more about this and what makes social support from family and friends different from what professional therapists do.

Social support

In times of crisis we will often turn to our family and friends for help. Barker et al. (1990) carried out a survey of over 1000 adults who were representative of the UK population with respect to age, sex, and social class. They asked: if you had a personal problem, who would you talk to about it? The most frequent answer was partner (68 per cent), followed by a close relative (54 per cent), a friend or neighbour (43 per cent), the family doctor (41 per cent), a workmate (20 per cent), and finally, a religious adviser (17 per cent). Some interesting differences were found between men and women. Men were more likely to seek help from their partner (71 per cent) compared to women (64 per cent). Women were more likely to seek help from a close relative (61 per cent) compared to men (45 per cent), and more likely to seek help from a friend or neighbour (52 per cent) compared to men (34 per cent). Men were more likely to seek help from a workmate (23 per cent) compared to women (18 per cent). But can social support from our friends and family really help?

Depending on the relationship between the people involved and the nature of the problem, social support from family or friends might indeed be sufficient in helping a person overcome his or her difficulties. Certainly, there is now a substantial body of research showing that people who have high levels of social support from friends and family are psychologically healthier than those who have low levels of social support. By social support, what is meant is the provision of emotional or practical aid to a person from others in their social network. Family and friends who are able to provide emotional reassurance, who can help us see things differently, or help us feel valued and esteemed, who are able to provide a loan of money or other practical help if needed, and who are able to offer advice on how to deal with a situation can help us cope with the most upsetting and stressful experiences in life. We know this, not only from accounts of what people tell us, but also from the numerous research studies that have been carried out. In these studies, the researchers have found ways of measuring social support and psychological health, through the use of questionnaires, interviews, or observing interactions between people. They then go on to test statistically whether or not there is an association between social support and psychological health. The results of the numerous studies show that greater levels of social support are associated with lower levels of psychological distress (Cohen and Wills, 1985).

Indeed, social support from family and friends has even been shown to be associated with better adjustment following the most horrific and traumatic events. After the *Herald of Free Enterprise* disaster – the ferry capsize which took place off the coast of Zeebrugge in 1987 – my colleagues and I asked survivors to complete a questionnaire, the Crisis Support Scale, which measured the amount of support received from family and friends. We found that those survivors who reported having higher levels of social support in the immediate aftermath of the Zeebrugge and similar disasters subsequently fared better than those who reported having lower levels of social support (Joseph et al., 1992; Joseph et al., 1993; Dalgleish et al., 1996). So, if social support from family and friends is so important, why might we need counsellors and psychotherapists? What is it that counsellors and psychotherapists are able to provide that our family and friends can't?

When our friends and family are not enough

Alex feels that he has alienated his friends through his aggressive behaviour and that he has no one that he can turn to for support. Helen has withdrawn from her family and friends who, although they want to help, feel shut out by her. Furthermore, family and friends are often unable to provide us with the support we need. They might not have the emotional or practical resources themselves to help us deal with our problems. Matt's family and friends would like to be able to help, but they just don't know what to do.

Not everyone has people around him or her to provide support. This is most evident, for example, in the case of people who have lost loved ones. Not only have they been bereaved and are in need of social support to help them cope with their grief, but they have also lost their main source of social support. This is the case for Tom. He also feels such shame as he was the driver on the night of the accident and that stops him seeking help from others. He feels others judge him and so he keeps his thoughts and feelings to himself. For those who have lost loved ones, bereavement counselling might provide a very valuable emotional resource which will help them to work through and accept their loss, and to find ways of dealing with their painful feelings.

Furthermore, family and friends might offer us support that we actually find unhelpful. For example, they might offer us advice when all we want is to be listened to. They might encourage us to talk when all we want to do is sit in silence. They might try to stop us crying when all we want to do is cry. In their attempts to be supportive, family and friends will often do things that we find unhelpful. Most of us will be able to find examples of when we felt that others' attempts to be supportive were unhelpful or even harmful.

Psychologists have studied these interactions, and one very interesting study investigated what types of social support are helpful and unhelpful to people with cancer. Dakof and Taylor (1990) asked their sample of people diagnosed with cancer to state the particular acts that others carry out that they found helpful or harmful. Based on the assumption that the ties of kinship, marriage, or friendship all create different obligations and constraints, Dakof and Taylor asked respondents about seven other people:

1. spouse
2. other family members
3. friends
4. support group members
5. doctors
6. nurses
7. acquaintances.

For each of these people, respondents were asked:

1. what was the most helpful thing?
2. what have they said or done to make you angry?
3. what have they done that nobody else could have?
4. what have you wished they did?

Dakof and Taylor then analyzed the answers to these questions, dividing helpful and unhelpful actions into three types of social support:

1. *esteem support*, in which the person was made to feel cared for, valued, and esteemed;
2. *information support*, in which the person was provided with advice, guidance, and information;
3. *instrumental support*, in which the person was offered practical help of some kind.

Dakof and Taylor found that 70 per cent of the cancer patients said that their spouse, family or friends were most helpful with regard to esteem support, and that their inappropriate attempts at esteem support were the most unhelpful. Other cancer patients and doctors were seen as the most helpful regarding information support, and the lack of this from them was seen as the most unhelpful. More specifically, partners were seen as helpful for expressing concern and affection, and for being accepting of the illness. Partners who were seen as critical of the person's response to cancer were seen as particularly unhelpful, as was their failure to express concern. Other family members were most appreciated for expressing concern, being there and providing practical assistance such as transport. However, criticizing and minimizing the impact of the cancer was seen as most unhelpful.

So, sometimes, friends and family, despite their best intentions, can be unhelpful in the way that they provide support. Indeed, other research with men with HIV found that having a partner was associated with poorer social adjustment (Pakenham et al., 1994). Pakenham and colleagues suggested that having a partner may have encouraged dependency and adherence to a sick role and, as a consequence, fostered ill health and impaired social functioning.

Defining counselling and psychotherapy

For a variety of reasons, therefore, friends and family are not always able to be supportive in the way that would help us deal with our problems, and sometimes it might be appropriate for a person to visit a counsellor or psychotherapist. Counsellors and psychotherapists are not simply substitutes for friends and family. Counsellors and psychotherapists will usually work with someone who has not been able to find the help that he or she needs from family or friends, or who is reluctant to approach others in their life, or whose problems go beyond the help that can be provided by family and friends.

Counselling

Unlike family and friends, counsellors and psychotherapists are trained in using particular skills derived from complex theoretical understandings of what causes problems in living. The help counsellors and psychotherapists offer is of a very different nature to that offered by family and friends. So, how can we define *counselling* and *psychotherapy*? The British Association for Counselling (1996) states that:

> The overall aim of counselling is to provide an opportunity for the client to work towards living in a more satisfying and resourceful way. The term 'counselling' includes work with individuals, pairs or groups of people often, but not always, referred to as 'clients'. The objectives of particular counselling relationships will vary according to the client's needs. Counselling may be concerned with developmental issues, addressing and resolving specific problems, making decisions, coping with crisis, developing personal insight and knowledge, working through feelings of inner conflict or improving relationships with others. The counsellor's role is to facilitate the client's work in ways that respect the client's values, personal resources and capacity for self-determination.

Psychotherapy

A useful definition of psychotherapy is provided by Norcross (1990):

> Psychotherapy is the informed and intentional application of clinical methods and interpersonal stances derived from established psychological principles for the purpose of assisting people to modify their behaviours, cognitions, emotions, and/or other personal characteristics in directions that the participants deem desirable. (p. 218)

What's the difference between counselling and psychotherapy?

Although the above definition of psychotherapy would seem to apply equally well to counselling, there are those who would argue that counselling and psychotherapy are different activities requiring separate definitions.

The term 'counselling' was first introduced by Carl Rogers in the 1940s because at that time psychologists were not permitted, as non-medical practitioners, to describe what they did as 'psychotherapy'. So Rogers used the term 'counselling' to describe what he was doing. Times have changed since then and psychotherapy is no longer the province of the medical profession. But, because of these historical reasons, the professions of counselling and psychotherapy developed separately for much of the twentieth century, and are understood by some to be different activities.

Historically, counselling was seen as a short-term activity, lasting only weeks or months, whereas psychotherapy was seen as a longer-term activity lasting up to several years in some cases. Also, some would argue that counselling tends to operate at a relatively superficial level of human experience whereas psychotherapy operates at much deeper levels. These two points – duration and depth – are the ones most often used to make a distinction between counselling and psychotherapy, and reflect the historical usage of the two terms specifically to refer to humanistic therapy and psychoanalytic therapy, respectively. More will be said of these approaches in later chapters.

For others, however, counselling and psychotherapy are interchangeable terms in recognition that Rogers would have used the term 'psychotherapy' if he had been able to. Today, counsellors often do longer-term work and psychotherapists shorter-term work (e.g., Anderson and Lambert, 1995; Cameron, 2007). One further important similarity between counselling and psychotherapy is that the person seeking help, the client, has control over the direction the therapy takes, that people are assisted in making changes that they themselves deem to be desirable. This is an important distinction, and sets counselling and psychotherapy apart from the more medically oriented professions in which people can be sectioned within the Mental Health Act and treated against their will. In such cases the treatment is likely to be drug-based rather than some form of psychological therapy.

The distinction between counselling and psychotherapy remains a contentious issue in professional circles (Pointon, 2004; Reeves, 2009; Rosen, 2004). However, for the purposes of this book, which is concerned with theory, I will use the terms 'counselling' and 'psychotherapy' interchangeably with the term 'therapy'.

Setting the scene

The reason why definitions of therapy are contentious is that the various professional groups who are involved in the practice of therapy all have very different visions of what it is. As van Deurzen (1998) wrote:

> As soon as one tries to reach an agreed definition there is immediately disagreement about whether psychotherapy is to be seen as a form of treatment or as a form of personal development. There is still no agreement about whether psychotherapy is primarily a medical, a psychological, an educational or a spiritual activity ... Psychotherapy for some is about priesthood, for some about parenting, for some about education, for some about healing, for some about friendship, for some about mental or moral exercise. (pp. 4–5)

The situation is exacerbated by the fact that there is much professional rivalry and political struggle between the various professional groups for the ownership rights to the field of therapy. Mahrer (1998) explained it as follows:

> Picture a gathering of all the psychotherapy-related professions and someone asking, 'who has a justified right to train psychotherapists?' Psychologists would raise their collective hand. So would social workers, nurses, and educators. The school of medicine would raise its hand. So would schools and departments of pastoral studies, human relations, rehabilitation, guidance, child development, family studies, philosophy, and many others. (p. 20)

More recently, as Totton (2003a) wrote:

> Every practitioner operates, consciously or not, from some position about what people *should be like*, indeed, what people 'really are' like: some vision, in other words, of human nature. For example, people are intrinsically loving and creative; people are intrinsically aggressive and envious; people are intrinsically ambivalent. Sex is at the root of everything: god is at the root of everything; relationship is at the root of everything ... Each of these simplified slogans represents one or more schools of psychotherapy and counselling. They also constitute what are essentially political positions. (p. 4)

These quotes set the scene very much for this book. Each of the theories of therapy offers a vision of human nature. Through this book I hope that the reader will begin to reach an understanding of how each of the theories of therapy offer a way of looking at how psychological problems develop, and how people can be helped.

Distress, deviance, dysfunction, and dangerousness

One helpful way to think about people's psychological problems is to consider whether the thoughts, feelings, or behaviour of the person in question are distressing, dangerous, deviant, or dysfunctional. These are terms used by Comer (1998) to think about the different ways in which people's problems in living are expressed.

At one time or another many of us will feel emotionally upset (*distress*), perhaps we will do something that is harmful to ourselves or to another person (*dangerous*), do something that seems really odd or strange to other people (*deviant*), or have difficulty functioning in our everyday lives (*dysfunction*). This is often a useful way to think about psychological suffering and it can be helpful to spend some time thinking about the concepts of distress, deviance, dangerousness, and dysfunction and how they apply to examples of behaviours that we might consider as psychological problems.

So, thinking back to Helen, we might say that her thoughts, feelings, and behaviours are problematic insofar as she is clearly emotionally upset (distressed), having difficulties holding down her job (dysfunctional), at risk of harming herself (dangerous), and behaving out of character (deviant). Alex, who explodes in violent rages, is clearly dangerous to others and deviant in terms of social norms. Tom is distressed by his upsetting memories. Matt does not consider himself to have a problem and he is less likely to seek out help voluntarily. However, he might be considered as dangerous and deviant by his parents and friends who are likely to bring Matt to the attention of psychiatric and psychology services. What this illustrates is that people's problems take different shapes. For some people, they are characterized by distress, for others dysfunction, dangerousness, or deviance. Questions are also raised as to who makes these judgements? And who determines that someone is in need of help? Generally speaking, counsellors and psychotherapists are more likely to work with people who are distressed and dysfunctional and who have sought help for themselves, whereas psychiatrists and psychologists are more likely to work with people who are a danger to themselves, are seen as deviant, and who are considered by other people to need help.

The more distressing, dangerous, deviant, or dysfunctional the thoughts, feelings, and behaviours are, and the more obvious these thoughts, feelings, and behaviours are to others, the more likely we are to consider them as problematic. The more extreme the behaviours, the more easily we can see them as problematic. Sarah, on the other hand, does not appear to have problems. She simply longs to do something different and more personally fulfilling with her life, and wants to find a way to pursue her passions to do something more creative.

Certainly, it would not be unusual for someone like Sarah, who is looking for a more restful life, to also seek some form of counselling or psychotherapy despite the fact that she is not in need of help in the very obvious way that Matt, Helen, Alex or Tom are. Counselling and psychotherapy are also useful to people whose levels of distress, deviance, dysfunction, and dangerousness are low. Counsellors and psychotherapists work with people across the spectrum of functioning, not just those at the extremes. Few of us could say that we have no problems in living whatsoever. Maslow (1970) used the term 'psychopathology of the average' to describe most people's level of functioning. Many of us will recognize something familiar in Sarah's experience. People often talk about how they feel that they are not living life to the full, using their potential, or not being true to themselves. Each therapeutic approach offers us its own vision of what it is to be human, how problems develop, and how they can be resolved. Each of the theories also gives us insight into what leads to healthy functioning.

Different therapeutic approaches

Broadly, the problems people bring to counselling and psychotherapy are either those that have their origin in the remote past of the person's life or those that arise from current stressful situations. It seems that Tom's problems have arisen as a result of the accident and his struggles to come to terms with his loss. Tom's feelings of guilt for what happened that evening seem to be important. But what sense can we make of Helen's mood, Alex's rage, or Matt's seemingly bizarre behaviour? There doesn't seem to be an obvious trigger that explains their difficulties. Does that mean that their difficulties arise from experiences in their remote past?

Theories of counselling and psychotherapy are concerned with understanding the mechanisms which lead one person and not another to develop psychological problems. Historically, psychological problems have been understood in many ways – the result of supernatural forces, the wrath of gods, demonic possession, the influence of the moon, for example. At different times, psychological suffering has attracted ridicule, fear, pity, and anger, and has been variously treated, from attempts to exorcize demons to taking cold baths (see Davey, 2008). Today, there are seven major ways in which we can understand how problems develop:

- biomedical model
- psychodynamic model
- behavioural model

- cognitive model
- humanistic model
- transpersonal model
- sociocultural model.

By 'model', what is meant is a particular set of shared assumptions underlying how we see the world. A model provides us with the boundaries of inquiry, a way of looking at the world, a shared set of assumptions about reality which allow us to communicate with each other. Another word, which is often used instead of model in this context, is 'paradigm'. Each of these seven models, or paradigms, has a consistent view of human nature, how it can go awry and lead to problems, and how the resultant problems can be prevented and treated. In the following chapters I will say a little more about the main ideas behind each model. I have tried to treat each model sympathetically. It is my understanding that each model can tell us something important about human experience.

A brief look at the models

The biomedical model suggests that psychological problems are the result of physical dysfunction; the psychodynamic model suggests that psychological problems are caused by conflict between unconscious forces; the behavioural model suggests that psychological problems are a result of maladaptive learning; the cognitive model suggests that psychological problems are caused by irrational or distorted thinking; the humanistic model suggests that psychological problems are caused by a failure to know oneself and accept oneself; the transpersonal model is concerned with spirituality; and the sociocultural model suggests that psychological problems result from social factors. Of course, these are superficial generalizations of what each model is about and more detailed accounts of each model will be provided in subsequent chapters. Each chapter will begin by outlining the model followed by a description of some of the therapeutic approaches associated with that tradition. In the final chapter, current perspectives on models, the role of evidence-based practice, and eclectic and integrative approaches to therapy will be considered. For the moment, however, the point is simply to show how each model contains assumptions about the driving forces behind human behaviour and how psychological problems develop, and how people can be helped to overcome those problems (see Table 1.1).

The biological and sociocultural models are not usually considered in books about counselling and psychotherapy. Neither model forms the basis for a psychological therapeutic approach, the sociocultural model emphasizing instead the need to change social structures and to rethink

Table 1.1 Different models of psychological distress

	Psychological problems are caused by:	*People can be helped with:*
Biological	Biochemical imbalances, genetic factors, brain defects	Medication, electric shock therapy, surgery
Psychodynamic	Internal psychological conflict between unconscious forces	Therapist interpretations which help to bring unconscious conflicts into consciousness
Behavioural	Maladaptive learning	Learning of new behaviours to replace old behaviours
Cognitive	Dysfunctional attitudes about the self and the world	Techniques which modify existing attitudes, schemas, thoughts
Humanistic	Thwarted personal growth	Therapeutic relationship
Transpersonal	Lack of touch with spirituality, the divine, God	Meditation, spiritual experience
Sociocultural	Adverse social and environmental factors, maladaptive communication patterns	Changing the nature of society, family and community psychology

how we perceive psychological suffering, and the biological model emphasizing anatomical structures and the need for physical treatment. Nevertheless, each of these two models promises to tell us something about human experience and how problems in living might develop, and should therefore also be of interest to counsellors and psychotherapists. We are biological beings who live in a social world and the importance of both biology and society should not be dismissed. We have to be alert to the danger of overlooking the possibility that distress can have biological or social causes. As therapists we must be careful not to overlook the fact that we live our lives within confines dictated by biology and society.

Today, we also see interest in the transpersonal model, which its adherents might argue reflects the developments over the last century in quantum physics which have made us stop and think about the very nature of the universe and its relationship with consciousness. Transpersonal psychology is concerned with those experiences which transcend, or go beyond, the individual, and therapists working from within the transpersonal model are concerned with using mystical, spiritual, or psychic experiences to increase human potential. Some might argue that the popularity of these ideas within the general population reflects people's need for a spiritual existence in their lives with the decline of traditional religious observation. Certainly, some of these ideas might seem bizarre and are not usually considered within texts on mental health, and often the exponents of transpersonal psychology are not taken seriously within the scientific community. Nonetheless, we must be careful not to overlook the spiritual aspects of human experience.

However, most counsellors and psychotherapists tend to work using ideas developed within either the psychodynamic, behavioural, cognitive, or humanistic models which emphasize the psychological aspects of human nature. A recent survey of members of the British Association for Counselling and Psychotherapy (BACP) found that 29 per cent adopted the most well-known of the humanistic therapies, person-centred therapy, 18 per cent the psychodynamic approach, and 4 per cent cognitive-behavioural therapy. While the majority of BACP members are humanistic in orientation, findings from the United Kingdom Council of Psychotherapists (UKCP) found that most (30 per cent) were psychodynamic in orientation, 3 per cent cognitive-behavioural and only 0.4 per cent person-centred (*Therapy Today*, 2006). While the 'pure' humanistic and psychodynamic approaches remain popular, the majority of therapists today describe themselves as eclectic or integrative – meaning that they draw on different approaches as the need arises, or somehow blend the different approaches. Eclectic and integrative approaches will be discussed in more detail later.

Inspecting the elephant

At first inspection the world of therapy is confusing. And it can be surprising to the novice therapist to discover this – who would have thought that counselling was so complicated? But for me this is one of the exciting things about therapy – the fact that it is about all the different ways of looking at what it is to be human. We are challenged to try to look at things from as many angles as possible, to constantly juggle the different perceptions, and to question our understandings.

The disputes between theorists have been compared to the well-known fable about philosophers who were sent by the wise king into the pitch-dark barn where there was an elephant. Never before had they encountered an elephant and each one, on touching a part of the elephant, assumed that they now had the key to understanding the whole animal. One of them, reaching out and touching the elephant's trunk, exclaims: 'I understand the nature of this animal, it is like a snake.'

Another, touching a leg of the elephant, cries out in reply: 'No, it is like a tree.' Different versions of the fable abound, but the point is, of course, to remind us of the folly in drawing conclusions on the basis of limited evidence and to remind us to question our own beliefs. When we try to understand the nature of psychological suffering we are sometimes like the philosophers standing in the dark around the elephant. The idea is that, although truth exists, our knowledge is limited and we can never fully know that truth.

Each of the models gives us a particular understanding of how problems arise, and what leads to well-being. Although humanistic therapists might be well-versed in the language and ideas of Rogers and Maslow, psychodynamic therapists in the ideas and language of Freud and Klein, and cognitive therapists in the language and ideas of Ellis and Beck, for example, they are not well-versed in each other's language and ideas. Furthermore, traditional counselling and psychotherapy training has not left its graduates well-versed in the language and ideas of psychologists and psychiatrists. At present the biomedical model is generally dominant and reflects our understanding of ourselves as organisms shaped through millions of years of evolution. Certainly the biomedical model is a particularly dominant force in psychiatry, where practitioners are medically qualified. Within the professions of counselling and psychotherapy, it is probably true to say that the humanistic and psychodynamic paradigms are the dominant ways of looking at psychological problems, and within the profession of psychology, the behavioural and cognitive paradigms are probably the most dominant ways of looking at psychological problems. Of course, there will be many that do not fit these generalizations, but, overall, the different mental health professions are fairly entrenched in these different theoretical camps.

The importance of theory for practice

Does it make a difference what the therapist believes? I think it does. Let me give an example to explain what I mean. Let us suppose that a person goes along to a friend and says that he has problems with alcohol. The friend, who is well-meaning, suggests that he gets in touch with Alcoholics Anonymous (AA). That would seem to be good advice and probably fairly typical of what many of us might do in that situation. But how many of us are aware of the underlying assumptions, or model, of the AA programme? The essence of AA's underlying philosophy is contained in its Serenity Prayer: 'God grant me the serenity to accept the things I cannot change, courage to change the things I can, and wisdom to know the difference.' Although there is undoubtedly much common sense in this statement, it also suggests that the ability to make these changes may depend on forces external to the person rather than internal to the person.

The AA have what they call the 12-step programme (see Table 1.2). The philosophy underlying the AA programme seems to be that people should accept that they are powerless over their behaviour, at least in regard to alcohol. The alcoholic's life is under the control and direction of powerful forces that may, depending on their understanding of God, reside outside of themselves. This belief system represents a way of looking at the world that is in direct contradiction to that held by many counsellors and psychotherapists, at least in Western culture. It is probably true to say that most counsellors and psychotherapists in Western society operate from the basic, and secular, assumption that positive therapeutic change will be evident when the client is able to take control of his or her life. Personal responsibility is fundamental to counselling and psychotherapy in Western culture (Nelson-Jones, 1984).

Table 1.2   The 12-step programme of Alcoholics Anonymous

1. We admitted we were powerless over alcohol – that our lives had become unmanageable.
2. Came to believe that a power greater than ourselves could restore us to sanity.
3. Made a decision to turn our will and our lives over to the care of God as we understood Him.
4. Made a searching and fearless moral inventory of ourselves.
5. Admitted to God, to ourselves, and to another human being the exact nature of our wrongs.
6. Were entirely ready to have God remove all these defects of character.
7. Humbly asked Him to remove our shortcomings.
8. Made a list of all persons we had harmed, and became willing to make amends to them all.
9. Made direct amends to such people whenever possible, except when to do so would injure them or others.
10. Continued to take personal inventory and when we were wrong promptly admitted it.
11. Sought through prayer and meditation to improve our conscious contact with God as we understood Him, praying only for knowledge of His will for us and the power to carry that out.
12. Having had a spiritual awakening as the result of these steps, we tried to carry this message to alcoholics, and to practise these principles in all our affairs.

This is not to say that a therapist would challenge such belief systems as those expressed in the AA programme. Counsellors are responsible for working in ways which promote the client's control over his or her life, and respect the client's ability to make decisions and change in the light of his or her own beliefs and values. The point here is not to criticize the AA programme (as we shall see later there are many other therapeutic approaches with a spiritual element), but simply to make explicit the idea that every therapeutic approach rests on some basic assumptions about human nature. How does the 12-step programme fit with your own views of what it takes to change behaviour?

So it matters what the theory says, because that will influence what we actually do in practice. And importantly, we are always practising on the basis of some theory whether or not we realize it!

Eclectic and integrative approaches

A question that has occupied many people over the years is whether any one model is sufficient to explain all the different ways in which psychological suffering is expressed. For example, can all psychological problems be attributed to sociocultural factors, or are all psychological problems a result of biological factors? Most mental health professionals today, of whatever persuasion, would probably agree that human experience is so diverse that no one model is able to offer the full explanation for all psychological problems for all of the people all of the time. For example, research suggests that people who are depressed have both lower levels of social resources (evidence for the sociocultural model), and lower levels of the neurotransmitter serotonin (evidence for the biological model) than people not suffering from depression.

Eclectism

For the reason that no one model seems to have all of the answers, many therapists working today do so in an *eclectic* way, that is to say, drawing on the techniques and interventions associated with one therapeutic approach when they see it as appropriate and then drawing on the ideas of another model when that seems appropriate. Indeed, many programmes of therapy training deliberately set out to show trainees different approaches so that they are able to practise eclectically. Clinical psychologists, for example, are trained in this eclectic way, learning about all of the different approaches.

Integration

Eclectism should not be confused with integrative approaches. Many therapists describe themselves as *integrative*, meaning that they have adopted and blended one or more of the models that they see as being consistent with each other. In a survey of members of the BACP, 26 per cent adopted integrative approaches, and in the UKCP, 17 per cent described themselves as integrative (*Therapy Today*, 2006).

Those working integratively endeavour to work in a more circumscribed and theoretically consistent way, drawing on the ideas from models that they see as reconcilable. Indeed, trying to find a reconciliatory path – one that is able to integrate the different paradigms – has been one of the greatest challenges of recent years for the professions of counselling and psychotherapy. Perhaps the most successful attempts at therapy integration have been the merging of ideas from the cognitive and the behavioural models to produce what is known as the cognitive-behavioural approach. In more recent years, the merging of ideas from the psychodynamic and the cognitive models have produced what is known as the cognitive-analytic approach.

In Chapter 7, views on integration will be discussed. However, most counsellors and psychotherapists undergo extensive training in the ideas and way of working associated with one of the psychological models, that is, the behavioural, cognitive, humanistic, or psychodynamic model. Although there are advantages to having a detailed and thorough training in one model of therapy (see Spurling, 2002) – and traditionally counselling and psychotherapy training has been of this nature – it means that counselling and psychotherapy graduates often lack a common language. In essence, the issue for training as a therapist is the tension between depth of understanding versus breadth of understanding. Is it better to have a broader but inevitably more superficial knowledge of several approaches, or is it better to have a thorough grounding in one approach?

Research mindedness

How we make sense of the world around us and what we believe about human nature is fundamental to how we practise as counsellors and psychotherapists. For this reason, as counsellors and psychotherapists we have a duty to reflect upon our own beliefs and to monitor the effectiveness of what we do. As therapists we like to think we help people. But how can we be sure?

Throughout this book I will demonstrate what research is about, why it is carried out, and why counsellors and psychotherapists should be interested in it. The reader will come to understand the scientific function of assessment, classification, and diagnosis in psychotherapy and counselling; why psychodynamic and psychoanalytic ideas have been criticized for their unscientific nature; how this has led to the rise of behavioural and cognitive approaches with their emphasis on observability and scientific testability; and how some theorists within the humanistic and transpersonal models question the relevance of the traditional quantitative scientific approach to their domains of interest, preferring instead a qualitative phenomenological approach.

Although more will be said about the role of research in later chapters, for the moment I want to say a little more about why it is thought to be important. Research allows us to check up on the validity of what we think is true. To illustrate, there is a well-documented area of psychological inquiry which shows that people may remember things or report events in a way that has been shown to be false. People will often make the wrong connections between events and distort evidence to make it fit their beliefs. Sutherland (1992) argues that the need to hold on to our expected ways of seeing the world is powerful and can often mislead us. For example, read the following three lines:

PARIS

IN THE

THE SPRING

This is a well-known example used by Sutherland (1992) to illustrate how we cling to what we think to be true and, unless you have encountered this before, you might have read it incorrectly as 'Paris in the spring'. We see what we expect. If we are working within a particular model of counselling or psychotherapy which we believe to be effective and we are not recording data on our clients' outcomes in a systematic way which is amenable to scientific scrutiny, we will, the argument suggests, see what we expect. Although the terms 'evidence-based treatment' and 'evidence-based practice' are relatively recent, the idea that we should use the methods of science to check up on what we think we know is not new. Rogers, the originator of the person-centred approach to counselling, made the following statement:

> Scientific research needs to be seen for what it truly is; a way of preventing me from deceiving myself in regard to my creatively formed subjective hunches which have developed out of the relationship between me and my material. (Rogers, 1961)

The point is simply that we can be irrational in our thinking (see Sutherland, 1992) and, according to Rogers (1961), we might be best advised to adhere to the principles of scientific investigation if we want to avoid deceiving ourselves. As Rogers said, 'the facts are always friendly'. The cases at the beginning of this chapter illustrate the difficulty in understanding how problems arise and how to offer help. As such, we turn to research to find answers. Research can help us to build up an understanding of what causes problems in living and which therapies are most effective in alleviating those problems. This is a compelling argument in favour of research.

While there is general agreement on the importance of research, we also have to be mindful of those who question the role of research. Can we always trust research? Not according to some exponents of the sociological approach who, as we shall see in Chapter 6, point towards the existence of implicit political agendas. Also, scientists, like anyone else, are not immune to getting things wrong, to deceiving themselves, and finding it difficult to relinquish what they think is true. Thus, it is important for therapists to be research minded in order make sense of the debates for themselves. In the subsequent chapters we will look at the research-related issues as they arise in each of the models of therapy.

Conclusion

The aim of this chapter was to describe what it is that therapists do that is different from the social support we receive from family and friends. Therapists mainly derive their ways of working from complex theoretical models about the nature of psychological suffering. Several models were briefly introduced: the biomedical model; the psychodynamic model; the cognitive model; the behavioural model; the humanistic model; the transpersonal model; and the sociocultural model. The role of research was briefly introduced as a way of preventing ourselves from engaging in self-deception regarding our beliefs. In the subsequent chapters a more detailed description of each of the therapeutic approaches will be presented.

Summary points

- Definitions of counselling and psychotherapy vary with some viewing these as interchangeable terms, and others seeing counselling and psychotherapy as distinct activities.

- A broad definition of counselling and psychotherapy is that they are activities concerned with assisting people to modify their behaviours, cognitions, emotions, and other personal characteristics in directions that the participants deem desirable using methods derived from psychological principles.
- Deviance, distress, dysfunction, and dangerousness are useful concepts for thinking about the different ways people experience psychological problems.
- There is no one agreed set of principles for how to assist people to change and there is disagreement among the various professional groups involved in counselling and psychotherapy as to what constitutes counselling and psychotherapy.
- Several approaches to therapy exist, from biologically-based treatments through various psychological and spiritual interventions, to considerations of the social forces acting on a person.
- Research can help us to understand what approaches to therapy are helpful.

Topics for reflection

1. Think about a high profile case of extreme behaviour that has been in the media. How would you explain that person's behaviour?
2. Do you agree that counselling and psychotherapy has only developed to help people because support from family and friends and the wider community is no longer able to support people in the way it traditionally did? If not, what is it that therapy is able to offer that supportive others can't?
3. Thinking about what you already knew about counselling and psychotherapy, how does what you have read in this chapter add to your knowledge?

Chapter 2

Biomedical and Medical Approaches

Introduction

Anyone who has ever had a few alcoholic drinks will recognize that human behaviour can be profoundly affected by biochemistry. As counsellors and psychotherapists we must be aware of the possibility that some of the psychological difficulties people experience are actually caused by abnormal workings of the brain and are best treated by practitioners who can address the problem biomedically. The biomedical approach has had a profound influence on how mental health professionals think about the nature of psychological problems. In this chapter I will introduce the biomedical understanding of how psychological problems develop and their treatment.

Within the biomedical model it is recognized that a person's behaviour and experience may change if there are physical or chemical changes in the brain and nervous system. For example, we know that a severe injury to the brain can have a profound effect on behaviour. There may be problems in concentration and memory, and the personality of someone who sustains a severe head injury can change dramatically. For example, someone who was once outgoing and sociable can become shy and solitary. We also know the effects on behaviour that result from taking alcohol. People are more likely to act aggressively, to lose their inhibitions, to slur their speech, and so on. So, it is not unreasonable to suggest that psychological problems might reflect disturbances in the physical make-up or the chemistry of the brain. The aim of the biomedical model is to understand the relationship between psychological difficulties and physiological processes. So, for example, if it can be shown that a certain way of behaving is related to a certain aspect of brain chemistry, then it might be possible to help that person change or control their behaviour through some form of chemical intervention. This way of looking at human problems is the dominant one among psychiatrists who are medically qualified and allowed to prescribe drugs.

22

History of the biomedical model

Prior to the biomedical model, people held beliefs about supernatural causes of psychological problems and there are accounts of the casting out of demons in people who today would be seen as suffering from some form of psychological problem. Beliefs in demonological possession were widely held in the Middle Ages; thousands of people were accused of being witches and many were executed for their supposed crimes. It was in the late eighteenth century and early nineteenth century that the biomedical model replaced the demonological model. This was the age of enlightenment in which it was argued that psychological problems were not the result of supernatural forces but rather the result of physical illness. It was a time when scientific medicine was beginning to develop and, with it, the emphasis on an experimental approach to understanding human behaviour. It was thought that psychological problems could be treated like any other illness using biomedical techniques. This was a huge advance over the demonological model.

But it was also a time when the working lives of people began to change because of the industrial revolution. Traditionally, people's problems in living had been dealt with by the family and community. We know from the previous chapter how important social support is, but as people moved from rural living to urban living communities became less cohesive and less able to offer support. Asylums were introduced to contain people who needed help. Here, they could be treated with the new so-called medical advances of the day, which, looking back, seem more like torture to us than humane care. These were the early days of scientific medicine.

But the biomedical model has a long history dating back to the father of modern medicine, the Greek physician, Hippocrates (hence, the 'Hippocratic Oath' taken by medical practitioners). In the fourth century BC when most people believed that psychological problems were caused by supernatural forces, Hippocrates, wrote this about epilepsy:

> If you cut open the head, you will find the brain humid, full of sweat and smelling badly. And in this way you may see that it is not a god which injured the body, but disease. (Quoted in Zilboorg and Henry, 1941)

Hippocrates believed that psychological problems resulted from bodily disturbances. He distinguished between forms of 'madness' which resulted from various disturbances in the brain. The brain's healthy functioning was, he thought, dependent on a balance of four bodily fluids, or humours as they were called. The four humours were blood, black bile, yellow bile, and phlegm. Each of these four humours corresponded to the basic elements of earth, air, fire, and water, all of which must be in a state of balance within the universe. Illness was thought to be caused by an imbalance of the humours within the body. Someone with too much blood was moody, someone with too much black bile was melancholic, someone with too much yellow bile was anxious, and someone with too much phlegm was sluggish. Treatment therefore consisted of attempts to achieve a balance in the four humours. Such views persisted into the nineteenth century when asylums were introduced and treatments included blood letting, abstinence from sexual activity, and immersion in cold water – all attempts to restore the balance of the humours (see Starr, 1982). Hence the phrase that someone is in good humour! So, the idea that psychological problems are caused by biological disturbances is not a new one – it can be dated back to Hippocrates.

One of the most important psychological studies of the late nineteenth century was the case of Phineas Gage (Harlow, 1868). His was an unusual story which illustrates clearly that disturbances in the brain can affect psychological functioning. Phineas Gage, a 25-year-old construction worker for the Rutland and Burlington Railroad in New England, suffered damage to his brain in 1848. He was working on the railway when a piece of metal almost four feet long was propelled into his skull by an explosion. The metal went into his left cheek and exited through the top of his skull. He was stunned but amazingly quickly regained consciousness and was able to talk. Subsequently, it was noticed that his cognitive abilities, intellectual functioning and so on, remained relatively unimpaired. However, his behaviour changed remarkably. Where he had previously been a responsible, and well adjusted man, he now was much less restrained, more impulsive, less patient, and less socially and emotionally appropriate. Psychologists began, through Phineas Gage, to understand how brain and behaviour were related.

Another example is the story of general paresis. Today general paresis has all but vanished from the psychiatric textbooks. Most people today will not have heard of it and might be surprised to learn that in the late nineteenth century about a quarter of people admitted to mental hospitals were diagnosed with general paresis (Dale, 1980). The symptoms of general paresis included problems with memory, impaired intellectual functioning, delusions of grandeur, and paralysis, generally leading to death within two to five years. But, despite the fact that general paresis was so common, the cause was not known. It was found to be more common in men, those who used alcohol, and among sailors, prompting suggestions that it was caused by something to do with being a man, using alcohol, or going to sea. Some suggested it might have some connection with sexual behaviour. Following this line of thought it was then hypothesized that general paresis was caused by untreated syphilis. In order to test this hypothesis, in 1897 Richard von Kraft-Ebing injected pus from syphilitic sores into nine patients who had general paresis. He reasoned that, because people who have already contracted syphilis cannot do so again, if general paresis was caused by untreated syphilis then the nine patients should be immune and would not develop syphilis in response to his injection. None of his patients went on to develop syphilis, confirming that all had previously had syphilis.

This study was important in showing an association between untreated syphilis and general paresis. Although such a study is ethically questionable by today's standards of medical research, it provided the first evidence that eventually led to the successful treatment of this condition. Once the cause of general paresis was identified as syphilis bacteria infecting the cerebral cortex of the brain, medical practitioners were able to develop a test to diagnose the presence of the bacteria and treat syphilis in the same way as any other infection. As well as serving as an historical illustration of how psychological problems can turn out to be rooted in biology, the story of general paresis also illustrates the emergence of scientific medicine. The general idea is that the scientist observes some phenomenon, attempts to explain its occurrence, and then finds ways to test out the validity of the explanation.

Scientific medicine

One consequence of the development of scientific medicine is that it encouraged the use of classification. We recognize, for example, that a sore throat is a different condition from a skin rash which in turn is a different condition from a broken leg. All three conditions have different causes and consequently different treatments are appropriate for each. So if a person goes to the doctor with a throat infection he might expect treatment with an antibiotic, whereas if he had a skin rash he might expect treatment with hydrocortisone cream, and with a broken leg he might expect a brace. If doctors did not distinguish between throat infections, skin rashes, and broken legs and their different causes they would not be able to provide differential treatment. What use would it be if you went to the doctor and were given indigestion tablets for a broken leg? We expect medical practitioners to provide us with whatever treatment is most suitable for our illness or injury. The need for differential treatment is the logic underpinning the biomedical model. While this might be perfectly appropriate for physical illnesses, the biomedical model assumes that mental problems are ultimately physical problems. Thus, in the same way that physical conditions can be classified and treated, so too can mental conditions. This is referred to as the medical model.

Diagnostic and Statistical Manual of Mental Disorders

Building on the logic of the medical model, the American Psychiatric Association have produced what is called the *Diagnostic and Statistical Manual of Mental Disorders* (DSM). Many of the terms used to describe psychiatric disorders may already be familiar. In the cases introduced in Chapter 1, Helen might be diagnosed as suffering from major depressive disorder, Alex from a disorder of impulse control, Tom from posttraumatic stress disorder, and Matt from schizophrenia. Other commonly known, so-called 'disorders' include panic disorder, obsessive-compulsive disorder, anorexia nervosa, and bulimia nervosa. The roots of this system go back to the turn of the twentieth century and a German doctor called Kraepelin who, in the late nineteenth century, observed that some symptoms tended to occur together, leading him to develop early classifications of mental disease. DSM was first introduced in 1952 (DSM-I), followed by revised editions in 1968 (DSM-II), 1980 (DSM-III), 1987 (DSM-III-R), 1994 (DSM-IV). It is now in its revised fourth edition (DSM-IV-TR) (American Psychiatric Association, 2000). It should be noted that there is another system of classification in use: the *International Classification of Diseases* (ICD) produced by the World Health Organization (WHO) which is now in its tenth edition (World Health Organization, 1992) and serves a similar function to DSM. Much of what will be said here about the use of the DSM system also applies to the WHO system. The DSM-IV-TR is a voluminous work running to many hundreds of pages. Although earlier editions of the DSM attempted to relate psychiatric disorders to their supposed *aetiology,* or causes, the more recent editions have not done this. Now each disorder, with a few exceptions such as posttraumatic stress disorder, is defined in terms of its observable signs and symptoms.

Axis of functioning

Psychiatrists use DSM to assess people on five different axes (areas of functioning). Axis I is a list of clinical syndromes from which a person might be suffering. Axis II is a list of life-long, deeply ingrained and maladaptive personality patterns. Axis III is a list of medical conditions. Axis IV is a list of psychosocial and environmental problems. Axis V is a global assessment of functioning on a 100-point scale extending from 1 (persistent violence, suicidal behaviour or inability to maintain personal hygiene) to 100 (symptom free, with superior functioning across a wide range of activities). So, for example, a person might be diagnosed with an anxiety disorder on Axis I, as having an obsessive-compulsive personality disorder on Axis II, no related physical disorders on Axis III,

Table 2.1　DSM-IV-TR classes of disorder

- **Disorders usually first diagnosed in infancy, childhood, or adolescence.** For example, conduct disorder and infantile autism. This category includes emotional, intellectual, and behavioural disorders which occur before adulthood although they often persist into adulthood.

- **Delerium, dementia, amnestic, and other cognitive disorders.** Problems associated with impairment of brain by injury or illness.

- **Substance-related disorders.** These disorders are identified by substance, for example alcohol, and are conditions in which there is psychological distress or physical damage.

- **Schizophrenia and other psychotic disorders.** Disorders in which the person has lost contact with reality; there may be delusions and hallucinations, as well as deterioration in social functioning. The person might become severely withdrawn from others.

- **Mood disorders.** Depression or bipolar mood disorder in which the person alternates between periods of severe depression and mania, i.e., increased excitement and activity.

- **Anxiety disorders.** For example, phobia, panic disorder, obsessive-compulsive disorder, and posttraumatic stress disorder.

- **Somatoform disorders.** For example, problems with physical symptoms but no organic cause. A person might suffer from paralysis without there being any clear organic cause.

- **Factitious disorders.** Physical or psychological problems that are deliberately produced or faked.

- **Dissociative disorders.** Problems in which there is a splitting of consciousness, memory, e.g., multiple personality disorder.

- **Sexual and gender identity disorders.** Problems involving sexuality, ability to perform sexually, inappropriate sexual orientation, cross-gender identification.

- **Eating disorders.** Problems involving unusual patterns of food consumption, e.g., anorexia nervosa and bulimia nervosa. Anorexia nervosa involves a preoccupation with being thin accompanied by extreme weight loss. Bulimia nervosa involves periods of binge eating followed by purging through vomiting and/or the use of laxatives.

- **Sleep disorders.** Problems in which the normal pattern of sleep is interrupted. For example, sleep terrors in which the person wakes up confused and in a state of panic.

- **Impulse control disorders.** Problems in which there is an inability to refrain from harmful behaviours, e.g., kleptomania (stealing), pyromania (fire-starting), and compulsive gambling.

- **Adjustment disorders.** Problems in which there is a maladaptive and excessive response to an identifiable stressor.

as having occupational problems on Axis IV, and as having functioned over the past year at a general level of 40 on the Axis V global scale. The purpose of having these five axes of functioning is to provide a comprehensive description of the client's difficulties.

DSM is the reference work used by psychiatrists as a basis for their diagnoses of psychiatric disorders. DSM-IV-TR lists almost 300 separate disorders defined in terms of their observable symptoms. The disorders are further grouped into several major categories. It is beyond the scope of this book to go into detail on all of the separate disorders, but to illustrate the system a little further it might be useful to look at each of the major categories on one of the axes. On Axis I, psychological problems are classified into major classes of psychiatric disorder (see Table 2.1).

Scientific use of DSM

Although a full discussion of the DSM-IV system is beyond the scope of this book, I want to emphasize why psychiatrists have adopted this system. In the same way as there is a need to distinguish between different physical illnesses, it is believed by those who adopt the medical model that we must be able to distinguish between the different psychological conditions in order to be able to prescribe the correct treatment. By observation of all the symptoms people experience, what symptoms always seem to occur together, and what symptoms do not seem to occur together, we should be able to sort all the symptoms into different categories. So, we are then able to say that in this category we have, for example, loss of sexual interest, loss of appetite, and loss of interest in other people, and these 'symptoms' are usually seen together, that is, they co-occur. In another category we have, for example, hallucinations, apathy, and lack of pleasure and motivation, and these 'symptoms' usually co-occur. Once this grouping has been achieved, labels are given to each of the categories. The examples above are symptoms from the psychiatric disorders of depression and schizophrenia, respectively.

The point of categorizing symptoms is that it facilitates communication between mental health professionals, and this in turn enables researchers to design effective research programmes into the causes of these different conditions and what therapeutic interventions work with particular client groups. If different psychological problems are caused by different factors then it is important for researchers not to throw all psychological problems together but rather to look at separate psychological problems in relation to the different factors. For example, from your own experiences you would probably agree that when you describe yourself or someone else as being depressed that you mean something very different from when you describe yourself or someone else as being anxious. By depressed you probably mean the person is sluggish, tearful, sad, and down in the mouth, whereas by anxious you probably mean the person is nervous, excited, scared, and worried. The question is whether or not feeling anxious and feeling depressed are somehow different in the same way that you might say that a sore throat is different from a stomach upset and requires different treatment. If they are different then a coherent research programme which is trying to look at, for example, the treatment of depression and anxiety must treat them as such.

One of the functions of classification, therefore, is to drive scientific enquiry by providing a common language among mental health researchers and clear operational definitions of the phenomena under investigation. For example, if you suspect that a particular drug will help to alleviate depression, you might plan an experimental research programme in which a group of people who you thought were depressed were given the drug and another group of people who you thought were equally depressed were given a placebo drug (i.e., an inactive substance which resembles the real drug so that those taking part in the study don't know whether they are being given the active or inactive substance). The allocation of the participant to the active substance or inactive substance group would be determined by chance. This is called random allocation and serves to make sure that there is as little bias as possible in the way that people are allocated to the groups.

To avoid the expectations of the researcher affecting the results, he or she will also not know if the participant in the experiment is being given the active or inactive substance. Then, when the drug is expected to have worked, the researcher looks again to see if the people given the drug are now less depressed than those given the placebo. If they are, it can be concluded that the research has provided evidence that the drug alleviates depression. This method is known as a randomized control trial (RCT) (Dyer and Joseph, 2006) and is commonly used to test out new drugs as well as the efficacy of other forms of therapy. This is a very simple example of an RCT and experimental designs can be much more complex than this, involving, perhaps, several groups for comparison. The researcher might also be interested in whether the drug was even more effective when it was coupled with psychotherapy; he or she would then also want to include a depressed group who were given the drug and psychotherapy for comparison. Although it is difficult and expensive to carry out such studies (Seligman, 1995), the results can be very useful in guiding practice.

In order to carry out this type of research the researcher must be able to define exactly what is meant by the term 'depression' (or whatever target problem has been identified for treatment), and must be able to measure depression. The researcher needs to be able to say that the people in the group given the drug were equal in their level of depression to the people given the placebo at the beginning of the study, and that the level of depression in the group given the drug decreased while the level of depression in the placebo group did not.

Also, the researcher needs to be able to communicate to his or her colleagues exactly what was done so that others can do the same and confirm the results. The nature of good scientific practice is that experiments should be replicable. It is only when an experiment has been replicated by different researchers in different parts of the world that we can say with confidence that the evidence is robust enough for us to accept. So, we must be able to define very precisely the phenomenon under investigation, to measure it, and observe changes in it over time. Thus, it is important that we are able to translate our psychological concepts into numerical scores so that we are able to conduct the relevant statistical tests.

This is a very brief account of the experimental method in the context of the medical model. First, the researcher must be able to clearly define the phenomenon under investigation and measure it in some way. Second, some intervention is carried out in such a way that any changes are directly attributable to the intervention. This is ostensibly the scientific purpose of psychiatric classification. There are, as you might expect, criticisms of the scientific method and of psychiatric classification which we will consider shortly. But first it is useful, given the above discussion, to look in more detail at two of the most common psychiatric disorders – depression and generalized anxiety disorder – and how they are defined in DSM-IV-TR.

Measurement

Classification serves to provide the scientific community with a common language; DSM-IV-TR (American Psychiatric Association, 2000) lists hundreds of psychiatric disorders. It is beyond the scope of this book to summarize all of these here but, to give a flavour of the nature of the DSM-IV-TR, Table 2.2 lists the symptoms of major depressive episode. Note that nine 'symptoms' are listed and, in order to be diagnosed with major depressive episode, a person must be seen to have experienced at least five of the 'symptoms'.

So, when two psychiatrists are talking about a patient who is diagnosed with major depressive episode, they both have a clear understanding of what this means. Similarly, someone who is diagnosed with generalized anxiety disorder (GAD) would have to meet the criteria listed in Table 2.3, which are also outlined in DSM-IV-TR (American Psychiatric Association, 2000).

Table 2.2 Symptoms listed in DSM-IV-TR for the diagnosis of major depressive episode

A. Five (or more) of the following symptoms have been present during the same two-week period and represent a change from previous functioning; at least one of the symptoms is either 1. depressed mood, or 2. loss of interest or pleasure.
   Note: Do not include symptoms that are clearly due to a general medical condition, or mood incongruent delusions or hallucinations.
   1. Depressed mood most of the day, nearly every day, as indicated either by subjective reports (e.g., feels sad or empty) or observation made by others (e.g., appears tearful). **Note:** In children and adolescents can be irritable mood.
   2. Markedly diminished interest or pleasure in all, or almost all, activities most of the day, nearly every day (as indicated by subjective account or observation by others).
   3. Significant weight loss when not dieting or weight gain (e.g., a change of more than 5 per cent of body weight in a month), or decrease or increase in appetite nearly every day. **Note:** In children, consider failure to make expected weight gains.
   4. Insomnia or hypersomnia nearly every day.
   5. Psychomotor agitation or retardation nearly every day (observable by others, not merely subjective feelings of restlessness or being slowed down).
   6. Fatigue or loss of energy nearly every day.
   7. Feelings of worthlessness or excessive or inappropriate guilt (which may be delusional) nearly every day (not merely self-reproach or guilt about being sick).
   8. Diminished ability to think or concentrate, or indecisiveness, nearly every day (either by subjective accounts or as observed by others).
   9. Recurrent thoughts of death (not just fear of dying), recurrent suicidal ideation without a specific plan, or a suicide attempt or a specific plan for committing suicide.
B. The symptoms do not meet criteria for a mixed episode.
C. The symptoms cause clinically significant distress or impairment in social, occupational, or other important areas of functioning.
D. The symptoms are not due to the direct physiological effects of a substance (e.g., a drug of abuse, a medication) or a general medical condition (e.g., hypothyroidism).
E. The symptoms are not better accounted for by bereavement, i.e., after the loss of a loved one, the symptoms persist for longer than 2 months or are characterized by marked functional impairment, morbid preoccupation with worthlessness, suicidal ideation, psychotic symptoms, or psychomotor retardation.

Reprinted with permission from the *Diagnostic and Statistical Manual of Mental Disorders,* fourth edn, text revision. © 2000, American Psychiatric Association.

Table 2.3   Symptoms listed in DSM-IV-TR for the diagnosis of generalized anxiety disorder (GAD)

A. Excessive anxiety and worry (apprehensive expectation), occurring more days than not for at least 6 months, about a number of events or activities (such as work or school performance).
B. The person finds it difficult to control the worry.
C. The anxiety and worry are associated with three (or more) of the following six symptoms (with at least some symptoms present for more days than not for the past 6 months). **Note:** Only one item is required in children.
     1. restlessness or feeling keyed up or on edge;
     2. being easily fatigued;
     3. difficulty concentrating or mind going blank;
     4. irritability;
     5. muscle tension;
     6. sleep disturbance (difficulty falling or staying asleep, or restless unsatisfying sleep).
D. The focus of the anxiety and worry is not confined to features of an Axis I disorder, e.g., the anxiety or worry is not about having a panic attack (as in Panic Disorder), being embarrassed in public (as in Social Phobia), being contaminated (as in Obsessive-Compulsive Disorder), being away from home or close relatives (as in Separation Anxiety Disorder), gaining weight (as in Anorexia Nervosa), having multiple physical complaints (as in Somatization Disorder), or having a serious illness (as in Hypochondriasis), and the anxiety and worry do not occur exclusively during Posttraumatic Stress Disorder.
E. The anxiety, worry, or physical symptoms cause clinically significant distress or impairment in social, occupational, or other important areas of functioning.
F. The disturbance is not due to the direct physiological effects of a substance (e.g., a drug of abuse, a medication) or a general medical condition (e.g., hyperthyroidism) and does not occur exclusively during a Mood Disorder, a Psychotic Disorder, or a Pervasive Developmental Disorder.

Reprinted with permission from the *Diagnostic and Statistical Manual of Mental Disorders*, fourth edn, text revision. © 2000, American Psychiatric Association.

The *Diagnostic and Statistical Manual* provides psychiatrists, as well as others who use the manual, with a shared frame of reference, a common language, and a fundamental tool for scientific enquiry. Based on DSM, psychiatrists and psychologists have developed a number of interview and questionnaire methods for measuring psychological problems such as depression and anxiety. These are used in such a way so as to give numerical scores which can then be used in research to show changes over time.

Some criticisms of DSM

The authors of the current DSM-IV system have tried to achieve greater reliability by focusing as much as possible on observable behaviours. Nevertheless, subjective factors still play a role in clinicians' evaluations. Consider, for example, the diagnostic criteria for major depressive episode or generalized anxiety disorder. What exactly does it mean to say that there is a markedly diminished interest or pleasure in activities? What level of anxiety and worry must there be for us to consider it excessive?

The current state of knowledge about the classification of psychological problems is not set in stone. In one hundred years' time people may look back and see our current knowledge as relatively primitive, as we do today when we look back to the turn of the twentieth century and the work of the phrenologists who studied personality through bumps and indentations on the head. One of the problems with the current system may be seen when we look at the criteria for depression and anxiety. Although the goal is to describe discrete categories of psychological disturbance, often it is not clear where one category ends and another begins, and where the boundaries between different disorders should be drawn. For example, both the diagnostic categories of depression and anxiety include symptoms of sleep disturbance, fatigue, and difficulty concentrating. This means that diagnosis can be an unreliable procedure. It is possible that a person with these symptoms would be diagnosed with depression by one psychiatrist and with anxiety by another. Criticisms about the reliability of the diagnostic system have been made for many years, with agreement between psychiatrists for some disorders being less than 50 per cent (Williams et al., 1992; Zigler and Phillips, 1961). One of the tasks of each revision of DSM has been to try and achieve a more reliable system and, although not perfect, most would agree that the present system seems to be more reliable than the previous ones.

Others have criticized the validity of the diagnostic system. Validity here refers to the extent to which the diagnostic category measures what it was designed to measure. This is more difficult because, as we shall discuss further in Chapter 6, these so-called psychiatric disorders are ultimately just social constructions that only exist in the same sense that other social constructions such as beauty, truth, or justice exist (see Maddux et al., 2005). They are not real in the same sense that a broken leg is real.

However, the idea of psychiatric classification and the DSM system has become so ingrained in the thinking of many health professionals that it is easy to forget that this is only one way of thinking about psychological problems. Each of the other therapeutic approaches considered in this book offers alternative ways of thinking about psychological functioning. Perhaps one way in which the current system of DSM will come to be seen as primitive is the way in which disorders are categorical, that is, someone either has or has not a particular disorder. Hans Eysenck suggested that it would be better to view psychological functioning continuously, ranging from one extreme to another, with most people somewhere in the middle (Eysenck, 1986). Although this model might better reflect reality, the fact that mainstream psychiatric services are based on the medical model idea of a dichotomous split between 'normality' and 'abnormality' means that problems in living continue to be viewed in an all-or-nothing way, that is, a person either has a so-called disorder or they don't. This way of thinking is implicit in the idea that mental disorders are an illness. Eysenck's views are interesting and perhaps his suggestion will eventually lead to a better classification system.

However, although Eysenck is not criticizing classification and diagnosis per se, over the years there have been and still are many critics of the medical model and the role of classification and diagnosis. From the sociological point of view, social constructionists hold that the social world does not have an objective existence – reality is socially constructed. Thus, disorders of the mind are fabrications that only make sense at a particular time in history (a topic to which we will return in Chapter 6). But for now I want to discuss some research which asks the question, how well has the biomedical approach fared? One avenue of research, which has attracted much attention, is the investigation of the association between psychological functioning and biochemical imbalances.

Biomedical approaches

Biochemical imbalances

A first assumption of the biological perspective is that biochemical imbalances in the brain result in abnormal behaviour. The brain is composed of a complex network of neurons (nerve cells) which communicate with each other by electrical impulses. The electrical impulses are transmitted using chemicals which are called neurotransmitter substances. If there is an excess or deficit of a neurotransmitter substance, or the transfer of a neurotransmitter substance between neurons is blocked in some way, then the normal processes for which these neurotransmitters are responsible will go awry. Different types of neurotransmitter serve different regions of the brain. Researchers working within the biological model have attempted to study the relationship between the different neurotransmitters and the different psychological problems (as defined using the DSM system). For example, researchers have investigated the relationship between one subset of neurotransmitter substances called monoamines and the psychiatric diagnosis of depression, finding that people who are severely depressed and suicidal often have low levels of monoamines called serotonin and noradrenaline (see Davey, 2008). The case for associations between biochemical and psychological functioning is good. Techniques have been developed which allow researchers to carry out 'brain scans' in order to see which areas of the brain are active in people with various psychological problems. Results seem to suggest that psychological states are mirrored in brain activity.

There would seem to be little reason to doubt that our biochemical functioning is associated with our psychological functioning. However, although we can say that biochemical functioning is associated with psychological functioning, the evidence that biochemical imbalances cause psychological problems is not so clear. Biochemical functioning is equally likely to be caused by psychological functioning.

Genetic factors

A second assumption of the biomedical model is that biochemical processes are affected by genetic factors. Research in developmental genetics has shown that abnormalities in the structure or number of chromosomes (the structures within cells that contain the genes) are associated with a range of malformations such as Downs syndrome. There is no doubt that Downs syndrome has a genetic cause. At locations on the chromosome there are long molecules of deoxyribonucleic acid (DNA) which are the genes (if the chromosome is the necklace then the genes are the beads on that necklace). We know that genes determine physical characteristics such as eye colour, but the relationship between genes and behaviour is less direct and also depends on the environment. A person's genetic endowment is known as his genotype and the characteristics that result from an interaction between genes and environment is his phenotype. Thus, two people might have a genetic predisposition to a particular behaviour (that is, the same genotype) but whereas one person goes on to develop that behaviour the other may not (that is, they exhibit different phenotypes).

The complexity of gene–environment interaction is such that scientists have actually identified faulty genes for only a few conditions. For example, Huntington's disease is thought to affect about one person in 15,000 and to be caused by a single gene (Gusella et al., 1983). This is a disorder in which a person's limbs and facial muscles undergo irregular spasms, there is impaired speech, difficulty swallowing, failing memory, attention difficulties, and progressive dementia, leading to death after

Table 2.4   Organic disorders

Huntington's disease	A progressive dementia, with movement difficulties, caused by degeneration of brain cells
Parkinson's disease	Loss of intellectual functioning, accompanied by tremors, caused by dopamine deficiency
Multiple sclerosis	Loss of intellectual functioning, accompanied by weakness and unsteadiness and spasticity of legs, caused by myelin loss
Alzheimer's disease	A progressive dementia caused by loss of neurons in hippocampus
Multi-infarct dementia	Dementia caused by series of strokes
Brain injury	Intellectual, cognitive, personality changes caused by blow to the brain
Tourette's syndrome	Multiple tics caused by neurochemical (acetylcholine/dopamine) imbalance
AIDS dementia	Cognitive impairment caused by AIDS
Korsakoff's syndrome	Memory and attention problems caused by damage to thalamus as a result of alcohol use and nutritional deficiencies

about 10–20 years. Other disorders of which we think we now largely understand the biological basis include Parkinson's disease, multiple sclerosis, Alzheimer's disease, Tourette's syndrome, AIDS dementia complex, and Korsakoff's syndrome (see Table 2.4).

The biomedical paradigm is extremely useful in investigating organic disorders. What problems now thought to be of a psychological nature might be included within a list of organic disorders in the future? As already mentioned, there is evidence that biological factors are associated with a range of psychological problems, but the direction of causality remains uncertain in most cases. A possible exception to this, it might be argued, is the so-called disorder of schizophrenia. Contrary to what many people think, a diagnosis of schizophrenia does not mean that a person has a split personality, but rather that there is a split between thoughts and emotions. DSM-IV-TR outlines the symptoms that must be present before a diagnosis of schizophrenia can be made:

1. psychotic symptoms lasting at least one month;
2. a marked deterioration in such areas as work, social relations, and self-care;
3. signs of some sort of disturbance for at least six months.

Twin studies

If schizophrenia has a genetic cause then one would expect that twins are both likely to be diagnosed as schizophrenic. This is indeed what the evidence shows. The most famous study was carried out by Gottesman and Shields (1972) who, from the histories of 45,000 people treated at two hospitals in London between 1948 and 1964, contacted 57 schizophrenics with twins who agreed to be studied. They found that 42 per cent of the identical twins had schizophrenia, as did 9 per cent of the non-identical twins. The prevalence of schizophrenia in the general population is about 1 per cent and so these results suggest that the closer two individuals are in biological relatedness, the more likely it is that, if one has schizophrenia, then so too does the other. Since the study by Gottesman and Shields there have been a number of such studies and a similar pattern is consistently reported (Heston, 1992). Of course, those who are biologically related are usually brought up together and so share similar environments. Consequently, it is not always clear in such studies that the high rate of concordance is attributable solely to genetic factors. But where investigators have tried to rule out environmental factors by comparing twins brought up together against those brought up apart, it is found that the high rate of concordance holds, even for twins who have been separated early in life (Gottesman, 1991). It is now generally accepted by most psychologists and psychiatrists that schizophrenia has a biological underpinning, although the nature of that underpinning, that is, the precise role of genetic and neurochemical factors, is not yet certain. But this is not to say that genes cause schizophrenia. What the studies suggest is that if one twin has schizophrenia then there is about a 50 per cent chance that the other twin has it too. What this also means is that if one twin has schizophrenia there is around a 50 per cent chance that the other one does not! This fact suggests that, although there may be a genetic vulnerability to the so-called disorder of schizophrenia, other factors seem to be equally important in determining whether or not a person goes on to develop this condition. The question of how factors interact in this way will be revisited in Chapter 7 when we will consider what is known as the diathesis-stress model. But are we able to identify which genes indicate those individuals who are at risk of schizophrenia?

Although some studies have provoked speculation that schizophrenia has a genetic basis, this remains a topic of research and controversy (Boyle, 1993). Scientists have not yet been able to pinpoint an exact gene in the way that Huntingdon's disease has been linked to one single gene. Also, we don't know precisely how genes influence behaviour, although there is much speculation and research on how genes might influence the neurochemistry of the brain. Interestingly, other thinking has led to alternative explanations for schizophrenia, such as the possibility that during pregnancy viral infections such as chickenpox or measles at a time when the brain is forming affect the development of the child (see, for example, O'Callaghan et al., 1991; 1993). Thus, the causes of schizophrenia remain a focus for debate.

Bipolar disorder, or what used to be called manic-depression, is a condition in which individuals experience mania, often alternating with periods of depression. Mania consists of an elevated and expansive mood, perhaps with inflated self-esteem and self-grandiosity, decreased need for sleep, increased talkativeness, racing thoughts, and flights of ideas. About 1 per cent of adults have this condition at some point in their lives and it seems to be equally prevalent among men and women, and across social class. If one twin has this, the other has around a 50 per cent chance of having it too (McGuffin and Katz, 1989). However, as with schizophrenia, at present medical scientists do not know which or how many genes are involved or what the mechanisms are, assuming that there is a genetic predisposition.

The evidence seems to suggest that biological factors are necessary in the development of some psychological problems. In particular, the psychiatric diagnoses of schizophrenia and bipolar disorder appear to be, at least in part, biologically-based. However, it is much less certain for other psychological problems whether biological factors are a cause or are themselves a product of the psychological problem. Psychiatrists and psychologists will be interested in obtaining a history of the client, and will enquire into their family background and whether there is a family history of psychological problems, particularly for patients for whom there is the possibility of a genetic loading (see the case of Matt in Box 2.1 (p. 40)).

Therapies based on the biomedical model

The biomedical model views psychological problems as resulting from physical factors. According to the model, treatment needs to focus on changing the physical state of the person. Three types of therapy will be discussed:

- drug therapy;
- electroconvulsive therapy;
- psychosurgery.

Drug therapy

We probably know more about depression than any other so-called psychiatric disorder. The reason for this is that it is one of the most common of all psychiatric problems and consequently has been the focus of much research interest. Antidepressants were first introduced in the 1950s and heralded the beginnings of psychiatry as we know it today. Drug therapy is now widespread in the National Health Service and millions of prescriptions for drugs to treat psychological conditions are issued every year.

It has already been mentioned that there is evidence showing that depression is associated with low levels of the monoamines serotonin and noradrenaline. Consequently, pharmaceutical companies have manufactured drugs which act to increase serotonin and noradrenaline activity, such as the monoamine oxidase inhibitors (e.g., 'Nardil') and tricyclic antidepressants (e.g., 'Tofranil'). However these drugs have a variety of side effects because, as well as influencing the level of serotonin and noradrenaline in the nervous system, they also influence the activity of other neurotransmitters which are not thought to be connected to depression. Side effects include cardiac arrhythmias and heart block, dry mouth, blurred vision, and urinary retention. For this reason, researchers have been interested in developing drugs that simply influence the level of serotonin and noradrenaline. These more recent antidepressant drugs are called *selective serotonin re-uptake inhibitors* (SSRIs) and *selective serotonin and noradrenaline re-uptake inhibitors* (SNRIs). The best known of these antidepressants is Prozac, which was first introduced in 1987. Around 15 million people worldwide now take this drug. But do antidepressants work? Certainly there is the belief that they are effective in the short term with people suffering from severe depression, but there are concerns about their long-term use and research does not always suggest that antidepressants are more effective than psychotherapy (Moncrieff, 2009).

Also, for those people diagnosed as suffering from bipolar disorder (manic-depression), lithium carbonate, a naturally occurring salt, is often prescribed. Another neurotransmitter, dopamine, has been implicated in schizophrenia. It has been found that drugs which increase the level of dopamine in the brain produce symptoms similar to those found in individuals diagnosed as schizophrenic (e.g., Lieberman et al., 1990) and antischizophrenic drugs which decrease the level of dopamine reduce the symptoms of schizophrenia (e.g., Kleinman et al., 1984). But even though the dopamine hypothesis has attracted much research support, the exact relationship between dopamine levels and schizophrenia remains uncertain.

Box 2.1   Matt

Matt was referred to a psychiatrist through his GP. From reading the referral notes the psychiatrist quickly came to the conclusion that it was possible that Matt was suffering from some form of psychotic illness, possibly a form of schizophrenia or bipolar disorder, with a genetic component. Following a detailed interview with Matt, the psychiatrist ascertained that he did indeed meet the necessary symptom criteria for a diagnosis of schizophrenia. Most prominent were Matt's grandiose and paranoid delusions that he was doing work which was vital to the safety and security of the world. Matt believed that there were governmental and alien forces operating to prevent him from telling the world the truth about the conspiracy between alien beings and Western governments. Matt found it hard to trust the psychiatrist, suspecting that he was in on the conspiracy and part of the plot to silence him. The psychiatrist took a detailed history of Matt's immediate context, finding out about his living arrangements, his relationships with other people, his experiences at school, as well as asking about difficulties that other members of his family had experienced. From careful and systematic questioning of Matt and his parents it turned out that Matt's elder sister had dropped out of university because of problems with her nerves and that an uncle of Matt's had also been hospitalized with a diagnosis of schizophrenia 20 years previously when he was around the same age as Matt. These details helped to confirm in the psychiatrist's mind that Matt was suffering from some form of psychotic illness to which he was genetically susceptible.

Drug therapies are a cornerstone of modern psychiatry. As well as side effects (Moncrieff, 2009), one of the concerns about drug-based treatments is that underlying problems can remain. For example, someone with a fear of flying might take a tranquillizer before a flight, enabling him or her to cope successfully with the journey. However, the effects of the drug will wear off and the fear of flying will remain (O'Sullivan and Marks, 1991). A full discussion of drug therapies is well beyond the scope of this book and interested readers might consult Moncrieff (2009) for a critical introduction.

For people suffering from a psychotic disorder some form of anti-schizophrenic medication would usually be prescribed. Matt was referred by his GP to psychiatric services where he was prescribed a course of neuroleptic medication. A patient with depression might be prescribed a course of Prozac (see Helen's case in Box 2.2 (p. 42)). One of the disturbing things about drug therapies is that they are often prescribed by people such as GPs who, although medically trained, have not trained in psychology or psychiatry and are not qualified as psychological therapists. People who present to the GP and who are put on a course of drugs might sometimes benefit at least as much from counselling and psychotherapy. However, fortunately, this situation seems to be slowly changing as more and more psychological therapists are being employed in community health centres and general practices.

Electroconvulsive therapy

The research discussed above has attempted to understand the cause of psychological problems with the aim of introducing treatments to alleviate the cause. However, other treatments are used to alleviate the symptoms without an understanding of the cause. Electroconvulsive therapy (ECT) involves passing electricity through the brain in order to induce seizure. It was originally introduced in 1938 by Ugo Cerletti and Lucio Bini, based on the observation that epilepsy was rare among schizophrenics and thus, the reasoning went, epileptic seizures might prevent schizophrenia. We now know that epilepsy is not as rare among schizophrenics as was then thought, and that the rationale for this treatment was therefore mistaken. As a treatment for schizophrenia, ECT has been ineffective. But, ECT continues to be used today for severe depression, either bilateral ECT in which electrodes are placed on both left and right temples and electricity is passed through both sides of the brain, or unilateral ECT, where electricity is passed through only one side of the brain. Initially ECT was a very dangerous treatment with patients suffering spasms leading to physical injury. However, during ECT as it used today, the patient is administered a muscle relaxant to prevent the dangerous jerking body movements that occur during convulsion (Weiner and Krystal, 1994). Although there are those who claim that ECT has been of great benefit to them, and there is supportive research evidence, ECT has received a great deal of criticism.

Notably, ECT has been criticized for its lack of scientific basis. It has been likened to hitting the television set when you can't get a clear picture. It has also been criticized for the side effects, for example that it causes memory loss. Furthermore, it has been criticized as being a barbaric and inhumane treatment. But, those who use ECT say that in cases of severe and chronic depression in which other treatments have failed, it is often an effective last resort. Most psychiatrists would probably agree that ECT is highly effective in the treatment of severe and suicidal depression and, unlike other treatments whose effects take time to work, particularly psychotherapy, the effects of ECT are immediate, and in that respect can save lives.

Box 2.2   Helen

Helen has recently broken up with her partner after a relationship of seven years and her GP determines that this event has played a major role in the onset of her depression. Although a short course of antidepressant medication is offered to Helen to help her cope better while she rebuilds her life, her GP also considers that Helen's problems are related to low self-esteem and the way she has appraised the break-up with her partner as proving that she is worthless and unattractive. In the longer term it is thought that she might benefit considerably from counselling and her GP also refers her to the practice counsellor. In the short term, however, Helen finds that Prozac helps her to feel better and more able to function on a day-to-day basis. She is able to continue with work and the GP recommends that she continues taking Prozac for the following six months during which time she also enters into counselling with a therapist at the GP's practice. The GP, in consultation with the counsellor, recommends at the end of the six-month period that she reduces the dosage and gradually comes off Prozac. Meanwhile the counsellor is helping Helen to understand how her self-esteem is tied to her perception of how other people perceive her and how much she succeeds in living up to their expectations of her.

Psychosurgery

As well as drug therapy and ECT, in extreme circumstances psychosurgery might be deemed appropriate. Psychosurgery involves the deliberate destruction of a small part of the brain. Although psychosurgery was once a fairly widespread treatment for psychiatric disorders, it is rarely carried out today. Modern technology means that the surgery is more precise than before, although, not surprisingly, it remains a controversial treatment which can lead to irreversible and negative side effects (Snaith, 1994).

Treatment–aetiology fallacy

One of the issues that all therapists need to be aware of is the *treatment–aetiology fallacy*. It is easy to conclude that, just because a treatment works, this tells us about the cause of the problem. Although this applies to all therapies, it is perhaps easier to see it in relation to medical approaches. For example, even if ECT or drug therapies are effective, this does not mean that the cause of the problem was biochemical. This is the big question. While there can be little doubt that our psychological state is associated with our biological state, what we don't know so well is whether there is a causal relation between the two. As Rowe (2001) put it, taking an aspirin can remove a headache, but it doesn't prove that it was the lack of aspirin that caused the headache! The same is true for psychological problems that are treated with medication. This remains a heated topic:

> We need to keep on remembering and reminding ourselves that scientists have been attempting to prove a biological basis for mental distress – in particular schizophrenia – for decades, but that, to date, no solid, reliable and reproducible evidence has been obtained. This is in spite of the fervent wishes and considerable funding of the pharmaceutical industry, who stand to gain hugely from such proof.
>
> (Gray, 2005a, p. 27)

Conclusion

In summary, the biomedical model suggests that psychological problems represent some underlying disease process, biochemical abnormality, or genetic difference. Forms of treatment considered under the biomedical model are drug therapy, ECT, and psychosurgery. But despite the growing evidence for the role of biological factors in the origins of several so-called psychiatric disorders, there is a saying that anatomy is not destiny. It is important to understand that, although there might be important biological factors in the causes and treatment of some psychological problems, this does not lead us to adopt an attitude of extreme biological determinism. Certainly, there are some who do seem to overemphasize the role of biological factors, but most theorists and researchers understand that it is only through an interaction of biological and environmental factors that psychological difficulties arise. We will return to this topic in Chapter 7 when we go on to look at the biopsychosocial model, and in particular the diathesis-stress point of view. The biomedical paradigm is the foundation block for the profession of psychiatry, although many of the medical model assumptions will also be shared by other mental health professionals such as psychologists. Although psychologists do not often take a wholly biological approach to understanding psychological problems, they will often adopt a medical approach; that is to say they might share the same assumptions about scientific practice and the need for diagnosis in order to formulate an appropriate form of treatment. The *Diagnostic and Statistical Manual* might be used in this respect as an aid to understanding the client's problems.

However, the system of psychiatric classification is not without criticism. For example, there are questions about its reliability and validity, that is, the extent to which different clinicians can reach agreement about what disorder a person is suffering from and exactly what the disorder consists of. As we shall see in Chapter 6, there are those like Szasz who claim that the medical approach to psychological problems also has other more covert social and political aims. One final issue worth considering in the context of medical treatments for psychological problems is the fact that there remains much stigma attached to mental health problems and for some people it is easier to perceive themselves as suffering from a physical problem than from a mental problem. Consequently, for those people, it will be easier to go along to a doctor for biomedical treatment than to a psychological therapist. Nevertheless, the question of whether some experiences represent abnormal workings of the mind is one that we must take seriously.

Summary points

- The biomedical model emphasizes psychological problems as resulting from biological abnormalities or neurochemical imbalance in the brain.
- The biomedical model adopts a medical perspective by attempting to classify the different forms of psychological problems that people may experience. The most widely used classification system is the *Diagnostic and Statistical Manual of Mental Disorders* (DSM) published by the American Psychiatric Association.
- Using DSM, people are assessed on five different axes (areas of functioning): clinical syndromes; life-long personality patterns; medical conditions; psychosocial and environmental problems; and a global assessment of functioning.
- Classification is the fundamental tool of scientific enquiry and the biomedical model has a rich history of experimental investigation. The main tool of scientific enquiry is the randomized control trial (RCT) which is used to test for the efficacy of new treatments.
- Much research evidence exists to support the idea that biological functioning is associated with psychological functioning. There is evidence that biochemical imbalances are associated with so-called psychiatric disorders such as depression, anxiety, schizophrenia, and bipolar disorder. However, the causal relationship between biochemical factors and psychological problems is less clear.
- There is also evidence from twin studies suggesting that there may be a genetic vulnerability for some people to develop psychiatric disorders,

although it is emphasized that scientists do not know exactly how genes are involved in the development of schizophrenia or other so-called disorders.

- Therapies based on the biomedical model are most often drug-based therapies which aim to redress the neurochemical imbalance in the brain. Evidence shows that drug therapies can be effective in alleviating symptoms and in helping people to cope, but symptoms can return once the person is no longer taking the drug and underlying problems are not addressed.
- Although drugs might help to alleviate psychological distress, this does not prove that the distress was caused by a biochemical imbalance.
- Other therapies include electroconvulsive therapy (ECT) and psychosurgery. These are more controversial treatments involving passing electric shocks through the brain and surgery to the brain, respectively, and are not commonly used today.

Topics for reflection

1. What do you understand by the term medical model?
2. The use of psychiatric classification is controversial. Make a list of the advantages and disadvantages of classification.
3. Some therapies such as ECT are claimed to be helpful, but we don't understand why they might work. Should we use treatments even if we don't understand why they work?

Chapter 3

Psychoanalytic and Psychodynamic Approaches

Introduction

Like the biomedical model, the psychodynamic model assumes that problems in living have causes which are internal to the person. But rather than emphasizing biological causes, the psychodynamic model emphasizes psychological causes. For this reason, the psychodynamic approach offered something very different from what went before, and it set the stage for the humanistic, cognitive, and behavioural approaches that were to follow. The psychodynamic model is the oldest and the best known of the psychological models. Psychodynamic theorists believe that unconscious dynamic forces largely determine behaviour, and that psychological problems are the result of conflict between these forces. Such conflicts, it is thought, have their roots in early life experiences and the relationship with the caregiver in the first years of life. Sigmund Freud has been called the grandfather of the psychodynamic approach and it is his ideas which chiefly concern us here. Freud's work was important because he was able to show that problems in living had meaning and pattern which could be understood by an observer.

Sigmund Freud and the psychoanalytic model

The psychodynamic model was introduced at the end of the nineteenth century in Vienna by Sigmund Freud (1856–1939). Freud first introduced this idea as a way of explaining *hysteria*, a condition in which physical symptoms are experienced but no organic cause can be found. For example, someone suddenly can't see or can't hear but yet there seems to be no physical explanation for these symptoms. In such a case, Freud would have said that the cause was psychological, perhaps the person is trying to block out something that is distressing to him or her, something that he or she can't bear to confront and to acknowledge. So, first, let us look at psychoanalytical theory and the work of Freud.

Psychoanalytical theory

In 1885 Freud studied hypnosis in Paris with the famous neurologist Jean Charcot, then returned to Vienna to work with Josef Breuer (1842–1925). Breuer, at that time, was conducting experiments on hypnosis and what was then called 'hysterical illness', that is, physical complaints which seemed to have no biological cause. In one of the most famous studies, Breuer had been treating a woman called 'Anna O' and it was through this case that psychoanalysis was born.

The case of Anna O

Anna O was a young educated woman who suffered from various symptoms including physical weakness, paralysis and deafness. She had fallen ill while caring for her father, who was severely ill. Over time she developed a dual personality. One personality spoke German and the other English. She would fall into a hypnotic trance during which her symptoms disappeared, she talked of past traumatic experiences, and was able to express strong emotions, which, Breuer argued, was therapeutic in her recovery. This was the important discovery that Breuer made: that physical symptoms could be removed through the verbal expression of feelings and ideas. An example of this phenomenon was Anna O's difficulty in swallowing water, which reportedly disappeared after she recounted to Breuer her disgust at seeing a dog drinking water from a glass. Anna O called this her 'talking cure' and the method became known as the 'cathartic method', a term derived from the Greek word *katharsis* meaning purgation. Also, what was important was that these observations implied that psychological problems had meaning which was determined by principles of cause and effect.

Breuer and Freud went on to investigate a number of other cases and together proposed that hysterical illnesses were caused by psychological conflicts outside of conscious awareness which had their roots in traumatic experiences that were most often sexual in nature. By bringing these conflicts into conscious awareness, Breuer and Freud argued, the symptoms of hysterical illness would diminish. Although Breuer and Freud later went on to disagree over these ideas, they provided the foundation stone for Freud's later work and he continued to explore the nature of the unconscious mind and the role of early experiences for the rest of his life.

Through his work with Breuer, Freud initially developed an interest in hypnosis, seeing it as a tool through which people could recall forgotten traumatic memories. However, fairly early on in his career Freud dropped hypnosis as a method of treatment, although he continued to have his patients lying on a couch, and focused on developing ways in which he could help patients bring to consciousness their previously unconscious conflicts. Over time, Freud came to see hypnosis as unnecessary in the recall of forgotten traumatic memories, developing other methods to accomplish this process. Freud discovered that people actively resisted remembering traumatic and unpleasant events. People 'repressed' their memories. It was in 1896 that Freud first used the term 'psychoanalysis' to describe his methods, and in 1900 he published what is perhaps the most well known of all his works, *The Interpretation of Dreams*, which was followed the subsequent year by *The Psychopathology of Everyday Life*. During the rest of his life, Freud published voraciously on psychoanalysis, with his last book, *An Outline of Psychoanalysis*, being published in 1940. Thus, Freud can be credited with introducing the first psychological theory of abnormal behaviour, a theory that drew attention to the role of early childhood experiences and unconscious mental forces within the person. Such an approach was a dramatic shift in perspective from the biological treatments that were dominant at the time.

Many would argue that the importance of Freud's work was to draw attention to the unconscious and how this part of the human mind influenced behaviour. Within the unconscious, Freud argued, are instinctual elements which are inaccessible to the conscious mind, along with other material which has been censored or repressed but which affects consciousness indirectly. Today, therapists of all persuasions make good use of this or some similar distinction between experiences that we are conscious of and experiences which lie outside our conscious recollection. Freud distinguished the unconscious from the conscious and the preconscious. The conscious is what we are aware of at any given moment and the preconscious is material that we are not consciously aware of but which is accessible to conscious introspection. Thus, the essence of psychoanalysis is that psychological problems are a result of unconscious conflicts between different parts of the personality. Freud viewed personality as being divided into three parts, which he called the id, the ego, and the superego.

The id, the ego, and the superego

Freud believed that human personality is composed of three structures – the *id*, the *ego*, and the *superego* – and that behaviour is the product of interaction between these structures. The id is that part of personality

that we are born with and which consists of basic biological, instinctual, urges towards sex, food, warmth, elimination; urges that are unconscious. Freud described the id as a 'cauldron of seething excitement'
(Freud, 1933, pp. 103–4). The id was further divided into two basic
instincts, an instinct towards life which Freud called *eros*, and an instinct towards death which Freud called *thanatos*. However, it was eros
that Freud was chiefly concerned with and he viewed this force towards
life as mainly consisting of sexual energy which he called the *libido*. It
was only later in his career that Freud began to explore thanatos. The
id seeks immediate gratification and operates on what Freud called the
pleasure principle (that is, always seeking gratification). Gratification is
achieved, Freud thought, through reflex activity such as when an infant
receives milk from the mother's breast. However, if immediate gratification is not forthcoming, then gratification is obtained through generat-
ing fantasies of what is desired (that is, the generation of an image or a
memory of the desired object, in this case the mother's breast) through
what Freud called *primary process* thinking. Gratification of id impulses
through primary process thinking is known as wish fulfilment. Thus, the
id is a deep reservoir of basic sexual and aggressive impulses and desires
that resides in the unconscious.

In contrast to the id, which operates at the unconscious level, the ego
resides in the preconscious and is part of conscious awareness. It begins
to develop, Freud thought, out of the id at around six months after birth.
The infant comes to recognize that not all instinctual needs are met. For
example, the mother is not always there to provide for the infant. So,
part of the id becomes differentiated into the ego which also seeks gratification. However, the function of the ego is to confront reality through
secondary processes of planning and decision making. The ego operates
on the basis of what Freud called the *reality principle* because it strives
to meet the constraints of what gratification is obtainable and the demands of the id.

The third part of personality – the superego – is concerned with social and moral standards. The superego consists of introjections from
caregivers and operates within the unconscious, preconscious, and, to a
greater extent than the ego, within the conscious (see Figure 3.1). The
superego develops out of the ego and has two parts. First, the conscience
which reminds us that certain thoughts, feelings, or behaviours are right
or wrong, good or bad. The second is the *ego ideal* which is a composite
of all the values we have acquired and an image of the type of person we
are striving to become. The ego ideal part of the superego rewards moral
or ethical behaviour with feelings of pride.

Thus, Freud viewed psychological problems as resulting from intra-
psychic conflict between these different parts of personality which form

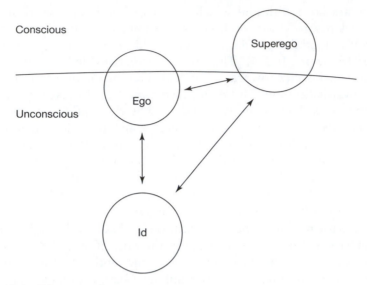

Figure 3.1   Id, ego, and superego

a closed energy system, with the three parts battling for their share of the id's energy. When we use the term 'psychodynamic' today we are referring to the interplay of these forces. For example, imagine the hypothetical conversation between the id, ego, and superego of a boy standing in a sweet shop:

Id	'I'll put the sweets in my pocket and just walk out of the shop.'
Ego	'I could do that, but tomorrow I get my pocket money and I could come back then.'
Superego	'And I know that it isn't right to just take things that don't belong to you.'

The conflict between the forces, Freud believed, is always there. It is when these forces are balanced that psychological health is present. The idea of balance between these instinctual forces is reminiscent of Hippocrates' humoural theory, which was discussed in Chapter 2.

Whenever id impulses demand gratification and the ego cannot allow these impulses to surface into consciousness, the ego experiences intense anxiety. The superego in turn can attempt to control id impulses by flooding the personality with guilt feelings. As well as producing psychological discomfort, unconscious processes can produce physical complaints. Most notably, Freud discussed what he called *conversion disorder*, which is a physical symptom, such as blindness, that has no biological cause but instead is the conversion of unconscious psychological conflict.

Psychosexual development

Freud also viewed personality as being formed through four separate stages of *psychosexual development*. In the first to second year of life, the principal erogenous zone, Freud argued, was the mouth. Thus, the first stage is the *oral* stage which occurs during the first year when the infant derives most gratification through id impulses of sucking and feeding. Between the second and third years of life, Freud argued, the anal area provides the major source of pleasurable stimulation. Thus, the second stage is the *anal* stage in which pleasure moves to the retention and elimination of faeces. The third stage is the *phallic* stage, which takes place between the age of three to six when pleasure comes mostly from genital self-manipulation and children notice that the genitals of boys and girls are different. At around five to six years, the child's sexual motivations, Freud argued, begin to recede in importance. It is as if the child's sexual drive has become inactive. Now the child is preoccupied with developing skills and engaging in new activities. The *latency* stage, as it is called, continues until around the age of 12 and the onset of puberty. After puberty, Freud argued, comes the *genital* stage during which adult sexuality emerges and most pleasure is derived from heterosexual relationships (see Table 3.1).

Healthy psychological functioning, Freud believed, was the result of successful and normal progress through each of these stages. Adult personality is determined by this process of development. So, for example, the age of toilet training will be related to later personality. If a child is toilet trained too early he or she will develop what are termed anal personality characteristics, that is, being overly tidy, orderly, mean, and obstinate. Likewise, early weaning is associated with what are termed oral personality characteristics, that is, a love of eating and drinking, pessimism, guilt, and dependence (see Table 3.2). Certainly, these are intriguing suggestions as to why some people seem to possess more of certain characteristics than others. Some researchers have developed questionnaires to assess these two personality types – the oral and the anal – and have tried to test whether people with more of one characteristic do

Table 3.1   Freudian psychosexual stages of development

Age (years)	Stage	Source of libidinal pleasure
0–2	Oral	sucking
2–3	Anal	retention and elimination of faeces
3–6	Phallic	self-manipulation of genitals
6–12	Latency	sexual motivations recede
12–	Genital	adult sexuality begins to develop

Table 3.2   Personality characteristics related to the failure to move successfully through the five stages of psychosexual development

Problems	Stage
Dependency, narcissism, guilt, depression, dependence on others, mistrust, eating problems, excessive smoking, drinking	Oral
Obsessive-compulsive behaviour, focus on tidiness, orderliness, obstinacy, stubbornness, sadomasochism	Anal
Gender identity problems, antisocial personality, self-depreciation, self-aggrandizement, problems in romantic relationships	Phallic
Problems of self-control, either inadequate or excessive	Latency
Identity diffusion	Genital

indeed have different childhood experiences. But the findings are mixed, with some studies providing evidence in support of Freud's ideas, other studies showing no associations, and yet other studies showing the complete opposite to what Freud claimed. So, there is no compelling scientific evidence to support these ideas.

The most difficult stage to move through, Freud believed, was the phallic stage. During the phallic stage, the child is filled with sexual desire for the opposite sex parent, a desire which is so threatening, because of fear of punishment from the same sex parent, that the child pushes the conflict into the unconscious. Freud referred to this conflict as the *Oedipus complex* when referring to boys and the *Electra complex* when referring to girls. As this element of Freud's theory is so central to psychoanalysis it is worth spending a little more time looking at it.

Oedipus complex

Boys at the phallic stage, Freud proposed, develop a sexual attachment to their mother and want to possess her sexually. The father is seen by the young boy as a sexual rival. This is what Freud called the *Oedipal dilemma*, after the Greek tragedy *Oedipus Rex*. Consequently, Freud suggested, the boy fears that his father wants to take vengeance on him, that the father will castrate him (*castration anxiety*) and in turn the boy also wants to kill his father. But the father is too powerful and so the boy must either disguise this desire by identifying with the father or by identifying with the mother. Identification with the father allows the boy to sleep with his mother in fantasy and so he obtains vicarious gratification. When the boy gives up his desire for his mother and instead starts to identify with his father, the conflict is resolved. The result is a strong superego as the boy identifies with his father and his father's values. If the conflict is not resolved, however, the foundations for psychological problems in adulthood are laid. The other way of resolving the conflict, identification with the mother, leads the boy to sleep with his father in fantasy. Although this disguises his jealousy of his father, the boy, in giving free rein to the homosexual tendencies which Freud believed all males have, is setting the stage for later disturbances.

Electra complex

For girls during the phallic stage there is the recognition that they do not have a penis. This results in horror and rejection of the mother as she too does not have a penis. Girls develop an attraction towards the father who they hope will provide the penis they lack. Freud called this the *Electra complex* after the character in Greek mythology who seeks to murder her mother to avenge her father. Because girls don't have a penis they don't suffer castration anxiety as boys do, and therefore are not similarly motivated to develop a strong superego. Hence, reasoned Freud, women are more emotional than men. These unconscious forces can be so distressing to the person that, Freud argued, there are a variety of defence mechanisms that are called into play to protect the person. Some of these will be discussed below.

Defence mechanisms

Neurotic anxiety, according to Freud, was a result of such repressed conflicts as those discussed above, and the fear of the consequences if a punishable id impulse was to be expressed. Neurotic anxiety was to be distinguished from objective anxiety – the ego's reaction to realistic danger – and moral anxiety – fear of the superego's punishment for transgressing moral standards. Freud went on to describe how neurotic anxiety and guilt were dealt with, by unconsciously distorting reality through the use of various *defence mechanisms* such as *repression*, *projection*, and *displacement*. The most important defence mechanism discussed by Freud was that of repression, that is, keeping unacceptable impulses unconscious. However, the repressed wish still exists and so can cause neurosis. Other defence mechanisms are therefore used to allow the repressed wishes to be released in a way in which they are not recognized. For example, projection might involve thinking that someone else wants to sleep with the mother. A range of defence mechanisms are listed in Table 3.3. Whether or not they have their roots in childhood experiences and represent the conflict between the unconscious forces discussed earlier remains uncertain, and perhaps even unlikely in some cases.

Table 3.3   Some ego-defence mechanisms

Denial
Refusing to face reality, behaving in a way that suggests the person is unaware of something he or she might be expected to know, e.g., refusing to accept that smoking is related to cancer, or blocking a painful experience from memory.

Repression
Prevention of painful, unacceptable, and dangerous thoughts and emotions from entering consciousness, e.g., a person who has been assaulted cannot remember what happened, or a man fails to recognize his attraction for his daughter-in-law.

Projection
Attributing one's own unacceptable negative thoughts and feelings to another, e.g., an employee who is angry at his boss because he is convinced that his boss is angry at him, or a teacher who is attracted to her student perceives that the student is attracted to her.

Reaction formation
Preventing the awareness of unacceptable desires by the adoption of the opposite behaviour, e.g., someone who is sexually attracted to another person acting towards them in a cold and hostile way, or someone who is strongly attracted to homosexual behaviour expressing strong homophobic attitudes.

Displacement
Venting feelings on less dangerous substitute people or objects, e.g., feeling angry with a colleague at work and then coming home to shout at the children, or smashing a plate during an argument with one's spouse.

Intellectualization
Cutting off from emotional awareness, e.g., a person talking about a life-threatening situation in a cold and calm way.

Regression
Reverting to an earlier developmental level in which behaviour is less mature, e.g., sulking like a child during an argument, or having a temper tantrum when things do not go the way we want them to.

Identification
Affiliating oneself with a group or another person often perceived to be of high standing, e.g., an insecure young man emulating a movie idol who is known for a particular style of dress.

Sublimation
Channelling frustrated energy into socially acceptable activities, e.g., an aggressive and conflictual woman who becomes a police officer.

Rationalization
Making socially acceptable explanations that are based on unacceptable motives in order to justify behaviour or to conceal disappointment, e.g., after being sexually rejected deciding that the other person was unattractive anyway, or after failing to be offered a job deciding that you didn't really want it anyway.

In the previous chapter, the psychiatric disorder of schizophrenia was described and the biomedical explanation discussed. So, how can Freudian theory explain the so-called psychiatric disorder of schizophrenia? One possibility is that, when the ego becomes overwhelmed by the demands of the id or is besieged by overwhelming guilt from the superego, the person regresses to an earlier developmental stage, that is, the oral stage of psychosexual development. Remember that this is the stage in which the child has not yet learned to separate itself from the world around it. At this stage, the infant is the centre of experience, and so the adult regressed to this stage might manifest what we would see as delusions of self-importance. Fantasy and reality become confused, which might manifest as unusual perceptual experiences, paranoid ideation, and magical thinking.

We also saw that the biomedical model proposes that depression is caused by an imbalance of certain neurotransmitters in the brain. How would Freudian theory explain depression? Freud (1917) noted that there was a similarity between grieving and depression, and argued that depression was a grief process in relation to a real or imagined loss that was reminiscent of losses incurred in childhood. In summary, Freud suggested that psychological suffering was due to inner conflicts of which the person is not consciously aware because of various defence mechanisms. Conflicts often date back to childhood and early sexual experience, and through psychoanalysis a person can become aware of these conflicts. Freud's view, therefore, was a psychological one. Freud's focus was primarily on the energy of the id and how this energy was either channelled or transformed.

Criticisms of psychoanalysis

Given the sexually repressive society that existed in Victorian times, we can see just how radical Freud's ideas were. However, they have since become part of the Western world's cultural heritage and inform the way we think about the nature of human personality and psychological suffering. Few would disagree that Freud's ideas, and those of his contemporaries (see Makari (2008) for an excellent historical discussion), have changed how we think about human nature, and at least in this respect he deserves to be credited as one of the most influential thinkers of all time. But this is not to say that everyone would agree that the model he developed to explain human behaviour is correct. Many theorists have proposed reformulations of the psychodynamic model, and others have rejected it outright. One of those who have rejected it is Sutherland (1998) who writes:

One must ask what is the standing of Freudian theory and practice today: I write 'theory and practice' advisedly, since it is important to separate the two. It could be that Freud's theories about human motives and the development of the personality are correct while the therapy has no value. It is also possible that his theories are nonsense while the therapy works – neurotics might, just possibly, be helped by being presented with mythical stories about the origins of their feelings and actions. (p. 139)

As with all of the models presented in this book, each of us must make our own decision on what to think about Freudian theory and psychoanalytical practice. The main criticism is that, contrary to Freud's own claims, his ideas are generally not considered to be scientific. Freud was himself a medical practitioner and was, therefore, well used to the scientific way of thinking that characterized the biomedical model at the time (see Chapter 2). As such, he set out to develop a scientific approach to the study of the mind. But as the profession of psychology developed throughout the twentieth century and the application of science became increasingly rigorous, it became obvious that psychoanalysis could hardly be described as scientific by these new standards. That was the claim of the behavioural psychologists who, as we shall see in Chapter 4, went on to develop the new science of psychology based firmly on observable behaviour. Before moving on to discuss the practice of psychoanalysis itself it is worth exploring this criticism of psychoanalysis further.

Popper and the concept of falsification

A little was said in the previous chapter about the role of scientific inquiry and how traditional research requires the processes that are hypothesized to occur to be measurable in some way. But this is not the whole story. The work of Freud provides an opportunity to say a little more about the nature of scientific hypothesis testing. Freud observed patients within a clinical setting, *then* developed theoretical ideas about how unconscious forces operated to produce disturbances, and then, through a series of further observations of patients who seemed to fit the expected pattern, concluded that there was support for his theories. But there is a major problem with this method: it has no logical basis. If you observe something to happen ten times, it does not follow that it will happen again on the eleventh occasion. What that means is that it is not logically possible to verify the theory.

Modern science is instead based on the concept of falsification developed by Popper (1959). Popper argued that hypotheses should be formulated in such a way that they are capable of refutation. He posited that science should consist of making a clear conjecture that can be shown to be false. An example of this would be the claim that all swans are white. It doesn't matter how many white swans are found; it only takes one black swan to falsify the claim. What scientists endeavour to do is to find the black swan. Thinking back to the previous chapter, this is what Kraft-Ebing did when he injected pus into his patients who had general paresis. If his patients had gone on to develop syphilis it would have shown his conjecture that general paresis was caused by untreated syphilis to be false. What Freud did was to find lots of white swans. This is what critics of Freud mean when they say that his work was not scientific. But is it fair to be critical of psychoanalysis because it is not scientific? Perhaps, as O'Carroll (2002) argues, working psychodynamically is about how people create a life for themselves. It is not about causes and effects and, as such, it is inappropriate to try to apply the same scientific thinking as we are used to in the biomedical approach.

However, some of Freud's conjectures can be tested scientifically. For example, Freud hypothesizes a relationship between toilet training practices and personality development, such that children who are toilet trained too early go on to develop more obsessive personalities. Overall, however, most of his theoretical formulations are complex and do not easily lend themselves to the process of scientific investigation (Fisher and Greenberg, 1996). Sutherland (1998) says that Freud's ideas are generally 'so flexible and imprecise that it is difficult to have faith in any of his detailed interpretations' (p. 140) and perhaps this is most evident when we look at Freud's description of movement through the phallic stage. Clearly, it is not possible to test out these ideas using scientific methodology, and we can see why some might refer to them as nothing but mythical stories. But does it seem so unlikely that a child could have such complex ideas about sexuality? Just because an idea can't be tested scientifically doesn't mean that it isn't true, only that it isn't possible to provide evidence in support of it. Freud's own evidence was from the dreams and free associations of his patients. But although sometimes seemingly convincing we must remember that this is not scientific evidence and, as Sutherland (1998) notes, 'with sufficient ingenuity any chain of associations or any dream can be interpreted in any way one wants' (p. 135).

Another criticism of Freud is that, although his theoretical formulations were thought to tell us about human nature, his observations themselves were largely restricted to middle-class Viennese women between the ages of 20 and 44. Should we therefore dismiss Freud's ideas altogether?

In defence of Freudian psychoanalysis it must be said that, although Freud did attempt to outline some broad inductive principles that apply universally to human behaviour, his work was chiefly concerned with the complex and very personal experiences that do not lend themselves to experimental inquiry. To dismiss Freud because his work falls short of fulfilling standards of inquiry derived from the more inductive physical sciences is to misunderstand Freud and the importance of his approach to practice.

Psychoanalysis

Turning now to practice, Freud's view was that the psychoanalyst's role was to uncover the unconscious conflicts that cause psychological distress, to bring formerly unconscious material into conscious awareness, and to achieve the reintegration of the previously repressed material into the total structure of the personality. Simply treating the symptom, as would happen in behaviour therapy, is not sufficient to lead to cure. Unless the underlying conflict is resolved, another symptom will appear. This is referred to as *symptom substitution*. The client, or analysand in psychoanalytic terms, must achieve insight. To do this, Freud reasoned, the psychoanalyst must encourage free and open expression, and the analysand must express whatever comes to mind. The conventions of ordinary conversation are set aside and the analysand is asked to be completely candid and to tell the analyst whatever comes to mind.

Free association

Free association is the name given to the technique through which the analysand says whatever comes to mind, any thoughts, feelings, or images, no matter whether they seem unimportant, trivial, or offensive. The psychoanalyst listens for clues to what is going on within the person. In response, the psychoanalyst has three main tools: *confrontation*, *interpretation*, and *reconstruction*. Using these techniques, the analysand is directed by the psychoanalyst, in a safe and secure setting, to re-experience repressed unconscious feelings and wishes which were frustrated in childhood.

Confrontation is when the psychoanalyst mirrors what the analysand is revealing through what they say, for example, 'you are denying your anger'. Interpretation is when the psychoanalyst explains the unconscious motives behind the behaviour, motives that often relate to past experience, for example, 'you are denying you are angry because I remind you of your father and if you express your anger you are scared that you will lose the love of your father that you so desperately seek'. Reconstruction uncovers those past experiences, for example, 'when you felt angry as a child your father would turn away from you'.

Resistance and transference

Using the tools of confrontation, interpretation and reconstruction, the psychoanalyst looks for *resistance* in the analysand. Resistance is when the analysand encounters a block in his or her free association, perhaps changing the subject of his or her dialogue to avoid a painful topic. For example, the analysand might be talking about his or her childhood when suddenly he or she changes the topic to some trivial event that happened at work the previous day.

The psychoanalyst is also on the lookout for *transference*. This is when the analysand acts or feels towards the psychoanalyst as if he or she was an important figure from their childhood. Thus, in classical psychoanalysis, the psychoanalyst often sits behind the analysand while he or she lies on a couch. The psychoanalyst uses this to maintain neutrality, an uninvolved stance, a blank screen, on which the analysand is most able to freely express whatever comes to mind. This encourages transference onto the psychoanalyst who in turn promotes insight into the transference. The idea is that the psychoanalyst, a shadowy figure traditionally sitting behind the analysand, becomes a focus for the analysand to transfer thoughts and feelings onto. For example, someone who has been brought up with parents who are rejecting and demanding will relate to the psychoanalyst as if he or she is rejecting and demanding. The psychoanalyst, in seeing this negative transference, will encourage it and explore it with the analysand. It is generally recognized that transference does occur in the psychotherapy setting, as in other contexts too, but it is only within the psychodynamic way of working that it is actively encouraged and made a focus for exploration.

Another method employed by psychoanalysts is the examination of what are known as Freudian slips, or *parapraxes*. Unconscious material sometimes slips out, and according to the psychoanalysts such slips of the tongue can tell us something about our unconscious desires.

Dreams

Another, and perhaps the most important, aspect of psychoanalytic work is the emphasis on dreams. Freud believed that during dreams the defence mechanisms, such as those described above, were less in operation and so dreams could be used to reveal more about the workings of the unconscious. Importantly, Freud distinguished between the *manifest content* and the *latent content* of a dream. The manifest content was consciously recalled whereas the latent content held the symbolic meaning. It was through understanding the latent content rather than the manifest content, Freud argued, that insight could be achieved.

Unconscious wishes, Freud thought, are expressed in dreams, but often these unconscious wishes are too distressing for the person to confront and so they are expressed in symbolic form. Freud described dreams as the royal road to the unconscious and psychoanalysts, as well as psychodynamic therapists, operate on the assumption that through our dreams we are able to catch glimmers of our unconscious and re-pressed fears and wishes. A large part of psychoanalysis is concerned with the interpretation of dreams. Free association is one technique used to uncover the latent content of dreams. Clients are encouraged to say whatever comes to mind, no matter how irrelevant or irrational it seems. The idea is that nothing is censored and through free association we are able to glimpse into the unconscious processes at work.

Psychodynamic therapy

Classical psychoanalysis is a lengthy and time-consuming process and psychoanalysts would argue that several sessions are required every week for several years for deep changes in personality to occur. For this reason, classical psychoanalysis is often impractical and overly expen-sive for most people. Psychodynamic therapists take their main influ-ences from the psychoanalytical and related literature but their way of working is not as time-consuming and lengthy as in classical psycho-analysis. Some of the concepts derived from psychoanalytical ideas also remain popular among therapists of other orientations. Understanding the client's use of defence mechanisms will, for example, be a focus for therapists from a wide variety of therapeutic orientations. But perhaps the psychoanalytic concept which enjoys most attention is transference. Although not all therapists will use the term, all recognize that the past has a way of repeating itself in the present (see Box 3.1).

Neo-Freudian psychodynamic models

A number of other influential thinkers were also involved in the early development of the psychoanalytical school. In this section we will con-sider other influences, beginning with Carl Jung (1875–1961).

Jung and analytical psychology

It was in 1907 that Freud and Jung first met and the two men quick-ly became close friends and collaborators in developing the psycho-analytic movement. Freud saw Jung as his successor as leader of the

Box 3.1 Alex

Alex began to realize that he had to change if he was to keep his friends and job, and after seeking advice from his GP he consulted a local psychotherapist. The psychotherapist worked with Alex for the next two years, helping him to understand how his early experiences were related to his current behaviour. Alex's parents separated when he was a small boy and he continued living with his father. Alex lost contact with his mother and his father remained hostile to her, always criticizing her in front of Alex. Alex found growing up painful and in therapy he struggled to recollect his childhood. He described how his father would drink heavily, coming back drunk at the weekends when he would often shout at Alex and belittle him. Sometimes his father behaved violently and Alex lived in fear of him. Alex's marriage of several years had been very tempestuous and had ended one night after a heavy drinking episode when he returned home to accuse his wife of sleeping with another man. In the ensuing argument Alex had put his fist through the window and threatened his wife. She left the following day.

At first Alex found it difficult to commit himself to regular therapy sessions, frequently phoning up to cancel the day before. He would often accuse the therapist of thinking belittling thoughts about him. The therapist was aware of how Alex was behaving towards him, as if he, the therapist, possessed the same characteristics as Alex's father. Through exploring this transference reaction, Alex began to understand how he often did this with people who reminded him of his father, how he expected to be belittled and teased and would react defensively to other people. In therapy, Alex began to understand how he dealt with this situation as a child through repressing his feelings, how he had used alcohol to help him regulate his emotions, and how as an adult his aggression was a way of displacing the feelings that would rise up in him. Through exploring his childhood, Alex began to understand how his feelings of rage were connected to his experiences of childhood, his anger with his mother for leaving and his fear of his father.

psychoanalytical movement and Jung became the first president of the International Psychoanalytical Society. However, Jung saw Freud as holding entrenched ideas and resisted the move to make him Freud's successor, simply to go on promoting Freud's ideas. Jung had his own ideas and around 1914 the collaboration and friendship ended. Jung resigned as the president of the International Psychoanalytical Society. The split was due, among other reasons, to a major point of disagreement on the nature of libidinal energy and infantile sexuality as the cause of neurosis. Whereas Freud saw the libido as essentially sexual in nature, Jung saw the libido as essentially spiritual. Also, whereas Freud saw libidinal energy as the primary motivating force, Jung saw libidinal energy as only one of several forces operating in the person (see Makari, 2008). For Freud, this was heresy.

Also, whereas Freud was concerned with the development of the child, Jung was also concerned with the development of the person across the life-span. Jung introduced the concept of *individuation*, a process which began at around the age of 40 and involved the person beginning to develop those archetypes within him or herself which up to that point had remained primitive. Individuation was the force for personal growth and the development of the self. The repressed unconscious conflicts discussed by Freud are no longer the central forces for development as they were in adolescence. Jung also wrote extensively about personality and introduced the idea that people differ in personality, some people being more concerned with the internal world, *introverts*, and others being more concerned with the external world, *extroverts*. After the split from Freud and psychoanalysis, Jung went on to develop his own ideas and formulated new techniques of psychotherapy which he called *analytical psychology.*

Although Jung is a major figure in the psychodynamic school, it is worth noting that we will meet him again when we come to examine the transpersonal approach. Jung also proposed the existence of what he called a collective unconscious, a record of human experience which is revealed in the myths that each culture creates, containing universal symbols, narrative themes, or archetypes, that occur time and again in art, religion, and literature. Much of this material, Jung argued, did not come through personal experience but rather through our psychological heritage. In the same way that the body has been shaped by evolution, so too, Jung believed, has the mind.

Alfred Adler and individual psychology

Another early collaborator of Freud and a president of the Vienna Psychoanalytical Society was Alfred Adler (1870–1937). As with Jung, Freud and Adler developed conflicts over theory, with Adler also criticizing Freud's emphasis on sexuality, while Freud criticized Adler's emphasis on the role of conscious processes (see Makari, 2008). Adler emphasized the role of the person's striving for control and power in his or her life, maintaining that early experiences of powerlessness in childhood can lead to later feelings of inferiority in adulthood. The way the person deals with his or her feelings of inferiority, Adler believed, could result

Box 3.2 Alex

The sense of powerlessness experienced by Alex while he was growing up with his father seemed to have played an important role in shaping his adult personality. As a child Alex was often belittled by his father and sometimes was hit quite violently. Alex grew up feeling powerless and inferior. As a child he could not understand his father's behaviour and made the assumption that in some way he must deserve to be treated in this way. Although he is able to look back and say that his father treated him violently for reasons that were nothing to do with Alex himself, even as an adult he still feels inferior to those around him. At work he feels that other people are more competent than him and that what he does is never good enough. Often he will feel criticized even if no criticism is intended, and will react aggressively and defensively to others.

in problems in living. For example, because of a sense of inferiority a person might become withdrawn from others. Alternatively, they might overcompensate by becoming abusive and bullying (see Box 3.2).

Adler and Freud parted company, splitting the membership of the Vienna Psychoanalytical Society, and Adler (1931, 1964) went on to develop a system of therapy which he called *individual psychology*. In individual psychology the core motive of human personality development is a striving for superiority, by which Adler meant that we all create goals for ourselves in life, which give us purpose and which we then strive to attain. We all create an ideal self which represents the perfect person we strive to become; feelings of inferiority in relation to our perfect self are normal and the drive to overcome the sense of inferiority is the stimulus for our striving towards superiority. Adler discussed how women are in an inferior social position to men and how they strive for status, how someone who felt intellectually inferior as a child may strive as an adult to be intellectually superior, perhaps becoming a university professor. Adler also discussed how the position in one's family – birth order – influences lifestyle. Adler emphasized the social nature of human beings and how interpersonal relations and the social context into which we are born, shape the personal goals we choose to strive towards. Problems in living were the result of becoming discouraged from being able to attain the sense of superiority. For example, families characterized by mistrust, resentment, neglect, and abuse produced children who would strive for perfection using selfish goals such as attention seeking, power seeking, and revenge seeking.

   Adlerian therapy involves the patient becoming aware of his or her destructive goals, through consciousness raising. The therapist endeavours to help the patient to become aware of how their behaviour works to make real the fictional goals created early in life. This is done using a lifestyle analysis which consists of understanding the patient's family background, his or her position in relation to siblings, and how the patient came to construct a view of the world. This aspect is similar in some ways to that of the cognitive approach of Ellis and Beck, whose work we will consider in Chapter 4. Furthermore, many of Adler's ideas have been highly influential in later psychological theories (Ellenberger, 1970).

Melanie Klein and object relations

Freud was chiefly concerned with the id and how control over id processes was the core organizing principle for personality, but later psychoanalytical theorists became more concerned with projective and introjective mechanisms. This became known as the *object relations* school of thought. Object relations is mostly associated with the work of Melanie Klein (1882–1960) who published *The Psychoanalysis of Children* in 1932. In this book she detailed the developmental process through which children introject (incorporate) the values and images of important caregivers who were viewed with strong emotional attachment. These object representations (introjected people) become incorporated within the child's ego, leading people to respond to the environment through the perspective of people from their past. Klein (1932) viewed infants as having a need to relate to others, first as part objects (e.g., the breast) and later as whole objects (e.g., the mother). Behaviour is a result of fantasies about these objects. Although several strands of object-relations theory have been developed, all share the idea that early relationships are central to personality and the development of psychological problems (e.g., Fairbairn, 1952; Kernberg, 1976; Kohut, 1971).

Splitting

Early childhood experiences involving, for example, inconsistent messages from parental figures (perhaps being warm and loving inconsistently), lead children to develop insecure egos. The person is unable to incorporate the object representation fully and as a protective mechanism the person uses the defence of *splitting*, in which he or she views objects as all good or all bad. For example, a teacher is seen as wise, caring and all good until she later fails the student, who reacts furiously that the teacher is incompetent, cold and all bad. Therapy involves attempts

> ## Box 3.3 Alex
>
> Splitting is characteristic of Alex's behaviour. The friend that Alex attacked on the evening out had been a close companion of his at work for the last year since he joined the company. At first, they had got on well together and Alex had thought that his companion, John, was a great guy – loyal, trustworthy, one of the best. But after John had been promoted to a position which involved him commenting on Alex's work, Alex had come to see him as critical, harsh, and someone who just could not be trusted. This was typical of Alex's relationships with other people.

to strengthen the weakened ego and help the client to understand how he or she uses such defences as splitting to regulate their emotions (see Box 3.3).

John Bowlby and attachment theory

Psychodynamic approaches to personality have continued to develop since Freud, and theoretical developments have tended to shift away from an emphasis on innate drives towards an emphasis on relationships. Perhaps most influential of all is the work of Bowlby (1969, 1973, 1980), whose attachment theory emphasized the importance of early relationships. The basic premise is that humans, like other animals, have an inbuilt need to form attachments. He was interested in the way in which the child forms attachments to others, and how these early attachments shape experiences in later life and can result in the development of psychological problems. Bowlby emphasized how parenting involved a delicate balance between neglect and overprotection so that the child was able to undertake appropriate exploratory behaviour and develop a sense of security in the world. A child who does not form a successful bond with his or her primary caregiver grows up to be lacking in trust and unable to form healthy relationships. On the other hand, a child who experiences his or her caregiver as a 'secure base' grows up to be able to trust and form stable relationships. Children, Bowlby suggested, form 'internal working models' that describe their mental representation of their social world.

Bowlby's ideas were further developed by Mary Ainsworth who used a methodology she called the 'strange situation' procedure (Ainsworth et al., 1978). This consisted of putting the child in a specially designed playroom so that observers could watch the child from behind a one-way mirror. The mother left the child in the room, returned, and then left again. By observing children, Ainsworth was able to classify their behaviour into four types:

1. Insecure-disoriented – the child shows a frozen behaviour pattern.
2. Insecure-ambivalent – the child becomes anxious, distressed, and angry, even when the parent returns.
3. Insecure-avoidant – the child seems not to miss the parent, and avoids the parent on their return.
4. Secure – the child shows initial signs of missing the parent, seeks contact when the parent returns, and relatively quickly resumes normal play.

The interesting feature, however, was how Ainsworth was able to link these four patterns to the behaviour of the mother. Insecure children had mothers who were unpredictable, rejecting, and insensitive to the child's needs, whereas secure children had mothers who were responsive and emotionally engaged. There is no single therapeutic school associated with attachment theory. Bowlby was a psychoanalyst and his work fed into the wider development of psychodynamic therapy, but it should be noted that these ideas are also appreciated by therapists across the range of disciplines.

Erik Erikson and ego psychology

Whereas Freud outlined a stage theory of psychosexual development (see Table 3.1), Erik Erikson (1902–1994) offered a psychosocial stage theory of development which emphasized social tasks and their associated conflicts throughout the life-span (Erikson, 1959, 1963) (see Table 3.4). Each of Erikson's stages is dependent on the development of the preceding stage, and the unfolding of each stage is based on two underlying basic assumptions. The first assumption is that:

> the human personality in principle develops according to steps predetermined in the growing person's readiness to be driven forward, to be aware of, and to interact with a widening social radius. (Erikson, 1963, p. 270)

The second assumption is that:

> society, in principle, tends to be so constituted as to meet and invite the succession of potentialities for interaction and attempts to safeguard and to encourage the proper rate and the proper sequence of their unfolding. (Erikson, 1963, p. 270)

Table 3.4 Erikson's psychosocial eight-stage theory

Age	Stage	Virtue
Infancy	Basic trust vs. mistrust	Hope
Early childhood	Autonomy vs. shame and doubt	Will
Play age	Initiative vs. guilt	Purpose
School age	Industry vs. inferiority	Competence
Adolescence	Identity vs. identity confusion	Fidelity
Young adulthood	Intimacy vs. isolation	Love
Adulthood	Generativity vs. stagnation	Care
Old age	Integrity vs. despair	Wisdom

The first stage, *basic trust vs. mistrust,* is one in which the infant develops a sense of trust in the self and the world that is dependent on the quality of care received. If the caregiver is sensitive and responsive to the needs of the infant, who at this stage of life is helpless and dependent on the caregiver, the infant learns to trust in the self and the world. The virtue that results is hope. In the second stage, *autonomy vs. shame and doubt,* the child begins to interact with the world and develops a sense of autonomy, thereby acquiring the virtue of will. In the third stage, *initiative vs. guilt,* the virtue of purpose develops. In the fourth stage, *industry vs. inferiority,* there is a shift from play to work, practical skills are developed and the virtue of competence is achieved. In the fifth stage, *identity vs. identity confusion,* there are questions about the real self as the person faces up to making choices about their values and goals, and the virtue of fidelity is achieved. In the sixth stage, *intimacy vs. isolation,* a sense of independence and adult responsibility develops and the virtue which is established is love. In the seventh stage, *generativity vs. stagnation,* there are concerns with productivity and creativity and the virtue which is established is care. In the eighth stage, *integrity vs. despair,* a perspective on life is sought, with wisdom as the resultant virtue.

Identity

As well as going through the psychosexual stages outlined by Freud, the child also, Erikson suggested, goes through these psychosocial and ego-development stages. Also, in contrast to Freud's stage theory, Erikson's stage theory was concerned with the complete life-span of the person. Furthermore, at each stage, Erikson suggested that there can be positive or negative outcomes. Erikson discussed the crises that occur in development, that is, turning points in a person's life where the person is between progression and regression. Successful resolution of the crisis, Erikson suggested, promotes the particular virtue, or strength, at each stage. Erikson coined the term 'identity crisis' to describe the experiences of the soldiers he was working with in San Francisco in the 1940s (Erikson, 1968). He described them as not knowing who they were and as having lost their shock-absorbing capacities. They were suffering from a range of psychological and physical problems which sound similar to what today's psychiatrists and psychologists would describe as posttraumatic stress disorder (American Psychiatric Association, 2000). According to Erikson, *identity* was a central concept composed of four facets: a conscious sense of one's existence as a distinct entity; continuity between what one has been and what one will be; a sense of wholeness; and a sense of meaning in relation to others (Evans, 1969).

Like the humanistic psychologists we shall consider in Chapter 5, Erikson recognized that the therapist should facilitate the growth and development of the client rather than impose his or her own views. Also, like the humanistic psychologists, Erikson has been criticized by some for the lack of empirical data supporting his observations. Is it really the case that everyone in all parts of the world progresses through the eight psychosocial stages? Erikson's approach is known as ego psychology. Whereas Freud's approach emphasized the role of the id (instincts and conflicts are seen as central in shaping personality and psychological functioning), ego psychology assumes that the ego functions not only as a defence against the workings of the id, but also that the ego strives for mastery of the environment and produces a separate and conflict-free driving force towards adaptation to reality. Perhaps this is most clearly illustrated by considering the Freudian latency period. Whereas Freud did not view the latency period as important in shaping personality, Erikson viewed the latency period as one in which the person strives to develop a sense of industry, the failure of which leads to a sense of inferiority. Failure and success at developing a sense of industry was largely determined, Erikson believed, by cultural forces, for example, through discrimination of race, sex, religion, some individuals grow up lacking a sense of industry (Erikson, 1963). There are therefore parallels with the sociocultural theorists, who we shall consider in Chapter 6. Other theorists who were important in developing ego psychology were Hartmann (1958) and Rapaport (1958), but Erikson is probably the best known of the ego psychologists.

However, returning to the central theme of this chapter on psychodynamic approaches, we are left with the question of whether or not the therapeutic techniques which have grown out of this model are indeed effective for clients in distress.

Does psychodynamic therapy work?

As we have seen, the psychodynamic approach has been mostly criticized for its lack of scientific rigour. Notable critics are Sutherland (1992) and the behavioural psychologist, Hans Eysenck, who argued that Freud's theories are not only sufficiently vague to make them scientifically untestable, but also based on the study of a limited number of people from whom it is not possible to generalize to all human beings (see Eysenck and Wilson, 1973). These are well-worn criticisms familiar to several generations of psychologists and, as we have seen, there is at least some validity to their arguments. However, even if the theories themselves are scientifically difficult to test, we can still ask, using the scientific method, whether psychodynamic therapy works.

Currently, the National Institute for Health and Clinical Excellence (NICE) – the independent organization that reviews evidence for treatments and provides guidelines for practice followed by the National Health Service (NHS) – recommends psychodynamically-based treatments for depression when there are complex comorbidities, eating disorders, and in helping health professionals to understand the experience of service users with a diagnosis of schizophrenia (Khele, 2008).

Traditionally, psychodynamic approaches have been concerned with helping people in distress, but in recent years they have also been applied to the new field of coaching psychology. As with therapy, it is important in psychodynamic coaching for clients to understand the unconscious drivers of their behaviour, and it is claimed to be particularly useful for clients who want to develop interpersonal skills, enhance self-understanding, and to overcome self-defeating behaviour (Roberts and Brunning, 2007).

Conclusion

It might be argued that the importance of the psychodynamic perspective introduced by Freud was that it showed that psychological processes rather than biological processes can result in psychological problems. The legacy of Freud is that we have an understanding that unconscious motives and defence mechanisms influence behaviour and that early childhood experiences influence adult personality adjustment. Freud argued that problems in living are the result of fixation at early developmental stages, and excessive use of defence mechanisms; and that, through psychoanalysis, repressed wishes and feelings can be brought to the surface and dealt with in a more mature way. Although Freud's ideas have attracted much attention, much of this has been critical. In particular, the idea that sexual and aggressive impulses are the basis for human behaviour has been questioned. Several subsequent writers in the psychodynamic tradition have offered competing theoretical approaches which emphasize other impulses. Furthermore, it has been suggested that any theory must be falsifiable; otherwise it is scientifically of little value. Much of Freud's work does not lend itself to testing. For example, how are we to test whether there is the hypothesized psychic structure of id, ego, and superego? Others have suggested that the weakness of Freud's work was that he based his ideas on a small number of women living in a sexually repressive society. Many feminist theorists have been outraged at some of Freud's ideas, which they have seen as sexist.

Nevertheless, today many therapists would describe themselves as psychodynamic and there are a variety of different training courses available for people who are interested in working professionally in this area. Although training as a psychoanalyst is lengthy and requires one to undergo years of personal therapy, many therapists use psychodynamic techniques in their work. The concept of transference in particular remains a useful one to therapists from all orientations. Also, despite the various criticisms that are made of psychoanalysis and psychodynamic approaches in general, there is no doubt that they can provide those of us interested in human behaviour with a rich source of ideas.

Summary points

- Like the biomedical model, the psychodynamic model assumes that the causes of psychological problems are internal to the person. The psychodynamic model suggests that this is the result of conflict between unconscious forces.
- Freud introduced the psychodynamic model. He suggested that the human personality is composed of three structures: the id, the ego, and the superego. Problems resulted from conflict between these three forces.
- Freud also described stages of psychosexual development and how problems resulted if a person did not progress successfully through these stages. Many problems in adult life are thought to have their roots in the phallic stage of a child's life.
- Freud also discussed how people use defence mechanisms such as repression by which a person keeps unacceptable impulses or painful memories from entering consciousness.

- Freud's ideas have attracted many followers, as well as harsh criticism from scientific psychologists who are concerned that Freud's ideas are not capable of refutation, which is the foundation of the scientific method.
- Freud also introduced psychoanalysis, a form of intensive long-term therapy which aims to bring unconscious material into conscious awareness through the use of such techniques as free association and the exploration of the transference relationship between therapist and client.
- Although psychoanalysis in the form described by Freud is rare today, many therapists work using similar techniques and ideas drawn from psychoanalytical thinking, such as transference, and would describe themselves as psychodynamic therapists.
- Psychodynamic therapists are not only influenced by Freud, but by many other theorists subsequent to Freud such as Jung, Adler, Klein, and Erikson.
- Although many of the ideas generated by psychodynamic theorists lack scientific support, evidence suggests that psychodynamic therapy can be helpful.

Topics for reflection

1. The basic premise of the psychodynamic approach is that much of human behaviour is driven by unconscious forces. The conscious mind has been referred to as only the tip of the iceberg, so if we really want to understand our motivations in life we have to bring the unconscious to consciousness. Do you agree that this is true?
2. Critics of psychoanalysis have claimed that it is not scientific. Do you agree that this is a valid criticism? Is it important that therapy is scientific?
3. Looking at the range of defence mechanisms, can you think of instances in your own life when you have used one or more of these?

Chapter 4

Behavioural and Cognitive Approaches

Introduction

In this chapter the behavioural and the cognitive models will be introduced. In contrast to the psychodynamic model, which, as we have seen in the previous chapter, emphasizes unconscious forces, the behavioural model emphasizes the observable behaviour of people. The reason for this shift in emphasis, as I shall go on to describe in more detail, came partly as a response to the early criticisms of psychoanalysis. A major criticism was that psychoanalysis had failed in its aspiration to be a science of the mind. Thus, the founders of behavioural psychology were concerned that their approach should be grounded securely in scientific thinking, and that their theories would be amenable to measurement and scientific testing. Despite their differences, however, both the psychodynamic and behavioural models present a deterministic view of human functioning. In the behavioural model environmental factors are thought to shape our behaviour and our behaviour is the sum of all we have learned. However, over time many began to think that the behavioural model was limited in its explanatory power and so cognitive determinants of behaviour began to be introduced, resulting in a synthesis of the two approaches – what is known as the cognitive-behavioural model.

Behavioural model

The behavioural model has its roots in academic psychology. Understanding the processes through which learning took place increasingly became a main concern of psychologists in the first half of the twentieth century. As we have seen in the previous chapter, the argument that there was a need for research into the effectiveness of psychotherapy and counselling came about in part because of criticisms of the psycho-dynamic model for its unscientific nature and lack of effectiveness as a therapeutic approach (Eysenck, 1952, 1965). In response to Eysenck's criticisms of psychoanalysis, psychologists began to apply the principles of learning that had been discovered in the laboratory to clinical prac-tice. In contrast to psychoanalysis, which focuses on the internal proc-esses of the person, the behavioural model focuses on the environmental conditions that shape our behaviour. Theorists in the behavioural tradi-tion have emphasized two types of conditioning: classical conditioning and operant conditioning.

Ivan Pavlov and classical conditioning

Ivan Pavlov (1849–1936), a Russian physiologist, is credited with the discovery of a process called *classical conditioning* (sometimes called *Pavlovian conditioning*). Essentially, this is a process of learning by tem-poral association. Simply, what this means is that if two events occur in close succession they become associated and eventually we come to re-spond to one as we do to the other. Pavlov (1928) came across this phe-nomenon while he was studying the digestive process in dogs. As part of his research the dogs were given a meat powder, and Pavlov noticed that after a while the dogs began to salivate when the researchers were about to feed them. Later, it was noticed that the dogs began to salivate when they heard the footsteps of the researchers coming to feed them. Pavlov went on to experimentally test this observation by ringing a bell before the food was brought, finding that the dogs came to associate the sound of the bell with the food and would begin to salivate.

In the language of classical conditioning theory, an unconditional stimulus (UCS) (e.g., food) is a stimulus that automatically produces the unconditional response (UCR) (e.g., salivation). The conditioned stimulus (CS) (e.g., bell) when paired with the UCS (e.g., food) comes to produce a conditioned response (CR) (e.g., salivation) (see Figure 4.1). Although seemingly a simple process, it is one which has far-reaching implications for understanding how psychological problems develop and for therapeutic intervention.

The behavioural model suggests that problems can develop as a re-sult of classical conditioning and that through modifying environmental stimuli, problems can be extinguished. Classical conditioning has been put forward as an explanation for a number of psychological problems, and is now generally accepted as one explanation of why some people develop phobias. The earliest study to demonstrate this was carried out

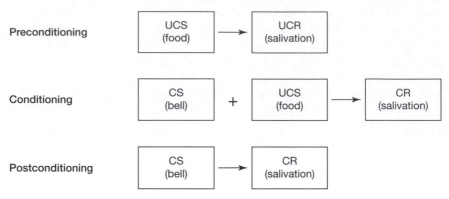

Figure 4.1   The process of classical conditioning

by J. B. Watson (1878–1958) who is today credited with recognizing, in his study of Little Albert, the importance of classical conditioning as an explanation for psychological problems.

The Little Albert study

In the most famous study to illustrate how classical conditioning might lead to the development of phobias, Watson and Rayner (1920) introduced an eleven-month-old boy called Little Albert to a tame white rat. At first, Albert showed no signs of fear and would reach out and touch the rat. However, Watson and Rayner then startled Albert with a loud noise made by striking a hammer upon a steel bar when he reached out to touch the white rat. This procedure was carried out over several days, with Watson and Rayner introducing the rat to the boy and observing his reactions. After a while, Albert showed fear of the white rat and would no longer reach out to touch it. Furthermore, Albert's fear spread to include a white rabbit, cotton wool, a fur coat and other objects similar to the white rat.

Although this study showed that classical conditioning could be used to induce fear, can classical conditioning explain all our fears? Wolpe and Rachman (1960) answer:

Any neutral stimulus, simple or complex, that happens to make an impact on an individual at about the same time a fear reaction is evoked, acquires the ability to evoke fear subsequently ... there will be a generalisation of fear reactions to stimuli resembling the conditioned stimulus.

Psychology as the behaviourist views it

Although by today's standards the study of Little Albert might be seen as ethically questionable and methodologically weak, it was an important study and drew attention to the role of conditioning. Watson (1930) believed that a person's history of conditioning was the main determinant of behaviour:

> Give me a dozen healthy infants, well-formed, and my own specified world to bring them up in, and I'll guarantee to take any one at random and train him to be any type of specialist I might select – doctor, lawyer, artist, merchant-chief, and yes, even beggar-man and thief, regardless of his talents, penchants, tendencies, abilities, vocations, and the race of his ancestors. (p. 104)

While we know that conditioning is important, most would now agree that this is an overly extreme view. Later work did not always find it possible to replicate the Little Albert study and it has been suggested that early writers on conditioning tended to ignore these data in their attempt to replace psychoanalysis with a science of behaviour (Samelson, 1980). As Watson and Rayner (1920) state, somewhat scathingly, towards the end of their paper on conditioned emotional reactions in Little Albert:

> Freudians, 20 years from now, if they come to analyse Albert at that age, will probably tease from him the recital of a dream which will be interpreted as showing that Albert, at three years old, tried to play with his mother's pubic hair and was scolded violently for it. Albert may be fully convinced of the truth of this interpretation of his fear if the analyst has the authority and personality to put it over convincingly. (p. 13)

Watson went on to revolutionize the field of psychology through his emphasis on the study of behaviour, and subsequent generations of psychologists have been taught to be scathing of psychoanalysis. Today, Watson's best-known paper was one he published in 1913 entitled 'Psychology as the behaviourist views it'. In this paper, Watson argued that the science of psychology could only progress if it was concerned with observable behaviour. By making observable behaviour into the focus of study, psychology could aspire to become a science. Mistakenly, however, behaviourism is sometimes seen as a school of thought whose adherents believe that there is no such thing as mental experience. Rather,

Watson's argument was that mental concepts were not observable and therefore were not properly the focus of scientific inquiry. This approach to the study of psychology was, of course, in direct opposition to the study of psychoanalysis. Behavioural approaches assumed that it was not necessary to be aware of one's behaviour or the factors controlling it in order to function effectively (Skinner, 1971). Many psychologists today would still adhere to the view that psychology should be concerned with observable behaviours that can be reliably measured, and, although it is also now common for psychologists to speculate on the unobservable processes of the mind, the influence of Watson in shaping modern psychology as a scientific discipline was great. Unlike psychodynamic therapies, the behaviourist is committed to providing scientific evidence for the effectiveness of the therapy. Other influences, aside from Pavlov and Watson, on the development of behavioural psychology were the important work of Thorndike and Skinner.

B.F. Skinner and operant conditioning

Whereas classical conditioning is concerned with the pairings of an unconditional stimulus with a conditional stimulus to produce behaviour, *operant conditioning* (sometimes called *instrumental conditioning*) is a process that is concerned with how that behaviour is maintained. Edward Thorndike, an American psychologist, noted that when something positive happens to us we tend to repeat what we were doing, and when something negative happens to us we tend not to repeat what we were doing. Thorndike (1898) demonstrated this process by placing a cat in a box that was carefully designed so that the cat had to press a certain lever to escape from the box. The cat was then deprived of food and a piece of fish was placed just outside the box where the cat could see it. Thorndike observed how, although at first its behaviour was erratic as it tried to find a way out of the box, the cat would eventually press the lever, escape, and get the fish. The next occasion the cat was placed in the box, the time it took to press the lever was shorter. On the next occasion, it was shorter still. Eventually, the cat would, on entering the box, very quickly press the lever and escape. Thorndike reasoned that when responses lead to positive consequences, in this case getting the fish, those responses are strengthened and are more likely to occur in the future. However, when responses lead to negative consequences the responses are not strengthened and are less likely to occur in the future. Thorndike called this the *law of effect* and it became a further theoretical cornerstone of behavioural psychology.

B.F. Skinner (1904–1990) took up the work of Thorndike and went on to describe in more detail the relationship between instrumental behaviour and its consequences. Skinner (1953) coined the term *operant conditioning* to describe the process outlined by Thorndike. The idea is that operant behaviour is controllable and voluntary, and that this behaviour can become conditioned by what he termed *reinforcers*. Reinforcers are those environmental situations that increase the frequency and strength of behaviours. There are two types of reinforcement: positive reinforcement and negative reinforcement. Positive reinforcement comes about when the behaviour is followed by the occurrence of a positive event, and negative reinforcement comes about when the behaviour is followed by the omission of a negative event. These two forms of reinforcement are distinguished from punishment, which occurs when the behaviour is followed by the occurrence of a negative event, and which aims to decrease the strength and frequency of a behaviour. Various psychological problems have been approached from the behavioural perspective, and operant conditioning helps to explain the persistence of maladaptive behaviours. Learning contingencies operate over time so that complex behaviour patterns are slowly shaped from childhood onwards (Gewirtz and Pelaez-Nogueras, 1992).

Mowrer's two-factor theory

So, operant conditioning explains the persistence of maladaptive behaviour and classical conditioning explains the formation of the behaviour in the first place. Mowrer (1947) proposed the *two-factor* model of fear and avoidance, in which fear is acquired through classical conditioning (first factor) and maintained through operant conditioning via negative reinforcement (second factor) as the person avoids his or her fear. We can see therefore how these processes can be applied to understanding how problems in living occur. Importantly, operant conditioning and classical conditioning also provide a theoretical framework for developing therapeutic interventions.

Behaviour therapy

The terms 'behaviour therapy' and 'behaviour modification' are sometimes used to refer to treatments based on classical conditioning and operant conditioning, respectively. Historically, the term 'behaviour therapy' was employed by British therapists and 'behaviour modification' by

American therapists, reflecting the different emphasis given to the two forms of conditioning in the two countries. Here, for simplicity, I have used the term 'behaviour therapy' to refer to all forms of therapy based on principles of learning. In behaviour therapy there is seen to be no need to uncover unconscious forces as in the psychoanalytic approach. Rather, the task of the therapist is simply to eliminate those unwanted behaviours which are the result of learning. Behaviour therapy is concerned with: first, removing specific symptoms; second, developing new adaptive behaviours; and third, changing environmental reinforcement contingencies.

Behavioural analysis

The first task of the behaviour therapist is to conduct a *behavioural analysis*. The therapist endeavours to describe the client's maladaptive responses in objective terms and to generate hypotheses about the behavioural and environmental factors that are controlling and maintaining those behaviours. On the basis of the behavioural analysis, the therapist proceeds to design a treatment programme which will consist of manipulating the controlling and maintaining factors in such a way as to modify the maladaptive responses. In classical conditioning, as we have seen, behaviours are controlled by stimuli that come before the response, and in operant conditioning behaviours are controlled by stimuli which come after the response. Based on these theories, behaviourists have attempted to explain a variety of psychological problems.

A classic example of behaviour therapy is that used by Mowrer and Mowrer (1938) to treat children with bed-wetting problems. Using the principles of classical conditioning, Mowrer and Mowrer developed the 'bell and pad' method to treat nocturnal enuresis. It was hypothesized that nocturnal enuresis resulted from the child not associating a full bladder with waking up, so Mowrer and Mowrer developed a moisture sensitive blanket which triggered an alarm bell when urination took place. Thus, over time, the child came to associate having a full bladder with waking up.

As we will see, however, behaviour therapies seem most applicable to anxiety-related problems. First, let us look at some of the specific therapeutic techniques which have been developed on the basis of learning theory, notably, systematic desensitization, flooding, aversion, and modelling. These techniques are based on the principle of classical conditioning. The principle of exposure to the feared or threatening situation, either in imagination or in reality, is the theme that runs throughout these behavioural approaches.

Joseph Wolpe and systematic desensitization

Joseph Wolpe was a South African psychiatrist who developed a technique called *systematic desensitization*. Wolpe viewed neurotic behaviour as consisting of persistent habits of conditioned behaviour, acquired in anxiety-generating situations. Systematic desensitization is based on the principles of classical conditioning. Recall the case of Little Albert, the child whom Watson and Rayner (1920) used to show that a fear of white rats could be conditioned. Shortly afterwards, another study was published by Jones (1925) regarding a boy called Little Peter, showing that once fears had been conditioned, they could also be alleviated using the principles of classical conditioning – for example, by pairing the feared object with a desirable response such as food. Following this line of enquiry, Wolpe (1958) assumed that fears could be unlearned and set out to devise a technique, which he called systematic desensitization, to help people unlearn their fears. Systematic desensitization has three stages:

1. Relaxation training;
2. Construction of a fear hierarchy;
3. Learning process.

The idea behind systematic desensitization is that feeling anxious is incompatible with feeling relaxed, so the client is first taught to use relaxation techniques. Once these have been learned, the client is helped to develop his or her own hierarchy of fear. So, for example, a person with a phobia is asked to construct a list of things he or she finds frightening, starting with the thing that he or she is most fearful of and ending with the thing of which he or she is least fearful. An example of a fear hierarchy is shown in Table 4.1 for a person who is fearful of social situations.

The learning process requires the person to maintain his or her state of relaxation and imagine the least fearful event. When this has been accomplished successfully, the client moves on and repeats the process, imagining the next most fearful event while in a state of relaxation. Eventually, the client learns to maintain his or her relaxed state even when imagining the most fearful event in the hierarchy. When desensitization is carried out in this way it is called *imaginal desensitization*, which is in contrast to *in-vivo desensitization* which involves the person gradually being exposed to real-life fears. For example, someone with a fear of going outside (agoraphobia) might, with the therapist's help, start off by opening the front door, progress through taking a few steps outside, right up to going on a trip to the shops. Many studies have been carried out to assess the effectiveness of this treatment for different fears

Table 4.1   Systematic desensitization hierarchy

	Degree of fear experienced
Saying hello to someone you know on the way to the shops	very low
Stopping to have a five-minute conversation with someone	low
Giving a short and informal talk to some colleagues at work	moderate
Attending a job interview	high
Giving a talk to a large group of people you don't know	very high

and phobias, and the evidence suggests that it does indeed seem to work (e.g., Kazdin and Wilcoxin, 1976), although research has shown that the relaxation component of the treatment may not always be necessary (Wolpe, 1990). It is the element of exposure to the feared or unwanted situation that seems to be most effective in helping people to overcome their difficulties and which, as we shall see, has come to be an important element running though behavioural procedures.

Flooding

Another treatment based on classical conditioning is that of *flooding*. Like systematic desensitization, flooding involves exposure to the feared object, but in contrast to systematic desensitization, flooding does not involve gradual exposure to the feared object. Instead, the person is exposed to the feared stimulus at full intensity without relaxation. The rationale is that this eliminates anxiety through the process of extinction, that is to say, the conditioned stimulus is repeatedly presented without avoidance until the unconditioned response is no longer produced (Wolpe, 1990). Usually, when we have a fear of something, we avoid it and so extinction does not take place. Flooding can be extremely anxiety provoking, and for some a form of graded exposure can be used to avoid the intense anxiety. Graded exposure is essentially the same as flooding except that exposure to the threatening or feared object is carried out in a series of small steps. This is similar to the process used in systematic desensitization except that relaxation is not used and, whereas systematic desensitization is often conducted imaginally, graded exposure is conducted in real-life settings. Such exposure techniques have been used successfully with people suffering from phobias (e.g., Marks, 1990; Mattick et al., 1990; Menzies and Clarke, 1993), posttraumatic stress (e.g., Foa et al., 1991), and obsessive-compulsive problems (e.g., Marks and O'Sullivan, 1988).

Aversion therapy

Classical conditioning theory is also employed in *aversion therapy*. Here, very simply, the idea is to take an unwanted behaviour and pair it with an unpleasant consequence so that the unwanted behaviour becomes associated with the unpleasant consequence and thus becomes less frequent. Aversion therapy was first used by Kantorovich (1930) with people with alcohol problems. Electric shocks were administered, accompanied by the smell, sight, and taste of alcohol. Similarly, aversion therapy might be used to help someone to stop smoking. People who want to stop smoking might be required to take a pill which makes them feel nauseous (an emetic). Once they feel nauseous they would then be required to smoke. Smoking becomes associated with feeling nauseous and so the frequency of smoking decreases. Although aversion therapy has been subject to ethical objections, and the evidence for its effectiveness is not consistently strong, there are occasions when it can be very beneficial. Classic studies were carried out by Bucher and Lovaas (1967) who used electric shocks to decrease self-destructive behaviour in an autistic boy, and by Lang and Melamed (1969) who used electric shocks to the legs of an infant to successfully decrease persistent life-threatening vomiting behaviour. Aversion therapy was also used in the past with people with so-called sexual disorders (e.g., Marks et al., 1970). However such approaches are less widely used today and clinicians would recommend the use of non-punitive forms of treatment where possible (e.g., Russo et al., 1980).

Albert Bandura and modelling

Albert Bandura described the process of *modelling*. This involves learning behaviour through watching others, i.e., learning by imitation (Bandura, 1969; Bandura and Walters, 1963). Interestingly, Freud (1940/1969) had also discussed the process of learning through identification and how children usually come to identify with the same-sex parent. For example, Alex may have learned through modelling of his father to control his emotions through alcohol (see Box 3.1, p. 61). In a series of famous studies conducted by Bandura, children watched adults behaving either in an aggressive or a non-aggressive way. Then, the children were allowed to play and it was found that those children who had watched the aggressive adults were more likely to play in an aggressive way than those children who had watched the adults behaving non-aggressively. Modelling can be used to help clients with a variety of anxiety-related problems. Essentially, the client watches the therapist model the appropriate behaviour and through doing so learns to do it for himself or herself. Often, the modelling will be conducted using a graded hierarchy of increasingly aversive behavioural performances involving the feared object or situation. Bandura's approach, although a behavioural one in that it relies on social learning, also relies on cognitive processes. Bandura claimed that the technique worked because it increases the person's sense of *self-efficacy*, that is to say the confidence with which they are able to perform the task. However, self-efficacy is an internal construct not amenable to observation in the strict behavioural sense.

Exposure to the unwanted or feared object seems to be the effective therapeutic ingredient common to these techniques (Marks, 1990). Exposure-based therapies are now the treatment of choice for many anxiety-based problems. There seems little doubt that approaches based on exposure can be useful in the treatment of fears and phobias (e.g., Barlow, 1988), and that they are at least as effective as biomedical therapies in these cases (e.g., Margraf et al., 1993). However, their application to the wider arena of so-called psychiatric disorders is now seen to be fairly limited (see Davey, 1992).

Reinforcement-based techniques

Other therapies are based on operant conditioning and use *reinforcement* schedules to shape behaviour. First, it is necessary to conduct a functional analysis in order to understand which conditions are responsible for maintaining the behaviour, why and when the behaviour occurs. Then, armed with this information, the therapist can intervene by changing the conditions in such a way as to modify reinforcement schedules to increase the frequency of desired behaviour and decrease the frequency of undesired behaviour.

Token economy

The use of operant techniques was first demonstrated by Allyon and Azrin who observed eating problems on a ward of chronic psychotic patients and hypothesized that these problems were functionally related to the reinforcements provided by the staff. At mealtimes patients who had difficulties were approached and helped by staff. Allyon and Azrin hypothesized that this increased social attention was rewarding for the patients and served to maintain the maladaptive behaviour. Thus, they changed the reinforcement contingencies so that staff ignored the eating problems and instead allocated their attention to other more socially desirable and prosocial behaviours. Within days it was reported that much of the disruptive and maladaptive behaviour had been extinguished. Then Allyon and Azrin introduced a monetary token system which staff could use to reward the socially desirable behaviours of the patients, such as making their beds and washing. Tokens could also be fined for socially undesirable behaviours. Tokens could be exchanged for goods and privileges such as watching television or trips outside. This too had a positive effect on increasing adaptive behaviours (Allyon and Azrin, 1968).

In summary, the behavioural model was most strongly promoted by the psychologist Watson who, as we have seen, argued that observable behaviour was the only appropriate subject matter for the relatively new science of psychology. Thoughts and feelings, Watson argued, could not be measured objectively. In behaviour therapy, the focus of treatment is the behaviour itself and the therapist will endeavour to change that behaviour using a range of techniques such as aversion or flooding. Techniques drawn from behaviour therapy were developed and used with a variety of client groups, those with eating disorders (e.g., Greenberg and Marks, 1982), neurotic problems (e.g., Stravynski et al., 1982), and phobias and obsessive-compulsive problems (e.g., O'Sullivan and Marks, 1991). A wide variety of health professionals are now trained in the use of behaviour therapy techniques (e.g., Duggan et al., 1993).

Recently, the behavioural model has provided a theoretical base for the development of coaching psychology approaches (Passmore, 2007). One of the most widely used approaches in behavioural coaching is the GROW model (Passmore, 2007). GROW has four stages:

- goals – what do you want to achieve?
- reality – what is happening?
- options – what options do you think there are?
- way forward – can you summarise what you are going to do and by when?

See Box 4.1 for an example of GROW in action.

As already mentioned, the behavioural approach, because of its emphasis on observable behaviours, lends itself well to traditional scientific research. However, the behavioural approach has been criticized for being inadequate to grapple with the complexities of human behaviour. Much human behaviour, many would argue, is a product of unobservable thoughts and feelings. This can be seen in Bandura's approach. Behaviour therapy is not often used in its pure form today, and many of the principles of learning have become incorporated with the cognitive approach, leading to what is known as cognitive-behavioural therapy. One reason for this is that behavioural techniques, although successful in the

Box 4.1   Sarah

Through word of mouth Sarah contacted Carol, who works as a life coach. Carol had worked for many years as a psychotherapist but had recently expanded the services offered by her private practice to include coaching clients. With Sarah it seemed appropriate to begin with the GROW model. Sarah was challenged to think about what she wanted to achieve. At first, Sarah's goals were quite fuzzy and about what she didn't want, such as commuting so many hours to work each week. Carol worked with her to be more specific and to pinpoint what it was that she did want, such as to be more creative and to use her strengths more. Carol also kept Sarah on track to be realistic. After years of working as an estate agent Sarah had progressed well in her career but was now looking for new exciting challenges. Sarah was frustrated that she couldn't just make a change there and then. As a result that kept her feeling stuck. Carol helped Sarah to grasp the idea that change could be achieved but it would possibly take time, and that it may take a lot of small steps, not just one big step. Having put it like that, Sarah was quickly able to begin thinking about her options, the small steps that she could begin to take. Carol then helped Sarah to work through the small behavioural steps that she needed to take to achieve her goal. Sarah remembers Carol's words that a small tilt of the rudder now is all it needs to take you to a very different destination.

treatment of various anxiety problems, did not seem to lend themselves as well to the treatment of depressive problems. In contrast, the cognitive approach did seem to lend itself well to understanding depression as well as a wider range of other psychological problems. We will go on now to consider the cognitive model.

Cognitive model: Albert Ellis and Aaron Beck

The cognitive model emphasizes how aspects of cognition, thinking and reasoning contribute to the development of psychological problems. The cognitive model is the most recent of all the psychological models, introduced in the 1950s by Albert Ellis (1913–2007) and popularized in the 1970s by Aaron Beck. But it has a long history. Epictetus, the Greek philosopher, is often quoted as saying that people are disturbed not by events, but by the views they take of these events. Similarly, Shakespeare's Hamlet says that 'there is nothing either good or bad but thinking makes it so' (*Hamlet,* Act II, Scene ii). So, the idea that our behaviour is shaped

by the way we think about ourselves and the world is not a new idea. But it was not until the second half of the twentieth century that these ideas were promoted by Ellis and Beck, who introduced cognitive approaches to therapy. The popularity of these approaches to therapy was accompanied by a movement within academic psychology towards an adoption of the cognitive model. Researchers began to investigate humans as information processors, and how psychological problems can result when this process goes awry.

Within the cognitive model, for example, the symptoms of schizophrenia are seen as representing faults in the way that information is processed. We are constantly bombarded with information from the external environment and if we are to function appropriately in the world we must selectively attend to the information. While I'm writing this I am focused on the words on the page and I am able to ignore for the moment the sound of the traffic outside, the sound of voices somewhere, a radio playing, and so on. But a breakdown in a person's ability to selectively attend in this way would result in him or her being overwhelmed by information. It has been suggested that people diagnosed with schizophrenia suffer such a breakdown and that their symptoms reflect the subsequent internal confusion. Their withdrawal into themselves is their way of keeping the bombardment of sensory stimulation to a manageable level.

If maladaptive behaviour is the result of the way we process information and perceive ourselves, then there are clear implications for therapy. Simply, people can be helped to see themselves and the world around them differently.

Albert Ellis and rational emotive behaviour therapy (REBT)

A-B-C model

Ellis's approach was known as *rational-emotive therapy* (RET), which he later renamed *rational emotive behaviour therapy* (REBT), in recognition that it contained strong elements of behavioural training as well as cognitive elements. Famously, Ellis is said to have first developed his ideas as a young man by staking out a park bench and forcing himself to speak to 130 women in one month as a way to overcome his shyness. Ellis proposed that maladaptive behaviour is the result of irrational beliefs (Ellis, 1962). Some examples of the type of irrational beliefs discussed by Ellis are given in Table 4.2. Ellis argued that it is not what happens to us that causes psychological problems, but rather it is how

Table 4.2   Examples of irrational beliefs

It is a dire necessity for an adult human being to be loved or approved by virtually every significant person in his community.

One should be thoroughly competent, adequate, and achieving in all possible respects if one is to consider oneself worthwhile.

Certain people are bad, wicked, or villainous, and they should be severely blamed and punished for their villainy.

It is awful and catastrophic when things are not the way one would like them to be.

Human unhappiness is externally caused and people have little or no ability to control their sorrows and disturbance.

If something is or may be dangerous or fearsome one should be terribly concerned about it and should keep dwelling on the possibility of it occurring.

It is easier to avoid than to face certain life difficulties and self-responsibilities.

One should be dependent on others and need someone stronger than oneself on whom to rely.

One's past history is an all-important determiner of one's present behaviour, and because something once affected one's life, it should indefinitely have a similar effect.

One should become quite upset over other people's problems and disturbance.

There is invariably a right, precise, and perfect solution to human problems, and it is catastrophic if this perfect solution is not found.

Source: Ellis, 1962.

we come to understand these events. It is, according to Ellis, our beliefs (B) about activating events (A) that determine the consequences (C). This is called the *A-B-C model* (see Table 4.3). For example, a student with a strong belief that she must succeed at everything she does (B) is likely to become depressed (C) on failing an exam (A). Irrational beliefs, such as those described above, lead to what Ellis has called a '*musta-batory ideology*', that is, they have a strong 'must' quality that places heavy demands on people who hold such beliefs (see also Warren and Zgourides, 1991).

Table 4.3   A-B-C model of Ellis

	Example
Activating event (A)	Achieve a poor exam mark
Irrational belief (B)	I must do everything well or I am a failure
Consequences (C)	Feel depressed

Disputing

Likewise, a person who holds a strong belief that she must be liked by everyone (B) is likely to become depressed (C) if someone doesn't like her (A). In Ellis's REBT, the therapist would endeavour to help the client modify his or her irrational beliefs and to replace them with new and more rational beliefs. For example, someone who has the need to be liked by everyone might come to adopt a new belief such as: 'It's good to be liked, but I can't expect everyone to appreciate me in the same way. Some people might not like me, and that's OK; it's not essential for me that everyone likes me.' The therapy is active, challenging, and directive. The basic idea behind Ellis's approach to therapy, therefore, is to challenge the client's irrational beliefs so that, in this case, the client no longer believes that she has to succeed at everything or be liked by everyone. The central technique in REBT is *disputing*. Ellis (1973) described the REBT therapist as employing:

> a fairly rapid-fire active-directive-persuasive-philosophic methodology. In most instances, he quickly pins the client down to a few basic irrational ideas which motivate much of his disturbed behavior; he challenges the client to validate these ideas; he shows them that they are extralogical premises which cannot be validated; he logically analyses these ideas and makes mincemeat of them; he vigorously and vehemently shows why they can't work and will almost invariably lead to renewed disturbed symptomatology; he reduces these ideas to absurdity, sometimes in a highly humorous manner; he explains how they can be replaced with more rational, empirically based theses. (p. 185)

Ellis also encourages the client to behaviourally check out their irrational cognitions. For example, much dysfunctional behaviour is thought to stem from feelings of shame, and Ellis also promotes the use of shame-attacking exercises in which the client is encouraged to engage in behaviours which provoke feelings of shame. Ellis describes the case of Myra, a client with a fear of appearing foolish. Ellis describes how he encouraged Myra to walk down the street with a banana on a dog leash. By doing this, she was able to learn that nothing bad happens even when she does look foolish.

Although Ellis's approach might seem harsh, it is not the client themself or the values that the client holds that are attacked, but rather it is the 'mustabatory' element of those values. This is an important point. The aim of the therapy is not to diminish the client but to modify his or her irrational beliefs. Also, some people question the use of the term irrational, believing that people's beliefs, even if they are irrational, can sometimes be helpful to them and therefore it would be better to think of beliefs as maladaptive or as dysfunctional (e.g., Arnkoff and Glass, 1982).

Aaron Beck and cognitive therapy

Another prominent thinker within the cognitive approach is Aaron Beck who also suggested that psychological problems result from faulty thinking. Like Ellis's REBT, the aim of Beck's cognitive therapy is to change the way in which a person thinks about a situation and to challenge maladaptive ways of thinking which are thought to contribute to the development and maintenance of psychological problems.

Beck proposed that people begin to formulate rules for living early on in life. Originally writing about depression, Beck (1963, 1967, 1974) argued that depression has its roots in the way in which people think about themselves and the world they live in. Depressed people, Beck argued, possess illogical ways of thinking. He discussed the way people might magnify their difficulties and failures, minimize their accomplishments and successes, arrive at conclusions based only on a selection of evidence, arrive at conclusions despite the absence of supporting evidence, or arrive at conclusions based on a single and trivial event. For example, if someone you know who is usually friendly hurries past you on the street without saying hello, would you conclude that he probably hadn't seen you or would you conclude that he had taken a dislike to you? Beck's theory says that it is the person who would reach the conclusion that he is disliked on the basis of such an event who is more prone to developing depression than the person who concludes that the other person just hadn't seen him or her. Some of the illogical ways of thinking discussed by Beck are shown in Table 4.4. Illogical ways of thinking are also characteristic of Helen (see Box 4.2).

Table 4.4   Illogical ways of thinking described by Beck

Magnification	magnifying difficulties and failures
Minimization	minimizing accomplishments and successes
Selective abstraction	arriving at a conclusion based on a selection of the evidence only
Arbitrary inference	arriving at a conclusion despite the absence of supporting evidence
Over-generalization	arriving at a conclusion based on a single and trivial event

Box 4.2 Helen

Helen was referred by her GP to a counsellor who uses the cognitive-behavioural approach. In the first session the counsellor interviews Helen to find out more about her relationship, and her family background, and in listening to Helen the counsellor soon picks up on the way Helen tends to arrive at selective conclusions and over-generalizes from single episodes. Although Helen did well at school and university, and now has a successful career in a large media organization, she tells the therapist how she feels like a failure. She has had many successes in her life, but she tends to focus on her perceived failures. One of the episodes she dwells on is her request the previous year for promotion which was turned down. On inquiry it turns out that the feedback Helen received from her line manager was actually extremely positive. She was told that she was not awarded the promotion because of budget constraints and that she was almost certain of promotion within the next year. It was after this episode that Helen began feeling tired all of the time, started to lose interest in things, and to feel depressed. Robert, her partner at the time, had been unable to provide Helen with the psychological support she needed and rows between them became increasingly frequent until they broke up. Helen says that there is something wrong with her and that she is not capable of being in a relationship, and that she can never see herself meeting anyone who could love her. Although Helen is an attractive woman with plenty of friends and admirers she sees herself as unattractive and unlikeable. Recently it was her birthday. Although she received cards and presents from many friends and colleagues, there was one friend who forgot her birthday and Helen dwells on this episode.

Negative cognitive triad

Beck argued that illogical ways of thinking lead to a negative view of the self, of current experience, and of the future. These negative views constitute, what Beck called, a *negative cognitive triad* underlying depression. The negative cognitive triad is experienced by people as *negative automatic thoughts,* that is to say, pessimistic ways of thinking, thoughts that come to mind like 'I'm useless, life is bleak, nothing will change'. Briefly, Beck and Weishaar (1989) noted five steps to cognitive therapy:

1. learning to monitor negative, automatic thoughts;
2. learning to recognize the connection between cognition, affect and behaviour;
3. examining the evidence for and against distorted automatic thoughts;

4. substituting more reality-oriented interpretations for these biased cognitions;
5. learning to identify and alter the beliefs that predispose a person to distort their experiences.

The cognitive therapist attempts to help the client to become aware of and challenge his or her negative automatic thoughts, and eventually replace them with more realistic and adaptive ways of thinking (see Box 4.3).

Box 4.3   Helen

The counsellor helps Helen to monitor her thoughts that she is unloveable and unlikeable, to explore the connections between her thoughts, her feelings, and her behaviours, and to examine the evidence for those thoughts. What evidence is there that the friend does not like her? Is it possible that she forgot to send her a birthday card because of some other reason? Over the coming weeks, the counsellor helps Helen to understand how she interprets events in such a way as to leave her feeling depressed, and shows her ways in which she can monitor her depressive thinking.

Collaborative empiricism

Furthermore, the cognitive approach encourages a collaborative relationship between the therapist and the client in which they both approach the client's problem using *collaborative empiricism,* that is to say, both work together to identify the problem and to formulate hypotheses about how change might be brought about (Hollon and Beck, 1994). Although there are clear similarities between the approaches of Ellis and Beck, Beck's approach to therapy is less directive and confrontational than that of Ellis.

Cognitive-behavioural approaches

However, as already noted in Chapter 1, many therapists recognize that no one model can give us the full understanding of how psychological problems develop or the best way of doing therapy. For this reason, many theorists have been interested in finding ways in which different models can be integrated. As such, therapists began to integrate these new cognitive ideas with the behavioural ideas, resulting in what is now generally known as *cognitive-behavioural therapy* (CBT). So, although the behavioural and cognitive models have been treated separately in this chapter, the distinction is not clear-cut. For example, a person suffering from panic attacks might be asked to engage in activities that lead to panic-like symptoms, such as taking exercise in order to stimulate cardiovascular symptoms, thus exposing themselves to panic symptoms in a safe environment. We have seen how exposure can be useful. The therapist might then use the sessions to help the client identify their automatic thoughts as they experience panic symptoms and, using educational techniques, show the client how to reinterpret their experiences as normal bodily processes.

One of the first CBT techniques was that of *self-instructional training* (SIT) developed by Meichenbaum (1977). This approach helps clients to focus on their thought processes and how these affect behaviour, with the aim of allowing clients to control their thoughts in such a way as to improve performance and decrease distress. In the same way that children use self-talk when they are learning new skills, Meichenbaum's SIT pays attention to internal dialogues, and in therapy clients are encouraged to externalize their dialogues and to change the instructions they give themselves. For example, think about learning to drive and how a person uses self-instructions, either silently or out loud, to learn: 'Check behind in the mirrors, put the car into gear, check again in the mirrors.' In SIT the client is retrained in the way he or she talks to himself or herself; dysfunctional self-talk is decreased and adaptive self-talk is increased. Initially, the therapist may model the new self-talk to the client, the client practises the new self-talk aloud, and over time comes to talk silently to himself in the new way. This continues until the new self-talk becomes habitual. As well as learning the new skills, the client is encouraged to practise using more positive self-statements, to reinforce himself positively, and to cope with failure using self-talk (see Box 4.4).

Box 4.4   Helen

SIT is one of the techniques taught to Helen by her counsellor. Now, when something happens at work she is able to monitor her negative automatic thoughts. Recently, Helen's line manager called her into her office. Immediately Helen was aware of how she automatically thought that she must have done something wrong, and was now able to use self-talk to calm herself down and to prevent herself going into a depressed mood: 'There I go again, blaming myself for things that haven't even happened, I'm not going to do that today.'

Today, the term CBT covers a wide range of approaches, some of which are more behavioural and some of which are more cognitive in their emphasis. Drawing on the range of cognitive and behavioural techniques that have been developed, particular CBT interventions have been developed for use with clients with particular psychological problems. Techniques drawn from CBT are also commonly used in group therapy approaches (see Box 4.5). Forms of group-based psychoeducational and training approaches are recommended in the NICE guidelines for drug misuse, and attention deficit hyperactivity disorder (Khele, 2008).

The cognitive-behavioural approach has also become popular within the self-help literature (e.g., Persaud, 1998). Such self-help books are useful to many clients in beginning to better understand how they can change the way they feel through changing the way they think about themselves and their roles and goals in life. Cognitive-behavioural approaches to coaching have also been developed which aim to help people achieve new goals, to resolve difficulties, acquire new skills and constructive ways of coping, modify beliefs, and develop new thinking skills in such a way that they are able to become their own 'self-coach' (Palmer and Szymanska, 2007).

Box 4.5   Matt

The clinical psychologist provided Matt and his parents with an educational package about the nature, course, and treatment of schizophrenia. The information was that schizophrenia was an illness with both physical and psychological components. Matt's parents were reassured that families do not cause schizophrenia but their role in helping him reach recovery was also emphasized, along with the importance of adherence to medication. The family attended for several sessions, and following this first educational session the psychologist helped the family explore their feelings, and learn new ways of coping with stress and dealing with family tensions. The psychologist drew heavily on behavioural skill-based techniques. During Matt's stay in hospital he attended several group therapy sessions with other patients. The main focus of the group was social skills training, using principles such as modelling drawn from the behavioural approach. The group was largely a psychoeducational one in which Matt and the other patients were instructed in aspects of day-to-day living that could cause them difficulties following discharge from the hospital. Role-play exercises were also used in which Matt would, for instance, play going into shops to ask for things. Through such exercises Matt greatly improved his interpersonal skills, learning, for example, how to make better eye contact, and to express himself more clearly.

Does CBT work?

The cognitive-behavioural forms of therapy have been subject to more research than any other of the psychological models. Although a comprehensive review of this literature is beyond the scope of this book, cognitive-behavioural approaches are now very well-established as a way of treating people for various so-called psychiatric disorders and physical health problems such as chronic pain (see Roth and Fonagy, 2005). Currently, the National Institute for Clinical Excellence (NICE) recommends various forms of CBT for people with problems of anxiety, depression, attention deficit hyperactivity disorder, bipolar disorder, eating disorders, obsessive-compulsive disorder, posttraumatic stress disorder, and schizophrenia (Khele, 2008).

Criticisms of cognitive-behavioural approaches

Although the research evidence is generally taken to support the effectiveness of cognitive-behavioural approaches to therapy, there have been critics of this approach. Some question the extent to which the research findings can be generalized to routine clinical settings and say that the approach has been overhyped (White, 2000). Results from experimental studies do not always translate into real life. Waller (2009) points out that a major aspect of CBT is behavioural change and as such it is important that therapists encourage clients appropriately through homework and other activities to make the changes. But CBT therapists in everyday practice may not be as rigorous in this respect as those who conduct the research trials into the effectiveness of CBT. This may explain why CBT doesn't always seem to work as well in real-life situations. Others are more critical. Smail (1996a), for example, writes:

> the ruling dogmas of clinical psychology, usually referred to loosely as 'cognitive behaviourism', embody an, in my view, extraordinarily simplistic collection of ideas about how people come to be the way they are and what they can be expected to be able to do about it ... Such ideas, acceptable enough perhaps to undergraduate students learning the experimental ropes, ring particularly hollow when they come to be applied in the clinical setting, where people's difficulties are often complicated and intractable. (pp. 29–30)

Certainly, many psychodynamic and, as we shall see, humanistically oriented therapists would agree with Smail's comment. Other commentators might note that behaviour therapies have traditionally been neglectful of the social setting in which therapy takes place and of the relationship which develops between the therapist and the client, although more recent writers in the behavioural tradition have begun to recognize the importance of the therapeutic relationship, and to question the stereotype of the behaviour therapist as someone who is cold and mechanistic (Schaap et al., 1993).

But it is not just theorists from the humanistic and psychodynamic models who have been critical of the cognitive approach. Skinner (1990), writing from the behaviourists' perspective, has argued that the cognitive model is a return to *unscientific mentalism,* that is, speculating about unobservable and unmeasurable phenomena which are outside the domain of scientific inquiry. However, despite Skinner's reservations about models which speculate on internal processes, most theorists would agree that it is indeed useful to do so, although, as we have seen, there remains disagreement about the nature of those internal processes: for example, the different ways of looking at internal processes as described by psychodynamically oriented therapists as opposed to cognitively oriented therapists.

Finally, one of the factors that has been important in the development and popularity of the cognitive-behavioural model is that research psychologists have adopted the medical model, and the language of psychiatrists, that is to say the use of the American Psychiatric Association's *Diagnostic and Statistical Manual of Mental Disorders,* and have therefore tested the techniques of CBT in relation to the various categories of so-called disorder. Psychologists' adoption of the medical model has been important in gaining respectability for CBT within the medical profession and the health service.

Conclusion

In this chapter the behavioural and the cognitive models were introduced. Behaviourism was developed following criticisms of the psychodynamic model for its lack of scientific rigour. Although successful in many respects, particularly it seems with anxiety problems, the behavioural model also became subject to criticism as theorists began again to emphasize the importance of internal cognitive processes. The idea that we can ignore thoughts and feelings and develop an understanding of psychology based solely on observable behaviour now seems incomplete. However, at the time, the behavioural model was a reaction to psychoanalysis and its emphasis on hypothetical unobservable mental constructs. The cognitive model, which first became popular in the 1960s, has received the greatest amount of research support and is widely used today to provide the theoretical basis for a number of therapies which research suggests to be effective for a variety of psychological problems. However, the cognitive approach to therapy is itself subject to criticism. Some see it as an overly simplistic approach to understanding human problems, and others see it as a return to unscientific mentalism.

Summary points

- The behavioural model developed in response to criticisms of psychoanalysis in an attempt to provide a scientific approach.
- Two principles of learning theory form the basis for the behavioural model – classical conditioning and operant conditioning. Based on these principles, several behaviour therapy techniques, such as systematic desensitization, flooding, and aversion, have been developed.
- Exposure to an unwanted or feared object without escape seems to be the effective ingredient common to many behaviour therapy techniques, and more recent exposure-based therapies have been used successfully with clients suffering from a range of anxiety-based problems.
- Although successful in helping people with anxiety, the behavioural model does not seem to lend itself as well to understanding depression as the cognitive approaches to therapy which were introduced by Ellis and Beck.
- The cognitive approaches of Ellis and Beck emphasize not just what happens to us but rather how we appraise and make sense of it. People with particular ways of thinking, such as those who magnify their difficulties and minimize their successes, are thought to be more prone to depression.
- Ellis's approach to therapy involves disputing with the client and directing the client to newer and more rational ways of thinking. Beck's approach to therapy is less confrontational and the therapist works in a more collaborative way, helping clients to examine the evidence for and against their distorted thoughts.
- Modern cognitive approaches tend to combine elements of behaviour therapy, resulting in what is known as cognitive-behavioural therapy (CBT).
- CBT has attracted much research and its supporters claim that it has a good evidence base for treating a variety of different so-called psychiatric disorders.

Topics for reflection

1. It seems common sense that if we change how we talk to ourselves we can make ourselves feel better. Can you see any problems with this?
2. One of the main issues in cognitive therapy is who decides what is an irrational thought? How do we know when a thought is irrational or not? Should we always want to rid ourselves of such thoughts?
3. Many of us have our own illogical ways of thinking. Considering Beck's list of illogical ways of thinking, do any of these sound like something you do? Think about times when your own beliefs have caused you difficulties.

Chapter 5

Humanistic and Transpersonal Approaches

Introduction

Humanistic psychology has been referred to as the third force in psychology, after psychoanalysis and behaviourism. It emerged in the middle of the twentieth century as a reaction against the previous ways of looking at human experience, which were seen as overly deterministic. Psychoanalysis was seen as painting a bleak and pessimistic view of human nature, in which people are basically selfish and driven by sexual and aggressive impulses which must be restrained. Behaviourism was seen as objectifying and dehumanizing the person and emphasizing environmental forces as determinants of behaviour. In contrast, the humanistic approach emphasizes human nature as essentially positive. The humanistic model emphasizes choices, values, and purpose in life. Problems are seen as resulting from not accepting personal responsibility for one's actions. Humanistic therapies therefore strive to enable people to accept responsibility for their actions, to become aware of their subjective experiences, and to fulfil their potential for personal growth. Like behaviourism, early humanistic psychology took a scientific stance but, unlike behaviourism, began to question the traditional medical model. Rather than seeing the client as a passive recipient of expert help, therapeutic approaches in the humanistic tradition emphasized the choices made by the client and the client's inner resources for change, as opposed to the techniques of the therapist.

As Szasz says:

> People seeking help from psychotherapists can be divided into two groups: those who wish to confront their difficulties and shortcomings and change their lives by changing themselves; and those who wish to avoid the inevitable consequences of their life strategies through the magical or tactical intervention of the therapist in their lives. Those in the former group may derive great benefit from therapy in a few weeks

or months; those in the latter may stand still, or sink ever deeper into their self-created life morass, after meeting with psychotherapists for years, and even decades. (Szasz, 1974, pp. 108–9)

The most well-known name associated with humanistic psychology is that of Carl Rogers (1902–1987) and it is his work we will first consider.

Carl Rogers and the person-centred approach

Carl Rogers was a psychologist by training. One of his earliest achievements was to pioneer the recording of therapeutic sessions which he then used for research (Rogers, 1942). Throughout his life Rogers was a prolific writer, publishing numerous academic papers and books, many of which are still widely read today. In his book *Client-centred Therapy*, Rogers began to outline his approach to therapy (Rogers, 1951). He went on to describe his ideas in more detail in later papers as he elaborated on his theory of personality and therapy (Rogers, 1957, 1959). Over the years, Rogers began to apply his ideas derived from therapy in wider contexts, such as education, conflict resolution, and encounter groups (see Thorne, 1992). In order to recognize the broader applicability of his model the term *person-centred* came to replace the term *client-centred*. These terms are often used interchangeably, although some prefer to use 'client-centred' when referring to therapeutic work and 'person-centred' when referring to the broader applications. Sometimes client-centred therapy is referred to as Rogerian therapy. However, Rogers disliked the use of this term, maintaining that he did not want to see a school of therapists who were modelling themselves on him, but rather to see therapists who were able to find their own ways of working within the person-centred approach.

Actualizing tendency

The foundation of Rogers' theory is what he called the *actualizing tendency*, which is the one natural motivational force of human beings and is always directed towards constructive growth and development:

> It is the urge which is evident in all organic and human life – to expand, extend, to become autonomous, develop, mature – the tendency to express and activate all the capacities of the organism, to the extent that such activation enhances the organism or the self. (Rogers, 1961, p. 35)

This tendency towards growth and development, however, can become thwarted. The developing infant seeks positive regard from his or her caregivers. But positive regard takes two forms, either unconditional or conditional. The need for positive regard is so strong that the child does not distinguish between the two forms of regard, but seeks out what is available. While unconditional regard facilitates the child's intrinsic direction for growth and development, conditional regard thwarts this intrinsic direction. Instead, the child introjects *conditions of worth* which operate in tension to the actualizing tendency, producing later problems. Rogers wrote:

> This, as we see it, is the basic estrangement in man. He has not been true to himself, to his natural organismic valuing of experience, but for the sake of preserving the positive regard of others has now come to falsify some of the values he experiences and to perceive them in terms based only on their value to others. Yet this has not been a conscious choice, but a natural – and tragic – development in infancy (Rogers, 1959, p. 226).

For example, a child grows up introjecting from the adults around the belief that to be valued he or she must always please others. That child internalizes those beliefs as his or her own conditions of worth (see Table 5.1). Thus, rather than the driving force of development being the actualizing tendency, this life force is thwarted by the child's need to please others. Such people would then develop a conditional positive self-regard, that is to say, that they only find value for themselves to the extent that they live up to how well they please others. On the other hand, full functioning results when the developing infant received unconditional positive regard from his or her caregivers, and

Table 5.1   Example conditions of worth

We grow up internalizing messages. Do any of the messages below sound familiar to you? Are there any you would add to the list?

- Do as you are told
- Make sure other people are happy
- Work hard at school
- Don't cry
- Don't get angry
- Put other people first
- Girls are not as important as boys
- Never let anyone see weakness

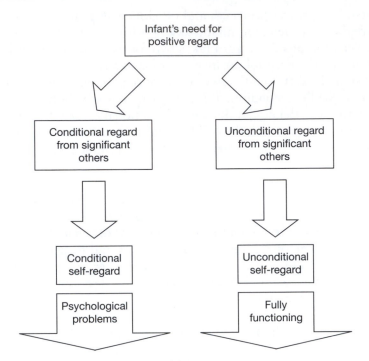

Figure 5.1   Person-centred model of functioning

the actualizing tendency is the driving force towards growth (see Figure 5.1). 'Fully functioning' is:

> synonymous with optimal psychological adjustment, optimal psychological maturity, complete congruence, complete openness to experience ... since some of these terms sound somewhat static, as though such a person 'had arrived', it should be pointed out that all the characteristics of such a person are process characteristics. The fully functioning person would be a person-in-process, a person continually changing. (Rogers, 1959, p. 235)

In terms of therapeutic practice, it is the therapist's trust in the client's actualizing tendency which makes the person-centred approach, and those other humanistic approaches which adopt this stance, so radically different from other therapeutic approaches (see Bozarth, 1998). In practice this means that the person-centred therapist works in such a way as to attempt to be a companion to the client on his or her journey to understand himself or herself. The therapist endeavours to provide a facilitative environment in which the client can become his or her real self. Rogers (1957) describes how he found that, whatever the problem was, whether it was to do with distressing feelings or troubling interpersonal relations, all of his clients were struggling with the same existential question of how to be themselves.

Necessary and sufficient conditions

Rogers described in detail the nature of the facilitative environment which, he believed, would allow the person to become his or her real self. When the client perceives the therapist to be congruent, empathic, and providing of unconditional positive regard, the process of actualization is promoted and therapeutic personality change will take place. Thus, congruence, empathy, and unconditional positive regard are viewed as the core conditions for constructive therapeutic personality change (Rogers, 1959). Given unconditional positive regard from significant others, the person increasingly develops positive self-regard and the actualizing tendency is promoted. Dysfunctional behaviour on the part of the client decreases. Rogers states that, for constructive personality change to occur, six conditions must exist and if they exist for a long enough period of time they will be sufficient to produce constructive personality change (see Table 5.2).

The first condition – psychological contact – is a precondition which if not met would mean that the following five conditions were redundant. All Rogers means by psychological contact is whether or not the two people are aware of each other, and that the behaviour of one impacts on the other. So, for example, with someone who is in a catatonic state it would be difficult to judge whether there was psychological contact. In

Table 5.2   Rogers' necessary and sufficient conditions for constructive personality change

1. Two persons are in psychological contact.
2. The first, whom we shall call the client, is in a state of incongruence, being vulnerable or anxious.
3. The second person, whom we shall call the therapist, is congruent or integrated in the relationship.
4. The therapist experiences unconditional positive regard for the client.
5. The therapist experiences an empathic understanding of the client's internal frame of reference and endeavours to communicate this experience to the client.
6. The communication to the client of the therapist's empathic understanding and unconditional positive regard is to a minimal degree achieved.

Source: Rogers, 1957.

the second condition, the client is in a state of anxiety and incongruence. Incongruence consists of an incompatibility between underlying feelings and awareness of those feelings, or an incompatibility between awareness of feelings and the expression of feelings (Mearns and Thorne, 1999). For example, someone who appears anxious to an observer but has no awareness himself of feeling anxious would be said to be incongruent in terms of his underlying feelings and his awareness of those feelings. Someone who is aware of her anxiety but says that she is feeling relaxed would be said to be incongruent between awareness and expression. In the third condition, the therapist is congruent; that is to say, he or she is aware of his or her inner experience, for example, feelings of anger or sadness, and is able to express this openly if thought to be appropriate. In the fourth condition, the therapist is able to provide unconditional positive regard; that is to say, he or she is able to accept the client for who he or she is without imposing conditions of worth on the client. In the fifth condition, the therapist has empathic understanding; that is to say, he or she is able to sense what the client's experience must feel like. Finally, in the sixth condition, the client perceives the therapist's empathy and unconditional acceptance (see Box 5.1).

Rogers (1957) believed that if these six conditions were in existence then constructive personality change would occur, but only if all six were present. He also stated that the stronger their presence, the more marked the constructive personality change of the client would be. His view was that this hypothesis applied to all clients, regardless of the presenting problems (as long as the first condition was met, that is, psychological contact). He argued that this was true regardless of which type

---

Box 5.1   Alex

For Alex, who had grown up experiencing criticism from his father, it was important that he was able to feel unconditionally accepted by his therapist. It was only over time that he began to trust that his therapist would not respond to him in a critical way. For the first few sessions Alex did not reveal his true feelings about himself to his therapist. Behind his seemingly confident appearance, Alex felt shame that he wasn't good enough and that he was inferior to other people. The therapist had a sense of this but did not question Alex in these first sessions about his feelings towards himself. Instead he gave Alex the space to talk about what he wanted, even if he was avoiding more troubling issues. It was when this sense of safety had become established for him that Alex felt able to trust his therapist. He then began to explore his inner conflicts and feelings openly and honestly and to admit to other people that he felt shame.

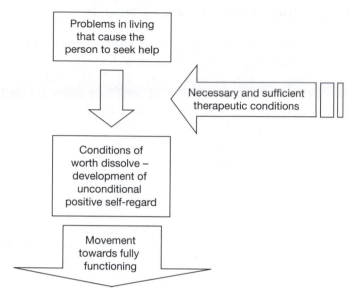

Figure 5.2 Person-centred therapy

of therapy was being delivered, and that these six conditions were able to produce constructive personality change in all relationships and not simply within the therapeutic relationship (see Figure 5.2). The therapeutic relationship was simply one that tried to maintain these conditions at a heightened level of intensity. Contrary to other theoretical approaches, Rogers also claimed that these qualities did not require special intellectual knowledge and training in techniques of how to treat people, but were qualities of the person which could be acquired through experiential training.

The person-centred therapist does not attempt to change the client in some way, that is to say, he or she does not set out to cure the client's depression or alleviate his or her anxiety, for example. Rather the therapist's task is to maintain the attitudinal qualities described by Rogers, to hold unconditional positive regard, to be empathic, and to be congruent in the relationship. By doing just this, the therapist is thought to provide the client with the conditions necessary and sufficient for him or her to change in his or her own direction. It is believed that change will, because of the actualizing tendency, be in a positive, social and constructive direction. One of the most important aspects of the person-centred approach was, however, Rogers' proposition that the best vantage-point for understanding behaviour is the internal frame of reference of the individual. Rogers (1951) argued that the only way we could understand another person's behaviour was to see the world through his eyes. Then, even the most seemingly bizarre behaviour would make sense.

Criticisms of the client-centred approach

The main criticism of the person-centred approach is focused on the concept of the actualizing tendency itself, which is of course the foundation block of Rogers' theory. Some have called this assumption naive (Ellis, 1959). Like Freud's concepts of id, ego, and superego, and other abstract psychological concepts which cannot be directly observed, it is not possible to ascertain whether an actualizing tendency as described by Rogers actually exists in people. Others, although accepting the general principle of the actualizing tendency, have viewed it as an insufficient basis on which to build a theoretical framework and approach to therapy, and consequently see a need for therapists to introduce other more directive cognitive and behavioural techniques. But, as we will see in Chapter 7, the fundamental assumptions underpinning therapy, no matter which brand of therapy we choose, are just that – assumptions – and there is no way to prove them right or wrong! As Schmid wrote:

> People who think that directivity is necessary in therapy and counselling have a different image of the human being, a different concept of how to deal with knowledge and a different ethical stance from those who work with their clients on the basis of non-directiveness. Since it is of no use to argue over beliefs (they precede acting, thinking, and science), there is no way to say who, ultimately, is right (Schmid, 2005, p. 82).

Rogers has been criticized as presenting an overly optimistic view of human nature. Critics of the client-centred approach often point to the range of human suffering and ask how there can be so much suffering if people are basically trustworthy, social and constructive in nature. In response to such criticisms Rogers said:

> I am certainly not blind to all the evil and the terribly irresponsible violence that is going on ... There are times that I think I don't give enough emphasis on the shadowy side of our nature, the evil side. Then I start to deal with a client and discover how, when I get to the core, there is a wish for more socialization, more harmony, more positive values. Yes, there are all kinds of evil abounding in the world but I do not believe this is inherent in the human species any more than I believe that animals are evil. (Cited in Zeig, 1987, p. 202)

Other criticisms of Rogers' approach are the looseness of his language and the vagueness of his concepts, which do not lend themselves to empirical testing. These criticisms are, however, somewhat misplaced because, although correct in terms of Rogers' more popular writings, his scientific writings were much more precise. For example, his early theoretical statements about the necessary and sufficient conditions for personality change were certainly presented as empirically testable hypotheses. Rogers was a psychologist and because of this background his earlier writings stressed the importance of subjecting the client-centred approach to empirical testing. However, although the early development of the client-centred tradition was fuelled by the results of scientific inquiry, later in his career Rogers moved away from working in academic psychological settings and the person-centred approach became less of a focus for research attention. Meanwhile, within academic psychological settings the cognitive-behavioural approach was gaining in popularity and attracting the interest of clinical research scientists. Consequently, the person-centred approach has been subject to less research in recent years than some other treatments, notably those from the cognitive-behavioural approach.

Also, many of those who became interested in the person-centred approach were not only less interested in conducting empirical research into the effectiveness of the therapy, but took the view that an empirical statistical approach was inappropriate, preferring instead phenomenologically-based qualitative research. It might therefore be argued that it is because of the anti-science approach of many of the humanistic practitioners that the person-centred approach has become less influential in recent years within academic psychology and psychiatry. Nevertheless, the approach remains popular within the fields of counselling and psychotherapy (see Thorne and Lambers, 1998).

Also, others have seen Rogers' understanding of how problems in living develop through the internalization of conditions of worth as simplistic. Going on to discuss the therapeutic implications of this, Nelson-Jones writes:

> Rogers' simplistic explanation of the genesis of people's problems has led to a unitary diagnosis: namely that of being out of touch with the valuing process inherent in the actualizing tendency. Consequently, he has restricted himself to what is essentially a single treatment approach. This is an inadequate way to approach the range of difficulties that people have in being personally responsible. (Nelson-Jones, 1984, pp. 15–16)

Although this is an oft-cited criticism, it misses the point. Person-centred therapy rejects the medical model (Sanders, 2005). As such, client-centred therapy does indeed question the assumption that there are specific treatments for specific problems (e.g., Bozarth, 1998). People's problems may manifest differently because of different circumstances, but the cause of psychological distress no matter how it manifests is ultimately the lack of unconditional regard earlier in life, and so there is no need for specific treatments for specific problems.

Humanistic attitudes towards the medical model

In the previous chapter we saw that the cognitive-behavioural model, although not concerned with biological causes of abnormal psychological conditions, largely adopts the medical model in its attempt to understand the most effective forms of therapy for specific conditions as defined in DSM. In contrast, the humanistic approach is generally thought of as being antagonistic to the medical model of therapy. Maslow summed this up in describing the use of words such as 'patient':

> I hate the medical model that they imply because the medical model suggests that the person who comes to the counsellor is a sick person, beset by disease and illness, seeking a cure. Actually, of course, we hope that the counsellor will be the one who helps to foster the self-actualisation of people, rather than the one who helps to cure a disease. (Maslow, 1993, p. 49)

The humanistic approach has been less influenced by the use of diagnostic systems than the cognitive-behavioural approach, recognizing that often any judgement of what is 'normal' or 'abnormal' is highly subjective and will rely on the clinician's own frame of reference (e.g., Garfinkel et al., 1995). Humanistic psychologists therefore tend not to use diagnostic systems such as DSM in their work. The role of the therapist is to let clients be themselves, to grow and to unfold in their own way, to break through their own defences and discover themselves. Some are wary of the implications of a medical model within counselling and psychotherapy. Mearns (1994), for example, is sceptical of the idea that working with particular client groups or issues requires prior training in that group or issue.

Does client-centred therapy work?

Humanistic therapists have not generally adopted the language of psychiatry, the *Diagnostic and Statistical Manual of Mental Disorders* published by the American Psychiatric Association. For this reason, in contrast to CBT, person-centred therapy does not have the weight of evidence behind it. For this reason client-centred therapy receives relatively limited attention by NICE (Khele, 2008), and humanistic approaches have failed to gain credibility within the psychiatric and medical profession in the same way as cognitive and behavioural therapies (see Joseph and Worsley, 2005).

Most outside commentators on the person-centred approach have concluded that there is a lack of evidence that person-centred therapy is effective for treating psychiatric disorders. But those studies that do exist are generally supportive. For example, Greenberg and Watson (1998) have shown that humanistic person-centred therapies are effective for the treatment of depression. A randomized controlled trial conducted by King and colleagues (2000) found no difference between cognitive behaviour therapy offered by clinical psychologists and client-centred psychotherapy offered by person-centred counsellors in the treatment of depression. Both were equally effective. Other evidence showed person-centred therapy to be effective in primary care when outcome was assessed five years later (Gibbard and Hanley, 2008), and as effective as more structured CBT approaches in real-world contexts for helping people with generic psychological problems (Brettle et al., 2008).

Current directions

Despite the lack of research, most commentators take the position that client-centred therapy is less effective for severe and chronic conditions. However, Rogers (1957) was of the opinion that the most essential ingredient for therapeutic change was the quality of the relationship between therapist and client, no matter what the client group was, and that client-centred therapy was useful even for psychotic clients. Until recently the use of client-centred therapy with psychotic clients had not received a great deal of attention. But this too is beginning to change.

Pre-therapy

Recent writers in the person-centred tradition have begun to explore the use of client-centred therapy with psychosis and so-called personality disorders (Lambers, 1994a, b, c). *Pre-therapy* has been introduced as a way of working with clients who have difficulty maintaining contact, which is the first necessary condition according to Rogers for therapeutic change to take place (Prouty, 1976, 1990; Prouty and Kubiak, 1988; Sanders, 2007a). Pre-therapy involves the therapist reflecting to the client his or her awareness of the client's external world. For example, the therapist will reflect to the client about his or her facial expressions, body postures, and communication. By doing this the therapist is able to facilitate the client in engaging with the therapist so that more conventional client-centred therapy can take place.

Process-experiential approach

Several alternative therapeutic approaches based on Rogers' client-centred therapy have also been developed. One is the *process-experiential approach* pioneered by Greenberg and colleagues (Greenberg et al., 1993). The process-experiential approach emphasizes an information-processing perspective, attempting to synthesize ideas from the client-centred tradition with those of the cognitive tradition.

Other variations include the experiential approach of Rennie (1998) which accepts the principle of non-directivity over the content of the client's material, but proposes a more directive approach to the process, using a range of experiential techniques to increase the client's self-awareness. Although not all therapists would agree that the conditions described by Rogers are necessary and sufficient for constructive personality change, most would probably agree that empathy, unconditional positive regard, and congruence are important therapist qualities which are perhaps necessary if not sufficient for change. Indeed, studies show that these qualities are often evident in other therapists from psychodynamic and behavioural traditions, and some have argued that it is these factors which are important in promoting successful therapeutic change in all therapies. We shall go on to look at the common and non-specific factors in therapeutic healing in more detail in the final chapter.

Motivational interviewing

Another more recent approach is that of *motivational interviewing* (Rollnick and Miller, 1995). Motivational interviewing is based on the finding that the person-centred qualities of the therapist are important ingredients of therapy. However, motivational interviewing adds a more directive element by skilfully helping the client to explore the pros and cons of change in order to motivate him or her towards making the necessary changes. Motivational interviewing has been described as a brief and directive form of person-centred counselling. It has become popular as a form of coaching (Passmore and Whybrow, 2007), and has been shown to be effective with clients with substance-use problems (Ford et al., 2006; Miller et al., 1992) (see Box 5.2).

Box 5.2 Alex

Although Alex found his experience in psychotherapy useful in understanding how his early and violent upbringing had led him to become the person he had become, he found it difficult to stop drinking, and through the advice of his therapist he entered into therapy with someone specializing in motivational interviewing. This therapist helped Alex to explore the pros and cons of his drinking and through this process Alex was able to make a decision to stop. Initially Alex was quite dismissive of the idea that therapy could help him, but one of the central features of motivational interviewing is that the therapist is not confrontational. Rather the idea is to facilitate self-confrontation. Alex's therapist avoided arguments with Alex – one of the things motivational interviewers learn to do is to roll with resistance, a sort of verbal judo, in which the therapist maintains momentum toward change.

As we have seen, the essence of person-centred therapy is not what the therapist does but the therapist's attitudinal qualities, the relationship which is formed between the therapist and the client, and thus the promotion of the actualizing tendency. It is this trust in the ability of individuals to develop and grow in a positive direction that is the foundation of the humanistic approach, and which is the unifying theme throughout all humanistic therapies. As well as applications to individual therapy, person-centred philosophy is also used to inform group therapy approaches. Carl Rogers was a founder of the *encounter group movement* in the 1960s. Encounter groups, sometimes called T-groups (T for training), are groups of individuals who come together to heighten their self-awareness and promote their personal development. Members of an encounter group focus on the present and their interpersonal relations.

Other humanistic-existential approaches

Person-centred therapy is perhaps the best known of the humanistic approaches, but it is not the only humanistic therapy. Two other notable humanistic-existential therapies are Gestalt therapy and transactional analysis, which we will now consider.

Fritz Perls and Gestalt therapy

Fritz Perls (1893–1970), along with his wife Laura Perls and the philosopher Paul Goodman, founded what is known as *Gestalt therapy*.

The word 'Gestalt' is German and is taken to mean the total configuration of an object, the idea that an entity is more than the sum of the parts of which it is composed. The fundamental idea behind Gestalt therapy is that the client experiences and explores the total configuration of who they are. Gestalt therapy is a therapeutic approach which, like client-centred therapy, emphasizes self-determination, choice, and responsibility. However, in practice, Perls' ideas contrasted sharply with those of Rogers because he advocated a more confrontational approach. In therapy the client is helped to maintain awareness and full contact with the present situation and the therapist interacts with the client in such a way as to facilitate the client's focus on the 'here and now'. For example, the therapist might ask the client to say what he or she is aware of right now, and to 'stay with' that awareness in order to train the client in present-centred attention. Other techniques used by Gestalt therapists are those which heighten the client's experience; the client may be asked to repeat what she is saying in an exaggerated way so as to enhance her experience. For example, someone who says that she is angry might be encouraged to shout it louder. Perhaps the most well-known of all the Gestalt techniques is the 'empty chair', or 'two-chair', exercise which is often used to help clients resolve conflicts. Perhaps it is a conflict over an important decision that has to be made. The client sits facing the empty chair and imagines one part of the inner conflict to be sitting in the chair opposite. The client is encouraged to talk to that other part, to maintain a dialogue between the two parts of the inner conflict, until some integration between the two parts is achieved. The exercise can be used in a variety of ways; often people will use it to explore interpersonal conflicts (see Box 5.3).

Box 5.3 Alex

Alex's therapist helps him to explore his feelings towards his father using the two-chair exercise. Alex draws a picture of his father looking angry and sets it on the chair opposite and begins to talk to it. At first Alex is angry, shouting at his father for having treated him so poorly as a child. But as he switches seats and replies as his father, Alex begins to feel sadness too. Talking from his father's seat, Alex tells how he didn't want to hurt his son, how confused he was as a father, how he couldn't control his drinking and had no one to turn to himself, and how sorry he is for the pain he caused. Alex can still not forgive his father, although during this session he comes to understand for the first time how much psychological pain his father was experiencing after the separation from his wife and while he was struggling to bring up Alex on his own. At the end of the session, Alex goes over to the picture and redraws a sad face on the picture.

Although Gestalt therapists employ a variety of techniques to heighten emotional awareness, what is more important to the Gestalt therapist is the ability to stay present with the client:

> To practise the Gestalt approach means that the counsellor uses himself or herself actively and authentically in the encounter with the other person. It is more a 'way of being and doing' than a set of techniques or a prescribed formula for counselling. Gestalt is characterised by a willingness on the part of the counsellor to be active, present as a person and interventionist in the counselling relationship. This is based on the assumption that treating the client as a human being with intelligence, responsibility and active choices at any moment in time is most likely to invite the client into autonomy, self-healing and integration. (Clarkson, 1989, pp. 19–20)

In contrast to client-centred therapy, which has some scientific research base supporting its effectiveness as a form of therapy, Gestalt therapy has tended to attract little serious research interest.

Eric Berne and transactional analysis

Eric Berne (1910–1970) introduced a system of therapy known as *transactional analysis* (TA) (Berne, 1971). The practice of TA is founded on three assumptions (Stewart, 1989):

- At their core people are 'OK'. Although the therapist may not like the person's behaviour, the therapist values and esteems the client.
- The TA therapist holds that each person has the capacity to think and make decisions about their life.
- People can behave differently: the way we think, feel, and behave is our own choice.

These are fundamental assumptions common to the humanistic approaches and for this reason transactional analysis has been included in this chapter. However, Berne trained in classical psychoanalysis and some might instead include his work as a later development in psychodynamic theory.

Thinking Martian

Berne encouraged people to *think Martian* – to observe human behaviour without preconceptions about what it means, to listen to how people say things as well as what they say. This involves the recognition that messages from one person to another can operate on two levels; what Berne referred to as the social level and the psychological level. The social level refers to what we say to one another, whereas the psychological level refers to what we really mean. For example, at a social level we might greet someone with the words, 'It's nice to see you', but the tone of our voice, or our eye contact, might say something else, such as 'Oh no, I was hoping you wouldn't be here, it really isn't nice to see you at all'. When the social and the psychological levels are incongruent in this way, the psychological message is said to be *ulterior*. Berne (1964, 1966, 1972) maintained that the psychological message was always the real message and it was this level that always determined what happened. In practice the role of the TA therapist is to be aware of, and to make the client aware of, the psychological level in his or her communication.

Ego states

Berne outlined a complex theoretical framework which therapists use to discuss with clients the nature of interpersonal communication. He outlined what he called the *ego state model* which consists of three ego states: the child, the parent, and the adult. In our child ego state we think and feel in a way we did when we were children. In our parent ego state we think and feel in a way that resembles those of the significant parental figures in our childhood. In our adult ego state we think and feel in ways that are direct responses to the here-and-now environment. Any behaviour is driven by the ego state which is in control of the personality at that moment. Feelings of inferiority, as well as those of spontaneous joy, are associated with the child. Criticism and orthodoxy are associated with the parent. Unemotional appraisal of the environment is associated with the adult. Normally we move in and out of these different ego states. Problems are understood in terms of the functional breakdown of barriers between ego states. For example, delusional ideation occurs where there is a breakdown between child and adult ego states such that child imagery contaminates the adult appraisal of the world. We can also analyze interpersonal interactions in terms of the communication between individuals at an ego state level of analysis. Often at a social level it might appear that we are talking adult to adult, but at the psychological level something else is happening, for example, we are talking parent to child, or child to parent. Berne also described the pathological games that people play in terms of stereotyped ego state communication.

Life-script

Transactional analysis provides a very elaborate model, taking the view that psychological problems often have their roots in childhood.

Understanding their communication with others also involves exploring the client's *life-script*. This is the plan decided in early life by each person about the course of his or her life, how it begins, what happens in the middle, and how it ends. Berne said that the life script was laid down between the ages of three and seven, and reflects one of four possible judgements about the self and others:

1. I'm OK and you're OK
2. I'm not OK, but you're OK
3. I'm OK, but you're not OK
4. I'm not OK, and you're not OK.

Such feelings reflect parental introjections in infancy and form the basis of the way the child experiences his or her life. As the introjections of these parental messages takes place at such a young age they are not the product of reasoned and logical thinking. The life-script is likened to each person's own unfolding drama. In childhood, each of us develops our own personal life story, which is referred to as the life-script. We carry these life-scripts into adulthood and play them out unconsciously, finding ways to confirm our early decisions. The content of our scripts is unique to each of us, although common script themes have been identified. For example:

I mustn't grow up
I mustn't be important
I mustn't exist
I mustn't make it
I mustn't feel
I mustn't be me

The therapist endeavours to identify the client's script beliefs and to confront the life-script and encourage autonomy. The therapist aims to facilitate the client's recognition that he can now make different decisions in life (see Stewart, 1989). The life-script represents the infant's way of surviving and getting his or her needs met in what seems to be a hostile world. The child makes decisions, at an unconscious level, and as an adult the person plays out part of this script. For example, the child might perceive the parent as wanting him or her to be different. With parents who wanted a girl instead of a boy, for example, a child might come to decide that 'I mustn't be me'. This script belief might be expressed in a variety of ways, for example, a sense of the self as inferior, or through behaviour typical of the opposite sex. It might be that Alex's script was 'I mustn't feel'. Although transactional analysis has a wide appeal, it has not been subject to extensive scientific testing as a form of therapy.

Berne, despite being included here as a humanistic thinker, encouraged a medical perspective to psychotherapy. To illustrate what he meant he used the analogy of a man who gets a splinter in his toe. The toe becomes infected and the man starts to limp. This leads his back and neck muscles to tighten up and in turn he develops headaches, as well as a fever from the infection. How should we approach this person? What is needed, Berne argued, is a diagnosis of splinter in the toe followed by its removal, with the result that all the symptoms quickly disappear:

> Running through this I think you will hear the dread medical model of psychotherapy, which scares the hell out of people – gives them nightmares. But I think it's a very good model. That's because it works for other conditions, and if you are going to cure people's heads I think you should use the medical model. (Berne, 1971, p. 12)

Existential approaches

There is no doubt that Rogers' approach to therapy was influenced very much by his own personality and his experiences in life – particularly growing up in a strongly Christian family – as well as existential philosophy (see Thorne, 1992). Rogers often referred to the writings of two philosophers whose ideas he thought resonated with the person-centred approach, Buber and Kierkegaard. Indeed, to an extent, the person-centred approach, transactional analysis, and Gestalt therapy may be thought of as forms of *humanistic-existential* philosophy (Rogers, 1973). But perhaps the name most associated with the humanistic-existential approach is that of Victor Frankl.

Frankl (1905–1997) spent three years in the Nazi concentration camps during the Second World War, during which time he experienced the deaths of his parents, wife, and brother. His experiences led him to emphasize the search for meaning in people's lives and to conclude that a fundamental purpose in life is to find meaning in a world which seems meaningless (Frankl, 1963, 1967). Meaning can come about through achievement, transcendent experience, and through suffering. Frankl developed a system of therapy known as *logotherapy* in which clients are helped to become fully aware of their own responsibilities, to develop choice over what attitudes are held, and to look at the existential vacuum of life. Using persuasion and reasoning as well as interpretations and confrontation, logotherapists attempt to raise the consciousness of their client. One particular technique is paradoxical intention, in which the client is encouraged to do what he or she fears doing.

Other notable existential therapists were Ludwig Binswanger (1881–1966) and Medard Boss (1903–1991) who endeavoured to understand the meaning of the client's experience, and used the discipline of philosophy rather than psychology to understand the human predicament. In more recent years, Yalom (1980) and van Deurzen (1988, 1998) have helped to bring existential psychotherapy to our attention:

> Radical existential psychotherapy focuses on the inter-personal and supra-personal dimensions, as it tries to capture and question people's world views. Such existential work aims at clarifying and understanding personal values and beliefs, making explicit what was previously implicit and unsaid. Its practice is primarily philosophical and seeks to enable a person to live more deliberately, more authentically and more purposefully, whilst accepting the limitations and contradictions of human existence ... Existential psychotherapy has to be reinvented and recreated by every therapist and with every new client. It is essentially about investigating human existence and the particular preoccupations of one individual and this has to be done without preconceptions or set ways of proceeding. There has to be complete openness to the individual situation and an attitude of wonder that will allow the specific circumstances and experiences to unfold in their own right. (van Deurzen, 1998, pp. 13–14)

Issues raised in existential psychotherapy are bound up with questions about the meaning and purpose of life – what it is to be human (Jacobson, 2007). Existential therapy is also concerned with metaphysical issues to do with good and evil, life and death, and consequently existential therapy often overlaps with the field of transpersonal psychotherapy (Rowan, 1993) (see Box 5.4).

Transpersonal psychotherapy

Towards the end of his life, Rogers became interested in altered states of consciousness and began to advocate a more spiritual understanding of human experience. Rogers stated that he was attracted to Arthur Koestler's view that individual consciousness was a fragment of cosmic consciousness (Rogers, 1980). Talking about what happened in therapy when he was most effective as a therapist, Rogers wrote:

> At those moments it seems that my inner spirit has reached out and touched the inner spirit of the other. Our relationship transcends itself and becomes part of something larger. Profound growth and healing and energy are present. (Rogers, 1980, p. 129)

Box 5.4   Tom

Tom, who was involved in the car accident, was referred to psychological services by his GP. The psychologist diagnosed him as suffering from posttraumatic stress disorder and offered him cognitive behavioural therapy. Tom benefited from the help he received from the psychologist, who showed him ways of managing his distress and techniques to help him get to sleep at night. The treatment with the psychologist lasted for ten sessions, at the end of which Tom was managing much better and had returned to work. However, inside he was, in his own words, still screaming. A friend had been to see a therapist and suggested to Tom that he visit her too as she was very helpful. Tom, like many people who choose to see a therapist, didn't know that there were different types, and so he was unaware that his therapist, Barbara, was a client-centred therapist who integrated existential and transpersonal ideas. But, Barbara explained about her way of working and that she was there to help Tom to make sense of his experiences in his own way, and in his own time. She seemed so different to Tom from the psychologist he had seen, who had sat with a notebook on his lap and asked questions. At first Tom was confused, expecting Barbara to do the same, but by the end of the first meeting Tom was surprised at how quickly the session had gone, and how good it felt having someone listen to him, someone who seemed to be trying to understand things from his perspective. Tom didn't mention his feelings of guilt in the first session – he didn't know if he could trust Barbara yet. It was only several weeks later that he did – and he looked nervously at Barbara as he told her – and felt huge relief that she did not seem to judge him. Over the following months, Tom met Barbara weekly and he came to an understanding that there was nothing he could do to change the past but that he had to find ways to live with his experience.

Some writers have discussed spirituality within the person-centred approach (e.g., Purton, 1998; Thorne, 1991, 1994). Humanistic-existential approaches lend themselves more easily to integration with spiritual ideas than, for example, the cognitive-behavioural approaches (see Payne et al., 1992). But Rogers himself did not elaborate much further on a *transpersonal* approach, which is probably most closely associated with the work of Abraham Maslow, who is recognised as the founder of the transpersonal approach.

Abraham Maslow and the hierarchy of needs

Abraham Maslow, like Rogers, emphasized human beings as striving to fulfil their potential. But whereas Rogers saw behaviour as being driven

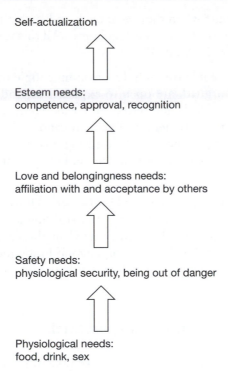

Self-actualization

Esteem needs:
competence, approval, recognition

Love and belongingness needs:
affiliation with and acceptance by others

Safety needs:
physiological security, being out of danger

Physiological needs:
food, drink, sex

Figure 5.3   Maslow's hierarchy of needs

by the self-concept, Maslow was concerned with the motives that drive
people. He suggested that there were two kinds of motivations, which
he called deficiency motivation, that is, the need to reduce physiological
tensions such as thirst and hunger, and growth motivation, that is, the
satisfaction of needs such as the need to be loved and esteemed. Maslow
described a *hierarchy of human needs* (see Figure 5.3).

First, a person must meet physiological needs. When these needs have
been met the person moves up to safety and security needs. When these
needs have been met, the person moves up to belongingness needs. Finally, when all the basic needs have been met, the person strives to meet
his or her needs for self-actualization. Achieving self-actualization is not
an all-or-nothing process – rather self-actualization comes about over
time by a matter of small changes. Maslow suggested that self-actualized
individuals are self-directed, creative, and independent, have an accurate
view of themselves and other people, are willing to try and understand
other people's points of view, and are open to new experiences:

> They listen to their own voices; they take responsibility; they are hon-
> est; and they work hard. They find out who they are and what they
> are, not only in terms of their mission in life, but also in terms of the

way their feet hurt when they wear such and such a pair of shoes and whether they do or do not like eggplant ... All this is what the real self means. (Maslow, 1993, p. 49)

Self-actualized people (or fully functioning people in the language of Rogers), Maslow argued, are open to experiences, and one form of experience that particularly interested him was what he called peak experiences. These are experiences that transcend ordinary human consciousness, often experienced as being religious or spiritual in nature. Such experiences are seen as existing beyond the person, hence the term, transpersonal:

> I should say also that I consider Humanistic, Third Force Psychology to be transitional, a preparation for a still 'higher' Fourth Psychology, transpersonal, transhuman, centred in the cosmos rather than in human needs and interest, going beyond humanness, identity, self-actualization and the like. (Maslow, 1968, pp. iii–iv)

Stanislav Grof and the transpersonal

Since Maslow's death, his colleagues have gone on to explore and map out the field of transpersonal psychology. One leading exponent is Stanislav Grof. Grof was a close friend of Maslow and together they helped found the International Transpersonal Association. Grof trained as a medical doctor, going on to conduct psychiatric research into schizophrenic experiences and the potential value of LSD. From this work he developed interests in the transpersonal and in his career attempted to integrate Western science with the wisdom of the great spiritual systems. Grof has written about how experiences in the womb and during birth provide psychospiritual blueprints which guide the way we experience life and can become reflected in psychopathology. Grof also draws on the work of Jung among others (e.g., Sheldrake, 1981) in linking our experience with those of a collective unconscious, one that exists beyond the boundaries of what we perceive as space and time:

> Over three decades of systematic studies of the human consciousness have led me to conclusions that many traditional psychiatrists and psychologists might find implausible if not downright incredible. I now firmly believe that consciousness is more than an accidental by-product of the neurophysiological and biochemical processes taking place in the human brain. I see consciousness and the human psyche as expressions and reflections of a cosmic intelligence that permeates the entire universe and all of existence. We are not just highly evolved

animals with biological computers embedded inside our skulls; we are also fields of consciousness without limits, transcending time, space, matter, and linear causality. (Grof and Bennett, 1990, p. 18)

Grof reaches his conclusions from his observations of people experiencing trance states and spontaneous psychospiritual crises, or those states achieved through meditation, hypnosis, psychedelic sessions, and experiential psychotherapy. Grof discusses Jung's concept of synchronicity:

In a mechanical universe where everything is linked by cause and effect, there is no place for 'meaningful coincidences' in the Jungian sense. In the practice of traditional psychiatry, when a person perceives meaningful coincidences, he or she is, at best, diagnosed as projecting special meaning into purely accidental events; at worst he or she is diagnosed as suffering from hallucinations or delusions ... As a result they may wrongly diagnose 'meaningful coincidences' as the result of serious pathology ... Had those experiences been correctly understood and treated as manifestations of psycho-spiritual crisis those same people might have been quickly helped through approaches supporting spiritual emergence, rather than undergoing all the problems that unnecessary hospitalisation entails. (Grof and Bennett, 1990, p. 178)

Jung described his experiences of states of non-ordinary consciousness and his communications with a spirit guide called Philemon. According to the criteria of the traditional scientific inquiry, the evidence for these views is restricted to anecdotal accounts which cannot be verified. But, as with the humanistic approaches, Grof argues that the therapist must accept and trust the spontaneous unfolding of the process. This is a view in line with Jung's, that there is an inner wisdom for healing which comes from the collective unconscious. What psychiatrists might view as mental illness can come to be seen in a different light. For example, one writer who has provided some very interesting insights from his personal experience is Chadwick, who writes:

'Schizophrenia', whatever it might mean, shows life in a blazing and terrifying light, it is difficult to believe that one is being enlightened at the same time as this cruel pain is searing through one's psyche. My argument here is that this is indeed the case ... The psychotic experience takes one to the crags and ridges of human life and to the precipices of what consciousness can permit. It is very difficult after this to take on board the model of reality provided by science, which is like providing someone with a shoe box when they want an enclosure for an elephant. (Chadwick, 1997, pp. 39–40)

Transpersonal psychologists often draw on quantum physics (e.g., Bohm, 1980) to provide a theoretical foundation for their work. For example, the ideas of Tart (1975) are important. Tart has argued that there are realms of awareness beyond those which we understand today. We can use science, he says, but:

> the world we spend most of our time perceiving is not just any segment of the physical world, but a highly socialised part of the physical world that has been built into cities, automobiles, television sets. So our perception may indeed be realistic, but it is only with respect to a very tailored segment of reality, a *consensus* reality, a small selection of things we have agreed are 'real' and 'important.' Thus, within our particular cultural framework, we can easily set up what seem to be excellent scientific experiments that will show our perceptions are indeed realistic, in the sense that we agree with each other on these selected items from our consensus reality. (Tart, 1975, p. 39)

Ken Wilber and levels of consciousness

According to Tart we are prisoners of our ordinary state of consciousness, and Western science is challenged to recognize that our normal state of consciousness is a state of samsara, the Buddhist word for the state of suffering. But perhaps the writer who has been most influential in recent years in helping to lay the foundations for transpersonal psychology is Ken Wilber, who has attempted to integrate the religious traditions of the East with the psychology of the West. Wilber, drawing upon many traditions, including Hinduism, has discussed how consciousness exists as a hierarchy of dimensional levels. Wilber describes six levels of consciousness:

1. Physical
2. Biological
3. Psychological
4. Subtle
5. Causal
6. Ultimate

The physical level is that of physics and chemistry; the biological level is concerned with living matter; and the psychological level is concerned with thinking and feeling, in much the same way as it was described in the previous chapters. Moving beyond these dimensions, however, we enter the transpersonal. There is the subtle level, which Wilber says is the level of visionary insight, archetypal intuition, clarity of awareness, and higher experiences; then the causal level, which is the realm of dissolution and transcendence of subject-object duality; and finally, the ultimate, the highest level of consciousness. Therapy is about facilitating a person's development within the transpersonal realm of experience (Boorstein, 1980; Rowan, 1993, 2005).

Translation vs. transformation

There are similarities here with Buddhism, because people come to cease identifying with their construction of themselves, to realize at a profound level that there is no self. Wilber draws an interesting distinction between *translation* and *transformation*. Translation is when we come to think differently, and therefore to behave differently in the world, as would be the case in cognitive therapy. Transformation, on the other hand, refers to completely and radically dismantling our way of seeing the world, shattering our perception of the world as we know it. Both translation and transformation are legitimate models of change, Wilber argues, each being concerned with a different level of consciousness (see Wilber, 1998). Similarly, other writers have also focused on the relationship between Western psychotherapy and the ideas of Eastern religious traditions. Eastern thought also emphasizes the interconnectedness of all things, and how it is an illusion to see ourselves as separate from the world around us. Drawing on Eastern traditions, Brazier (1995) discusses how Zen is a form of therapy:

> The challenge which Zen poses us is to reach deeply into the experience of being alive to find something authentic ... Zen is simply the awakening of one heart by another, of sincerity by sincerity. Although words can express it, and can point to it, they cannot substitute for it. It is the authentic experience which occurs when concern with all that is inessential drops away. (Brazier, 1995, pp. 12–13)

Eastern approaches to therapy, along with other transpersonal approaches, most often involve some form of meditation and altered states of consciousness. In discussing transpersonal therapy, Grof and Bennett write:

> In work with non-ordinary states of consciousness, the roles of therapist and client are quite different from those in traditional psychotherapy. The therapist is not the active agent who causes the changes

in the client by specific interventions, but is somebody who intelligently co-operates with the inner healing forces of the client ... It is also in agreement with C.G. Jung's approach to psychotherapy, wherein it is believed that the task of the therapist is to mediate for the client a contact and exchange with his or her inner self, which then guides the process of transformation and individuation. The wisdom for change and healing comes from the collective unconscious and surpasses by far the knowledge that is intellectually available to the therapist. (Grof and Bennett, 1990, p. 211)

Conclusion

Running throughout this book has been the theme of research and how it relates to therapeutic practice. However, when we begin to discuss the ideas of the humanistic and transpersonal psychologists, we can see how some theorists within these traditions have come to doubt the value of traditional scientific inquiry for understanding what goes on in their domain of interest. As we have seen in Chapter 4, psychological research often adopts the medical model to test for the effectiveness of therapy, but humanistic and transpersonal psychologists do not generally view therapy as akin to the administration of a drug and thus question the reliance on RCTs to make decisions about effectiveness. Rather, they are more concerned with understanding human experience. As such, interviews with clients which are analyzed using qualitative methods of research are often employed to find out about clients' experiences, what they find helpful and unhelpful, and to give a voice to clients.

The influence of humanistic psychology remains a major force within the professions of counselling and psychotherapy, and there seems to be a recent growth in interest towards the related transpersonal and existential therapies. Indeed, the British Psychological Society now has a section of its membership devoted entirely to transpersonal psychology. However, the influence of humanistic and transpersonal approaches within the field of psychology remains minimal, and perhaps even less influential in the field of psychiatry. The reason for this lack of interest is often stated as the reluctance of many humanistic practitioners to put their model and their ways of working with clients to the test using the methods of empirical psychological science. For this reason many academic psychologists have viewed the humanistic perspective with disdain. However, there is now a growing recognition that the discipline of psychology must also embrace more holistic approaches, and also of the importance of the positive psychology espoused by the humanistic writers.

Summary points

- Humanistic psychology has been referred to as the third force after psychoanalysis and behaviourism. Unlike these earlier approaches humanistic psychology emphasized personal responsibility and choice in people's lives.
- Rogers developed the client-centred approach to therapy which was based on the philosophical premise that there is a single motivational force towards constructive growth within each person, the actualizing tendency. Problems in living result when the actualizing tendency is thwarted.
- The client-centred therapist endeavours to create a facilitative environment which nurtures the actualizing tendency.
- In the early years of client-centred therapy the approach was subject to much research which supported its effectiveness, although in more recent years practitioners of the client-centred approach have tended not to emphasize the importance of traditional scientific research or to adopt the medical model.
- Other humanistic approaches include Gestalt therapy, developed by Perls, and transactional analysis, developed by Berne.
- After humanistic psychology, transpersonal psychology and psychotherapy has been called the fourth force. Transpersonal psychotherapy is about experiences which seem to transcend or go beyond the realms of ordinary human consciousness and experience.
- Leading figures in transpersonal psychotherapy include Maslow, Grof, and Wilber, who question our perceptions of reality.

Topics for reflection

1. The foundation stone of the person-centred approach is the concept of the actualizing tendency – the idea that people are intrinsically motivated towards growth, development, and optimal functioning. What do you think of this idea? Does it fit with your experience of people?
2. Transpersonal approaches are seen as a bit wacky by some. What do you think? Should therapy be concerned with spiritual issues and concepts which do not seem amenable to scientific understanding?
3. One of the most well known ideas from humanistic psychology is Maslow's hierarchy of needs. The fact of its enduring popularity is testimony to the deep truth this model contains about human existence. Would you agree?

Chapter 6

Sociological and Social Approaches

Introduction

Each of the psychological therapies discussed in the previous chapters is, in one way or another, concerned with processes internal to human beings. In contrast, writers in the sociological tradition draw attention to how a person's psychological problems are related to the workings of the social world. In this chapter we are not so much concerned with therapeutic approaches in themselves, but with looking at therapy from a sociological perspective. This can be thought of in two distinct ways:

- How therapy itself is a social phenomenon and how, therefore, what are considered to be psychological difficulties are *defined* by society. I refer to this as the social construction of therapy.
- How psychological difficulties are caused by society through poverty, conflict, inequalities, and so on. I refer to this as structuralism.

Social construction of therapy

In Chapter 1 we were reminded of the fable of the wise men sent into the pitch dark barn. Each, unable to see the elephant, reaches out. One, feeling the leg, exclaims that an elephant is like a tree. One, feeling the trunk, cries out, 'No an elephant is like a snake'. When we walk around the topic of therapy we are a bit like those wise men. Therapy is about changing dysfunctional thinking patterns. Therapy is about finding yourself. Therapy is about making conscious the unconscious. And so on. Which one of these ideas is right?

Berger and Luckmann and the sociology of knowledge

That's where sociology comes in. Sociologists have for years been concerned with how knowledge is socially constructed. In 1966, two sociologists, Berger and Luckmann, published *The Social Construction of Reality: A treatise in the sociology of knowledge*, which started a revolution in how we think about what we know. They argued that the social world does not have an objective existence. Rather, what we perceive as reality is socially constructed. It is a mistake, social constructionists argue, to attempt to understand the individual in isolation from other people. Through language and power we construct our realities. To the social constructionist, therefore, all of the models of therapy are simply ways of understanding human nature, how problems develop, and how help can be provided. Each model is equally valid, simply a way of thinking about human suffering. Therefore, rather than following the traditional scientific route and asking which one of the models is correct, we realize that they are co-existing perspectives. We can stand back from our assumptions about therapy and reflect on how the business of therapy is socially constructed.

While accepting that ideas are socially constructed, we don't need to deny that there is a reality at all. To do so is an extreme view. From what is called the *critical realist* point of view (Bhaskar, 1975), it is acknowledged that, although our systems of understanding may be imperfect, they are attempts to understand the reality of human nature. As such, each of the models of therapy has an independent legitimacy (Middleton, 2007). Staying with the wise men in the barn, we can agree that there is an elephant standing there, but it is dark and we can't actually see it. We can only reach out and touch parts of the elephant in the hope that we can build up a picture.

In each of the previous chapters, I talked about the problems people bring to therapy and what the therapist does to help the client. It's easy to see in the use of such language how our conversations about therapy are influenced by the medical model. Take, for example, the analogy that when people have a splinter in their toe they go to the doctor who carefully removes it. Sociologists draw our attention to how the therapeutic profession has been socially constructed in this way, not surprisingly because of its historical roots in medicine, through the influence of Freud who himself was a medical doctor, and into the present day where counselling and psychotherapy are generally seen as part of healthcare, as opposed to, for example, education (Hansen, 2007).

Thomas Szasz and the myth of mental illness

The medical model is currently the one that has become dominant, not because, social constructionists would argue, it is more correct than the others, but because it serves a needed social and cultural function. Such criticisms date back to Thomas Szasz (1961) who, in his famous book *The Myth of Mental Illness*, argued that the biomedical model, when applied to psychological problems, was simply metaphorical. Psychological problems are not, he argued, illnesses in the same way as flu is an illness. Szasz (1961) argued that to make such a claim was to make a metaphorical statement:

> I hold that mental illness is a metaphorical disease; that, in other words, bodily illness stands in the same relation to mental illness as a defective television receiver stands to an objectionable television programme. To be sure, the word 'sick' is often used metaphorically. We call jokes 'sick', economies 'sick', sometimes even the whole world 'sick' – but only when we call minds 'sick' do we systematically mistake metaphor for fact; and send to the doctor to 'cure' the illness. It's as if a television viewer were to send for a TV repairman because he disapproves of the programme he is watching. (Szasz, 1974, p. 11)

If this is the case, why would we choose to construe psychological problems in this way? The reason, Szasz argued, was that mental illness was a concept invented to control and change people whose behaviour threatens the social order. During the slave trade, slaves who tried to escape were diagnosed as suffering from *drapetomania*, which was a sickness that caused them to seek freedom (Szasz, 1971).

It may be easy in hindsight to see the social control functions of the diagnosis of *drapetomania*, but sociologists challenge us to examine the functions of our current ways of looking at the world. As we saw in Chapter 2, the American Psychiatric Association's DSM is widely accepted as providing a common language for research and practice into psychological problems. The DSM has become so widely used that we don't often stop to question it but assume that it correctly describes the range of psychiatric disorders that exist. But what the social constructionist view says is that this, as with any other way of understanding people's problems, is nothing more than a fabrication that reflects its historical and cultural context. In Chapter 2 it was mentioned that in past times witchcraft was often seen as a cause of a person's behaviour. That may seem strange to us today but remember the culture at the time accepted the existence of witches and it is understandable that people used the beliefs of the day to explain behaviour. Similarly, although we can look back and be critical of asylums, at the time they offered treatments in line with the belief that mental problems were medical. For example, blood letting involved drawing huge amounts of blood from the patient in the belief that problems were caused by a build up of excess blood. We need to be aware that our perceptions are bounded by our cultural context.

An example which shows us that this is not an issue confined to the distant past or other cultures concerns psychiatrists' views of homosexuality over the past 40 years. Many people ceased to be ill in 1973 when homosexuality was removed from the American Psychiatric Association's *Diagnostic and Statistical Manual for Mental Disorders* (DSM). The first edition of DSM had classified homosexuality as a sexual deviation within the category of sociopathic personality disturbances. Homosexuality remained a sexual deviation in the second edition of DSM published in 1968, under the category of personality disorders. However, in 1973 the second edition of DSM was modified when the board of trustees of the American Psychiatric Association voted to eliminate the general category of homosexuality as a mental disorder, unless it was distressing to the person concerned. The exclusion of homosexuality from DSM came about as a result of political pressure from gay activist groups who maintained that its continued inclusion was inappropriate and oppressive. Within the American Psychiatric Association this was a controversial decision and the debate about the proper place of homosexuality within psychiatric classification continued. But what this illustrates is that the way in which particular behaviours become socially constructed as problematic or not, and how psychiatric classifications are applied, is not necessarily value-free.

Structuralism, mental health, and therapy

In medicalizing, and even psychologizing, people's problems in living we ignore, sociologists claim, the importance of the reality of the social world. In the same way that psychological theorists sometimes criticize the biomedical model for being reductionist in its focus on the biological rather than the psychological, sociologists are critical of the psychological approach for its lack of analysis of the importance of the social world.

Structuralism

Structuralism refers to the view that our behaviour is largely dictated by our membership of social groups and the institutions of society, such as marriage, education, and the way in which the boundaries of society are defined in terms of sex, age, and social status, for example, and how these vary cross-culturally. Further, sociologists are interested in how these structures are maintained, for example, by the political and religious ideologies (Morrall, 2008). Sociology asks us therefore to understand the individual within the wider social context.

Emile Durkheim and suicide

Few who have lived through the economic roller coaster of the late twentieth and early twenty-first centuries, the ups and the downs, would fail to recognize that what's happening in the wider world does not connect to the individual (Pointon, 2008). One of the defining studies in this area was conducted by the French sociologist Emile Durkheim (1858–1917). Durkheim (1897) was concerned with the way society has a set of values and norms which we usually behave in accordance with. When our own values no longer match those of the society in which we live, then our ties with that society are weakened, resulting in what Durkheim called *anomie*. Durkheim related this loss of social cohesion to some forms of suicide.

Hollingshead and Redlich

Sociologists have subsequently been interested in how feelings of anomie and alienation affect mental health. They have often drawn on the work of Marx, who argued that capitalism led to alienation as industrialized workers became estranged from their creativity and connection to others (see Morrall, 2008). The publication of *Social Class and Mental Illness: A Community Study* by Hollingshead and Redlich (1958) was a landmark work which recognized that sociocultural factors external to the person are important determinants of thoughts, feelings, and behaviour.

Brown and Harris

Building on such work, Brown and Harris (1978) conducted their famous study of women living in London. They found that those women who were diagnosed as depressed were more likely to have young children at home, less employment, and fewer people to talk to about their worries than those women who were not diagnosed as depressed. This landmark study was important in drawing attention to the social origins of depression. This and subsequent evidence leaves us with no doubt that psychological problems are related to social factors, such as unemployment, economic hardship, poverty, ethnicity, and social class (see Argyle, 1994). This is most evident in psychiatric hospitals, where a large proportion of patients will usually be from lower social class and ethnic minority backgrounds (Banyard, 1996; Pilgrim, 1997; Shaikh, 1985). Why might this be?

How social factors cause problems

Several explanations are possible. On the one hand there are explanations based on methodology rather than any real group differences: for example, it has been suggested that psychiatrists, who are mostly white and middle class, misperceive what is normal behaviour within other cultural groups as abnormal (Banyard, 1996). On the other hand, there are explanations based on real differences between the groups. From the biomedical perspective, it might be suggested that there are genetic differences leading to an innate vulnerability to psychological problems. But from the sociological perspective, we must consider that higher rates of psychological disturbance in ethnic minorities are a response to racism and disadvantage (see Littlewood and Lipsedge, 1993).

It has been suggested that those who are less able to function in society end up in the lowest social strata (and those who are able to function effectively move up the social strata). This is called the *downward drift hypothesis,* and most commentators would agree that this process plays at least a part in explaining the relationship between social class and health (see Williams, 1990). However, the downward drift hypothesis does not seem to fully account for the relationship between social class and psychopathology. It is also thought that those with lower social status are subject to more life-stressors and are therefore more likely to experience psychological problems. Certainly, there is evidence supporting the idea that people of lower social status experience greater life-stress (e.g., Gunnell et al., 1995; McLeod and Kessler, 1990) and engage in poorer health behaviours, such as smoking and taking less exercise (e.g., Blaxter, 1990), which in turn might contribute to poorer psychological health. Such health detrimental behaviours are, of course, linked to wider social factors. When we look across cultures therefore we have to be careful to take into account the norms of that society, and how they influence people's thoughts, feelings, and behaviours. In particular we have to be sensitive to issues related to sex roles, ethnicity, and social class, and how these influence our perceptions of what is pathological.

Impress of power

Smail (1996) has argued that the working of social power is central to understanding psychological problems. He sees individual distress as the outcome of a social process in which psychological problems have their origin in powerful factors, often distant in the person's life history, of politics, economics, and culture. It is the misuse of power which is ultimately at the core of people's difficulties (see also Hagan and Smail, 1997a, b; Smail, 2005). Thus, what sets the sociological perspective so

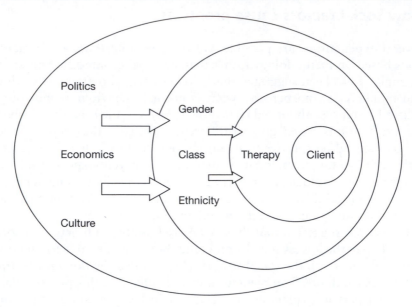

Figure 6.1   Impress of power

far apart from all the other perspectives considered in this book is that it is not focused on the individual, but on society and social processes (see Figure 6.1).

Cultural worldviews

Social constructionism and social and structural influences draw attention to the interplay between social context, how certain behaviours are viewed and experienced, and those therapies that are offered. Contemporary psychiatry and psychology embody the values of Western culture, affecting the way that forms of behaviour are perceived. One example is how society views bereavement and the expectations for how people ought to mourn the loss of loved ones. In Western culture we expect people to move on relatively quickly compared to other cultures where it is expected that people will openly grieve for significant periods of time.

Sociology challenges us to look across cultures and across history for the similarities and differences in human experience. What might be seen as a problem in one culture or at one point in time might not be seen as such in another culture or at another time. For example, in Victorian England, masturbation was seen as a cause of madness. Children who persisted in masturbating despite warnings and punishment would sometimes be 'treated' surgically, by castration in boys and the removal of the clitoris in girls. Such practices rarely exist in Western society to-day, although genital mutilation remains a practice in other parts of the world (see Walker, 1993).

Many psychological problems that are unfamiliar in the Western context have been described elsewhere in the world. *Koro* is a syndrome seen in Southeast Asia. In men, koro consists of anxiety and a fear that the penis is retracting into the abdomen, resulting in death. In women koro consists of a sensation that the breasts and labia are shrinking. In order to prevent koro, men may try to prevent the shrinkage of their penis by stretching it by, for example, tying weights to it. Koro is extremely rare in Western society and has only been observed in association with schizophrenia or drug use. However, in Asia there have been epidemics of koro, such as those in 1982 in India and in 1976 in Thailand.

A woman in Bali might suffer from what is called *bebainin*, a syndrome that includes abdominal pain, headache, ringing in the ears, screaming, weeping, and impaired vision. The onset of bebainin is sudden and the duration of an episode is short, after which the person has no memory of what has happened. Another syndrome traditionally not seen in Western cultures is *amok*. The Malayan word 'amok' means 'to engage furiously in battle'. In the condition of amok men erupt, following a period of depression and brooding, into a sudden state of frenzied and unprovoked indiscriminate violence ending in exhaustion and amnesia. The affected person may run wildly about with a weapon such as a knife, killing those in his way, until he is overpowered, commits suicide, or is killed. The condition has traditionally been associated with the Malayan people and was relatively common a few hundred years ago, although it is rare today. Theorists have speculated that amok was related to the cultural values which placed heavy restrictions on adolescents and adults, and the belief in magical possession by demons and evil spirits. In Western culture we have seen in recent years several well-publicized episodes of behaviour which bear similarity to the condition of amok.

With such examples it is easy to see how important cultural and historical context is in shaping how we think about psychological problems. But from the social constructionist perspective we have to be careful not to assume that our own cultural worldview is the more correct one from which to judge what is normal or abnormal elsewhere. Our task is equally to understand how our own cultural worldview influences our understanding.

The influence of our own cultural worldview is illustrated when we consider the increase in eating problems. DSM-IV-TR (American Psychiatric Association, 2000) lists two major subtypes of eating disorder – anorexia nervosa and bulimia nervosa. People with anorexia nervosa starve themselves. They have a fear of gaining weight and of becoming fat. This is despite the fact they are often very underweight. People with bulimia nervosa will eat an excessive amount of food in a discrete period of time during which they lack control over their eating. This is then followed by purging behaviour, that is, self-induced vomiting, misuse of laxatives, or excessive exercise. Such behaviour is recurrent, happening on average twice a week. While not claiming that eating problems have no biomedical or psychological component, it would surely be a mistake to overlook the sociological aspect. Both of these eating problems are about ten times more common in females than in males, and most common in young women in their teens and early twenties. Also, they are more prevalent in women who have careers that place importance on appearance, such as modelling. Furthermore, research which has looked at the risk of eating problems in different generations of women has concluded that it became more prevalent in the latter half of the twentieth century (see Kendler et al., 1991; Ogden, 2003). These findings have led some researchers to speculate that our cultural attitudes about appearance are central to understanding these problems. In Western culture, appearance is valued highly. Studies have found a high percentage of women are dissatisfied with some aspect of their physical appearance. For example, in one American survey, over 10 per cent were found to be dissatisfied with their face, over 20 per cent with their upper torso, over 40 per cent with their weight, and over 50 per cent with their mid torso (Cash and Henry, 1995).

Challenging medicalization

This interplay between society, how problems are viewed, and what might be done about them raises the important question of 'Is it something wrong with the person, or is something wrong in their lives?' These are questions about how we construe problems in living, and about the value of the medical model. Maddux et al. wrote:

> psychopathology and mental disorder ... are social constructions – abstract ideas whose meanings are negotiated among the people and institutions of a culture and that reflect the values and power structure of that culture at a given time ... it is time to acknowledge that science can no more determine the proper or correct conception of psychopathology and mental disorder than it can determine the proper and correct conception of other social constructions such as beauty, justice, race, and social class. (Maddux et al., 2005, p. 16)

Clients also bring their own understandings into the consulting room. How people think about their problems will influence how they go about seeking help, and whether or not they value the help that they are given. People come to therapy with their own models of what therapy is, and what the nature of their problems is. Terry Lynch, the author of the book *Beyond Prozac* (2004), for example, talks about his concerns regarding the biomedical model and how treating psychological problems as if they were medical problems disempowers people. He expressed this view in an interview with Penny Gray for *Therapy Today*:

> I meet many people who keep giving me their power because it's all they've known, and I have to gently feed it back to them. It can take a person a long time before they are ready to take it back. But then again, if you think of what most doctors do with medication, that in its own way is disempowering, because the message the person is getting is 'I need this tablet to make me OK', and that creates a psychological dependence on the medication that doctors don't often spot. (Gray, 2005b, p. 36).

Similarly, as Dorothy Rowe wrote in her discussion of depression:

> The kind of theory that says that depression has a physical cause has the advantage that the depressed person is not responsible for the depression ... There are many depressed people who prefer to see their depression as a chronic physical illness ... The illness is a nuisance, demanding regular pill-taking ... but, like epilepsy or diabetes, it is something you are born with and it is not your fault ... The theory that depression arises from the way we live our life has the disadvantage that we have to take responsibility for ourselves ... people are free to choose which kind of theory suits them best. (Rowe, 2001, p. 5)

George Albee (2000), a prominent American psychologist, has argued that there are major political differences between the medical and biomedical models and the social and structural model. The latter requires social change and seeks to end poverty, discrimination, exploitation, and prejudices as sources of stress leading to emotional problems. By not aligning themselves with the social model, professional groups such as clinical psychologists have joined the forces that perpetuate social injustice. Similarly, in the UK, Gillian Proctor (2005) also discusses how, in mopping up the problems of a sick society, the profession of clinical psychology has preserved its status and power.

This is not to claim that those in the mental health professions, such as clinical psychologists, set out to harm, but to raise the question of whether they unwittingly serve to maintain the status quo and collude in social control (Joseph, 2007). As Rowe wrote:

> Improving Access to Psychological Therapies and cognitive behaviour therapy do not attempt to deal with the real issues. Their use of the language of medicine only serves to obscure the way in which poverty, deprivation, inequality between the sexes, classes and ethnic groups, and cultural institutions like marriage create the conditions where depression and anxiety flourish, and protects the government of the day from having to deal with these issues. (Rowe, 2009, p. 560)

Similarly, Morrall writes:

> The institutions of therapy attempt to wield power in society, over their membership, and, by default, over those who wish to have no part in their power games. Such virulent power is inevitably open to abuse ... Specifically, the ability of an individual to change his/her personal circumstances through therapy is dictated, limited, or moulded by 'social power' which is external to, and beyond the influence, of the client ... To give the client the impression that he/she has the power to overcome these socially generated obstacles is as abusive as ... selling mock medication to the desperately ill. Furthermore, another significant abuse by the enterprise of therapy is the (heavily disguised) role it plays as an agency of social control. (Morrall, 2008, pp. 125–6)

This is not to say that therapy is a bad thing, but therapy should not be given at the expense of tackling social problems. As an analogy, if a roof has a hole and the rain is getting in, therapy is the equivalent of mopping the floor. Morrall refers to this as emotional offsetting, in the sense that we talk now of carbon offsetting through planting trees and so on while continuing to avoid dealing with the cause of the problem itself:

> the displacement of psychological distress through facile self-help programs and illusory professionalized helping, imparts absolution for those governments and corporations who seriously pollute the mind (through encouraging rampant consumerism, and not acting to stop inequalities and poverty), and does not deal with the essential causes of a malfunctioning global society. (Morrall, 2008, p. 164)

Labelling

The interplay between society, behaviour of people, and professionals' responses leads to labelling. Szasz had this to say about psychiatric classification:

> Psychiatric diagnoses are stigmatising labels phrased to resemble medical diagnoses and applied to persons whose behaviour annoys or offends others. Those who suffer from and complain of their own behaviour are usually classified as 'neurotic'; those whose behaviour makes others suffer, and about whom others complain, are usually classified as 'psychotic'. (Szasz, 1974, p. 26)

The most famous study to illustrate the difficulties of diagnosis, as well as difficulties in distinguishing normal from abnormal behaviour, was conducted by David Rosenhan (1973). Rosenhan's research team of eight 'normal' people visited twelve different mental hospitals saying that they were experiencing auditory hallucinations and hearing voices saying words like 'dull', 'thud', and 'empty'. They were not really hearing voices, and they proceeded to answer all the other questions they were asked by the medical staff honestly. However, most of Rosenhan's team were admitted to hospital and diagnosed as schizophrenic. Once inside, the task of the research team (now pseudo-patients) was to convince the hospital staff that they were 'sane'; they behaved 'normally' and insisted on their 'sanity'. The pseudo-patients were hospitalized for 7 to 52 days, with an average length of stay of 19 days. When discharged the members of the research team were diagnosed as schizophrenic in remission. But what was most interesting was that, while they were inside, their 'normal' behaviours were perceived by staff as indicating evidence of schizophrenia, although some of the other patients were able to identify the pseudo-patients as impostors.

The next step in Rosenhan's research was perhaps even more interesting. Rosenhan informed psychiatric hospitals that pseudo-patients would again present themselves over the next few months. This time, however, there were no pseudo-patients. But around one-fifth of patients admitted during this time were identified by staff as being pseudo-patients (Rosenhan, 1975). Rosenhan's studies are often taken as evidence for how diagnosis is uncertain and can lead to labelling, and how once a label is attached to a person it becomes a self-fulfilling prophecy. Not only does a label of mental disorder become a self-fulfilling prophecy, but it attracts stigma. A diagnosis of mental disorder or an admission of having had therapy is often seen as something shameful to be hidden away. Labelling theorists argue that behaviours are neither inherently 'normal' or 'abnormal' until society ascribes meaning to the behaviour.

Social approaches

Psychological therapy, whether it be psychodynamic, cognitive-behavioural, or humanistic, largely attempts to help the person to live in society as it is. However, as we have seen, sociocultural explanations emphasize the way in which we are products of our culture, and the fact that by changing our culture we are best positioned to create a healthy population (e.g., Newnes, 1996). Therefore the concern is not so much with therapy for changing the individual to fit better within the existing society, but with changing society itself.

Smail (1996a) discusses the alternative of a more ethically-based society in which people are cared for. In our society problems in living are largely a function of the social and environmental forces operating on us, and therefore psychotherapy, Smail argues, offers only a very limited freedom within the constraints in which we live. Acknowledging such arguments, and the need for therapists to take a public stance, several groups have been formed: the Radical Psychology Network; Psychotherapists and Counsellors for Social Responsibility (PCSR); Critical Psychology International; and the Critical Psychiatry Network (Middleton, 2007). We have to be cautious of thinking of therapy as the solution to people's psychological suffering, as Sanders writes:

> we have to be completely honest with clients if we think counselling is not going to help ... The use of counselling should be questioned if it is likely that their symptoms of distress are caused by:
> - Poor housing or homelessness
> - Poverty
> - Lack of opportunity due to discrimination or oppression
>
> Problems of this nature are best addressed by social action. (Sanders, 2007c, p. 3)

Sociocultural theorists are concerned with questions about what aspects of our culture need to change to create a healthy population. For example, how does our education system create and maintain divisions in society? What might an alternative education system look like? What about our working lives? How should we set about offering help to each other in society? In the 1960s therapeutic communities based on humanistic and existential approaches were developed to provide a safe and secure environment for clients to continue on what was seen as their voyage of self-discovery (see, for example, Cooper, 1967). The idea was to create small communities within society which provided the members of that community with acceptance, affirmation, and authentic relationships between persons. As an example, an Italian psychiatrist Franco Basaglia came to view psychiatric hospitals as instruments of social control and violence, and went on to help introduce community care (see Tansella and Williams, 1987). A more recent example is that of Soteria House, which was a residential psychiatric facility in a regular house in a multiethnic, working-class community in San Jose, California. It was staffed by people who often had supplementary skills in cooking, carpentry, musicianship, massage, yoga. The staff were not there to diagnose, interpret, or behave like psychotherapists. Rather they were trained to empathize, maintain patient autonomy, and encourage patients to stay connected to their usual social networks and environments (see Mosher, 1999; Sanders, 2007d).

Among the therapeutic community, person-centred theorists have recently begun to rise to the challenge of addressing the political dimensions. The person-centred approach is by its nature anti-authoritarian, and in this sense is political as it aspires towards changing society from the ground up. It also has an explicit sociological flavour in the sense that it takes a structuralist approach to understanding that dysfunction ultimately arises from the individual's relationship with his or her social world. While mainstream psychologists have been developing theories and conducting research based around DSM typology, person-centred psychology therefore offers an alternative vision of practice whose ultimate purpose would be in line with the aspiration expressed by Sanders (2005), to 'plan and organise a future where to be frightened, confused and overwhelmed is not considered to be an "illness"' (p. 38). Recent writers have emphasized the political stance of person-centred psychology, and how the approach is ultimately concerned with social change (Proctor et al., 2006).

One route to social change is of course changing how we think. As we have seen, ideas are socially constructed. When we talk about psychological disorders, we need to remember that these are metaphors. As with the example of homosexuality discussed earlier, we can begin to think differently. Sanders (2007b, d) argues that we need campaigning, social action, and the development of the social model. Such models make distress and how we handle it everyone's responsibility. A social model would embrace the social networks of distressed people, promote the need for empowerment and capacity building at a community level, and continue to develop understanding of the nature of power, privilege and hierarchy in creating inequalities in, and exclusion from, opportunities to live fulfilling lives.

Social systems

Understanding that we are social beings, and that our psychological problems may be a mirror of the wider social structures and the interpersonal interactions which take place within those social structures has led to an interest in social systems. In this book we have been largely concerned with individual therapy, but we must also look to the interpersonal level. Laing (1966, 1970) was concerned with the social and familial contexts in which psychopathology takes place, and used the following example to illustrate the idea behind family therapy:

> If one has a 'referral', say, from a hockey team, because the left back is not playing properly, one wouldn't think only of getting the left back round to one's office, taking a history, and giving a Rorschach. At least I hope not. One would also go to see how the team plays hockey. (Laing, 1976, p. 28)

In group therapies individuals who may not have met before come together and, by observing the relationships and ways of behaving that each member develops in the group, the therapist is able to understand more about how each person is in the world. There is no one single approach to group therapy. A variety of therapeutic orientations can inform the way the group is run. The choice of theoretical orientation might be guided by the goal of the group, whether it be to help people adapt better to their environment, for the reconstruction of personality dynamics, alteration of behaviours through mechanisms of conscious control, or the relief of specific symptoms. One example is the family systems theory, which suggests that psychological problems are the result of dysfunctional interactions within the family.

Family therapy

It is difficult to reject the general idea that the person can only be fully understood in context and that our families are important in shaping our personalities. Evidence shows that those seeking counselling are more likely to come from families which could be considered as dysfunctional (King and Mallinckrodt, 2000). According to the family systems model, each family is a unique social system in which all the elements are interconnected, and changes in one element of the system affect all other elements of the system. Families develop patterns of interacting and expressing themselves, and the psychological problems of any one member can be understood by stepping back and observing the family system and the dynamics of interaction. The family systems model has lent it-self to various forms of therapy in which families can be helped to find new and more adaptive ways of interacting. Although family therapists work in a variety of different ways, some employing psychodynamic, cognitive-behavioural, and humanistic approaches, they all share the same assumption that disturbances in the social and familial context are important to the well-being of the individual.

The idea that family members can contribute to psychological prob-lems dates back to Fromm-Reichman (1948) who first put forward the idea of the schizophrenic mother who is domineering, cold, rejecting, and guilt inducing. She suggested that such parents drove their children to schizophrenia. A similar theme was advanced by Bateson and colleagues (e.g., Bateson et al., 1956) who put forward the *double bind* theory of schizophrenia. According to Bateson, schizophrenia was the result of parents who send contradictory verbal and nonverbal signals to their children, for example, a parent who tells her child that she loves him but simultaneously looks at him with disgust. Children who experience such double binds, Bateson argued, are put in a no-win situation and begin to lose touch with reality. Unable to trust their own perceptions, they retreat inwards as a way of dealing with the situation, resulting in signs and symptoms characteristic of schizophrenia. Similar views have been put forward over the years by others (e.g., Wynne et al., 1977), although the idea that families, and mothers in particular, cause severe psychiatric conditions is largely disputed today.

More recent approaches to family therapy must be contrasted to the earlier approaches of Fromm-Reichman and Bateson and colleagues which implicated family structure and communication in the aetiology of schizophrenia. Family therapy recognizes that the elements of the family are interrelated and can be best understood not in isolation but in relation to the system. More recent approaches emphasize how ill-ness within the family can be stressful to all involved and how increased stress in turn can impair the family's ability to cope, which in turn can be involved in the relapse of the recovering person (Falloon et al., 1993).

The family therapist is therefore concerned with working with the family as well as the client. He or she will endeavour to understand the relationships between members of the family, and will treat the family as an organism, and attempt to change the family system. The thera-pist is interested in identifying problematic patterns of communication within the family, how misunderstandings arise, and who plays what roles in the family and why. Satir (1964), one of the founders of family therapy, developed an experiential approach known as *conjoint fam-ily therapy,* in which the entire family meet together and the therapist draws attention to the communication difficulties she or he observes. Satir viewed normal family functioning as consisting of open and clear communication with flexible and appropriate rules. The dysfunctional family, on the other hand, exhibits ineffective communication and incongruent non-verbal messages. The goal of therapy is to create a system with direct and clear communication and to provide an environment for growth through shared experience. Techniques such as family sculpting and genograms are used to explore family dynamics. NICE guidelines recommend family therapy approaches, along with other therapies, for bipolar disorder, depression in young people, drug misuse, and schizophrenia (Khele, 2008).

In *family sculpting*, each member of the family uses modelling materials to create a representation of the family, showing his or her view of personal relationships. The therapist can help the family to understand the meaning of the sculpture, and may modify it to show new forms that the relationships might take. Another technique associated with the Bowen model of family systems (Bowen, 1978) is the use of the *genogram*. Genograms are used to sketch out a map of the family over several generations, using specific symbols to represent individuals and the nature of their relationships. Therapists may also use sociograms and ecograms. Sociograms are diagrams used to sketch out the pattern of relationships between people in a system. Ecograms are like a social 'solar system' in which the family genogram is at the centre and other significant people and institutions are sketched out as concentric circles (see Neill, 2006).

Conclusion

According to the sociological theory, people's problems in living reflect the society in which they have been raised and are living. We are challenged to look across cultures for the similarities and differences in human experience, to think about how social context shapes behaviour, and how we can change society to benefit people's psychological health. Questions are raised about how we construe problems in living. Sociological perspectives therefore pose questions for a strictly medical view which holds that psychological problems are the result of physical or even psychological disturbances. Some sociological theorists warn of the dangers of psychiatric classification, and therapy itself has been seen as an oppressive force. Approaches to therapy which focus not only on the individual but on his or her social relationships and cultural context are encouraged.

Summary points

- Notions of what constitute problems in living vary depending on the historical and cultural context. Several culture-bound syndromes have been identified.
- Racial and sexual prejudice have been implicated in the development of psychological problems as well as in the way problems are perceived in psychological minority groups.
- Sociologists have brought to our attention the relationship between social factors, such as poverty and unemployment, and the development of psychological problems.
- Theorists such as Szasz have been critical of the biomedical model, claiming that mental illness is a concept invented to control and oppress people whose behaviour threatens the social order.
- Other theorists like Rosenhan have warned of the dangers of labelling and stigmatizing people with psychological problems.
- Sociological theorists are concerned with changing the nature of society as opposed to the idea of changing people to fit better within a society.
- Social constructionists argue that reality as we perceive it is a fabrication influenced by our social context.

Topics for reflection

1. Social constructionists argue that our perceptions of reality are not based on objective truth, but are fabrications that arise through social dialogue. When it comes to DSM and the psychiatric classification system, would you agree or disagree with the social constructionists' argument?
2. There is no doubt that social conditions are linked to distress and dysfunction, and that there is a need to deal with poverty and inequality as a way to improve well-being. But how big is this problem? Is it so big that therapists are in fact colluding with the maintenance of social inequalities?
3. How would you feel if you were given a psychiatric diagnosis? Does how you feel depend on which diagnosis? How would you feel about seeing a counsellor? What about a psychiatrist? Would you feel comfortable telling other people?

Chapter 7

Developments in Eclectic and Integrative Approaches

Introduction

Each of the models examined in the previous chapters provides a set of assumptions about human nature. Historically, proponents of each of the perspectives have tried to explain all psychological problems within their perspective. For most of the latter half of the twentieth century, psychologists were concerned with which of these models, or paradigms, was correct and some bitter conflicts between proponents of particular approaches resulted. However, most would now accept that all of the models tell us about human experience. In this final chapter, I want to say a little more about subsequent developments and current trends. How have subsequent theories developed to make sense of these competing approaches? First, I will discuss the commonalities across approaches. Second, I will introduce the biopsychosocial model which is the understanding that the biological, psychological, and social levels are different levels of analysis and can therefore be seen as complementary. Third, I will discuss eclectic and integrative approaches which provide therapeutic approaches that allow us to draw on several models. I will then ask whether it is possible to reconcile the different approaches. But first, let us ask what we actually know from research; Ernesto Spinelli sums it up nicely:

> While it is clearly evident that therapy 'works', it is also the case that we really don't know why it works as effectively as it does. To pretend that we do seems to me to be just bluff and bluster, smoke and mirrors. In like fashion, the overwhelming agreed-upon conclusion derived from plentiful research studies proposes that, as far as we know at present, no one model or theory of therapy can be shown to be demonstrably superior to any other. (Spinelli, 2001, p. 20)

Although evidence suggests that some therapeutic approaches may be more suitable than others for specific forms of suffering, no therapy stands out as greatly superior to any other in effectiveness overall. This was the conclusion originally reached by Smith and Glass (1977) who examined the results of 375 studies of therapy outcome, using a *meta-analysis* approach. They found that all forms of psychotherapy – humanistic, cognitive, behavioural, cognitive-behavioural, and psychodynamic – were equally effective. Meta-analysis is a statistical technique that allows one to reach a conclusion from reviewing the results of many separate research studies. A later study by Shapiro and Shapiro (1982) tried to improve on Smith and Glass's research design by only looking at studies with well-defined treatment and control groups, and found similar results. Although some questioned this conclusion (e.g., Prioleau et al., 1983), further research has confirmed the general equivalence of therapies from different schools (Stiles et al., 1986). It is now generally accepted that in terms of overall effectiveness no therapy is better than any other (Ahn and Wampold, 2001; Cooper, 2008; Lambert and Bergin, 1994; Stiles et al., 2006; Wampold, 2001), although people seem to do better with long-term treatment rather than short-term treatment (Seligman, 1995). These results support the idea that all therapies are, therefore, doing essentially the same thing, and that therapeutic effectiveness is the result of non-specific factors, that is, those factors common to all therapies. This is called the 'dodo bird verdict', after the dodo bird in *Alice in Wonderland*, who after the race around the lake declares that everyone has won and all must have prizes.

Commonalities across therapeutic approaches

It might be argued that similar processes occur in all psychological therapies regardless of what their proponents claim are the specific ingredients. For example, all forms of counselling and psychotherapy involve at least some level of self-disclosure. Is it simply that talking about distressing experiences is therapeutic?

Self-disclosure

Social psychologists have carried out very interesting research into the health benefits of self-disclosure, and there is now much evidence that talking about upsetting events is associated with better adjustment. For example, Pennebaker and O'Heeron (1984) found that spouses who had been bereaved through suicide or accidents and who talked with friends about the death had a lower rate of illness than those who did not talk to friends. Perhaps more surprising is the evidence that even writing about traumatic events when no one is going to read the accounts is associated with better functioning. Pennebaker and Beall (1986) asked students to write about either a trivial topic or a personally upsetting event for several consecutive days and then compared the number of visits to the health centre in the following months for the two groups. They found that those who wrote about the upsetting events made fewer visits to the health centre. Pennebaker and his colleagues' work on the expression of emotional material has a long history dating back to the Greeks, who believed that catharsis was an important means of alleviating psychological suffering. The idea was that emotional tensions built up inside and had somehow to be released or else the pressure would build up and result in somatic complaints. Thus, the expression of emotional material, even through writing, is psychologically helpful and this may be one reason for the success of all therapies (Pennebaker, 1997, 2004).

Therapeutic relationship

The identification of factors common to all therapies, and those which promote psychological change, has become the focus of much research interest (see Roth and Fonagy, 2005). Indeed, it has even been suggested that therapies might be developed on the basis of this knowledge (Garfield, 1992). We have already seen that Rogers' (1957) core conditions provide one common-factors model. Subsequently, there have been other attempts to delineate the factors that are common to all psychological therapies. For example, Jerome Frank (1961, 1971) also argued that it is through the non-specific factors common to all therapies that change comes about. The first non-specific factor identified by Frank was that of an intense, emotionally charged, confiding relationship with a helping person.

Most would now agree that one important commonality is the *therapeutic relationship* (Grencavage and Norcross, 1990). It has been argued that positive change is attributable to the healing effects of a benign human relationship (Russell, 1995). Research results certainly support the idea that the relationship between client and therapist is important (Cooper, 2008; Horvath and Luborsky, 1993; Horvath and Symonds, 1991; Krupnick et al., 1996; Lambert, 1992; Paley and Lawton, 2001). Estimates suggest that the therapeutic relationship accounts for between 17 per cent and 30 per cent of the variance in outcome (Cooper, 2008). Interestingly, the recognition of the importance of the therapeutic relationship as an agent of healing is clearly resonant with Rogers' person-centred approach to psychotherapy which sees the therapeutic relationship as the process which produces psychological change (Haugh and Paul, 2008). Rogers wrote:

> It is clear, however, that the stress is upon a direct experiencing in the relationship. The process is not seen as primarily having to do with the client's memory of his past, nor with his exploration of the problems he is facing, nor with the perceptions he has of himself, nor the experiences he has been fearful of admitting into awareness. The process of therapy is, by these hypotheses, seen as being synonymous with the experiential relationship between client and therapist. Therapy consists in experiencing the self in a wide range of ways in an emotionally meaningful relationship with the therapist. The words – of either client or counsellor – are seen as having minimal importance compared with the present emotional relationship which exists between the two. (Rogers, 1951, pp. 171–2)

What exactly are the common ingredients of therapeutic change remains a controversial question, although the therapeutic relationship would seem to be one important condition, if not the most important. As Mearns and Cooper (2005) argue in their relational depth approach, we are essentially relational beings, and it is in relationships that we are hurt, healed, and in which we become who we are. The relational focus of the person-centred approach is now widely acknowledged across therapeutic modalities (e.g., Duncan and Miller, 2000). Further, the American Psychological Association Division 29 Task Force on Empirically Supported Therapy Relationships found that empathy, positive regard, and congruence-genuineness were all either demonstrably effective or promising, and probably effective in terms of successful therapeutic outcome (Ackerman et al., 2001; Cornelius-White, 2002).

Psychodynamic therapists have also long emphasized the importance of the emotional bond between client and therapist – the therapeutic alliance is thought to comprise a collaboration on the goals and tasks of treatment (e.g., Agnew-Davies et al., 1998; Horvath and Luborsky, 1993). More recently, cognitive-behavioural therapists have come to recognize the importance of the relationship (Gilbert and Leahy, 2007). Looking across the literature at what works, overwhelmingly the weight of the evidence points to the role of the therapeutic relationship.

Non-specific factors

However, despite the importance of the therapeutic relationship, it may not be sufficient for therapeutic change. Thus, as well as emphasizing the therapeutic relationship, Frank (1961, 1971) also identified five other non-specific factors:

- Providing a rationale which explains the client's distress and strengthens the client's confidence in the therapist.
- Providing new information concerning the nature and sources of the client's problems and possible alternative ways of dealing with them.
- Strengthening the client's expectations of help through the personal qualities of the therapist.
- Providing experience of success that further heightens the client's hope and enhances his or her sense of mastery and interpersonal competence.
- The facilitation of emotional arousal.

Subsequently, other researchers have also sought to identify the common factors, and over 80 commonalities have now been suggested (Grencavage and Norcross, 1990). One of the most mentioned of these commonalities is positive expectations. This refers to the idea that those clients who expect to improve are more likely to do so. However, although it would seem that positive expectations are important, research would not lead us to believe that psychological change is the result of nothing more than the client possessing a positive expectation (e.g., Roberts et al., 1993).

While each of the therapeutic approaches has its own theory of why it works, common-factor arguments suggest alternative reasons. Proponents of the psychodynamic approach, for example, might say that person-centred therapy only works because it unintentionally provides insight and clarification. Alternatively, proponents of cognitive-behavioural approaches might say that person-centred therapy only works because it unintentionally provides a corrective learning experience or desensitizes the client to fearful experiences. On the other hand, proponents of person-centred therapy might argue that other therapies are effective, not because of what the therapist says he or she does, but because of the relationship and alliance that forms between therapist and client.

What all of this illustrates is that although there is research evidence for the effectiveness of different psychological therapies, it is often unclear why a particular therapy works. Although the various therapies might on the surface appear very different, perhaps the differences between the psychotherapies are only skin deep. It is likely that similar processes occur in all psychological therapies. A good example of this is the debate over the controversial therapy, *eye movement desensitization and reprocessing* (EMDR).

Eye movement desensitization and reprocessing therapy

EMDR was introduced by Shapiro (1989a, 1989b, 1995) who noticed that her own distressing and intrusive thoughts began to diminish while she was out jogging. She linked this to rapid movements of her eyes, and following further investigations she went on to develop the EMDR procedure. Briefly, the EMDR procedure involves the client creating in his or her mind a visual image of the upsetting event and then isolating a word or phrase which represents a belief about the visual image. For example, 'I am helpless' or 'I have no control'. The client then repeats these phrases while bilateral saccadic eye movements are induced by following the therapist's fingers which are moved rapidly back and forth across the visual field. The negative belief statements are then replaced with positive belief statements such as 'I am in control', or 'I am worthy'. After 20 or so passes, the therapist will ask the client to rest. Case studies testify that clients often report that their distress reduces, and the strength of upsetting images fades. It has been suggested that eye movements are connected to the way in which information is consolidated in the brain (e.g., Levin et al., 1999). For example, it has been suggested that EMDR activates a similar process to that occurring during rapid eye movement (REM) sleep, when it is thought that information is being processed and consolidated within the brain.

But while proponents of EMDR may speculate on the brain mechanisms that explain why it seems to work, others have argued for the role of non-specific factors. Hyer and Brandsma (1997) argue that EMDR works, not because it induces eye movements, but because it applies common and generally accepted principles of psychotherapy. Hyer and Brandsma argue that EMDR rests on the principle dating back to Carl Rogers that clients move towards positive growth given the right social environment. They suggest that EMDR, although directive over process, is non-directive with regard to content and allows the client to follow his or her own direction rather than that of the therapist. Furthermore, McNally wrote:

> the novel component of EMDR (eye movements) adds nothing to the traditional imaginal exposure component ... Therefore, what is effective in EMDR is not new, and what is new is not effective. (McNally, 1999, p. 619)

The strongest evidence that 'what is new' in EMDR is not the effective ingredient but that 'what is effective' is the role of more traditional behavioural principles comes from a meta-analysis of the EMDR literature by Davidson and Parker who concluded that:

In sum, EMDR appears to be no more effective than other exposure techniques, and evidence suggests that the eye movements integral to the treatment, and to its name, are unnecessary. (Davidson and Parker, 2001, p. 305)

These criticisms do not mean that people do not benefit in some way from EMDR; evidence suggests that they do (e.g., Chambless et al., 1998; Chemtob et al., 2000; Van Etten and Taylor, 1998; Vaughan et al., 1994). Indeed, EMDR has been included in the NICE guidelines as a recommended treatment for posttraumatic stress disorder (Morgan, 2006). But even if it is an effective treatment, the exact role of the eye movements remains a focus for inquiry and it is not certain why EMDR works – whether it is simply a form of exposure therapy by another name or a repackaging of therapeutic relationship (see, Joseph, 2002; Joseph and Linley, 2002). We should not necessarily conclude that just because a treatment works this tells us about the cause of the problem. This is the treatment–aetiology fallacy mentioned in Chapter 2. Evidence for effectiveness of therapies must not be confused with evidence for the model of therapy. It remains to be seen therefore whether Shapiro has in fact stumbled across something new or whether EMDR is a repackaging of existing therapeutic techniques.

Drawing it all together

Biopsychosocial model

Within psychology, there has been a move towards adopting a systems-based approach in which the understanding of human experience is based on different levels of understanding (see Schneider, 1998). Recognizing that psychological problems often have multiple causes – a combination of biological, psychological, and social factors – the challenge is to integrate what we know into a coherent approach to understanding psychological functioning. Biological, psychological, and social factors are conceptualized as different levels of analysis within the *biopsychosocial model*.

Holism versus reductionism

Thus, rather than viewing biological, psychological, and social context approaches as providing competitive explanations for human behaviour, we might view each of these approaches as providing a partial understanding of functioning at different levels of analysis. Therefore, a central principle of the biopsychosocial approach is holism, the idea that the whole is greater than the sum of its parts. Contrast this with reductionism, the idea that the whole is the sum of the parts and that explanations are found when problems are reduced to their smallest parts. Much of modern psychiatry is reductionistic in its search for bio-chemical causes of psychopathology (Cacioppo and Bernston, 1992). Therapists are often critical of psychiatry for this, but as we have seen in the previous chapter the same criticism of reductionism can be levelled at therapy because of its emphasis on the psychological at the expense of the sociological (Morrall, 2008).

Holism, however, views smaller units of explanation as subsystems within a larger system, such that no one explanation provides the correct answer. All levels of explanation are correct, but are concerned with different levels of analysis. The biological, the psychological, and the social are all different ways of analyzing the same problem and the challenge is to understand their interaction, and how changes at one level are reflected by changes at another level. For example, it has been shown that self-disclosure and talking about upsetting events is associated with healthier immune functioning (Pennebaker et al., 1988) and improved liver enzyme function (Francis and Pennebaker, 1992). Changes at one level in the system are mirrored by changes at another level, so that there are feedback loops that maintain and exacerbate psychological problems (see Figure 7.1). In recent years the connection between body and mind has become more recognized by therapists:

> The subject of body psychotherapy is neither the mind alone, nor the body alone, nor even the two linked in parallel – *but the bodymind …* much of our pain, neurosis and unhappiness is anchored in the bodily aspects of our existence. Problems may present directly through the body – symptoms of stress, emotional suppression, and trauma … Problems which are expressed primarily in psychological or relational terms also have a crucial bodily aspect: habits of posture and movement reflect and reinforce our attitudinal habits. (Totton, 2003b, pp. 8–9)

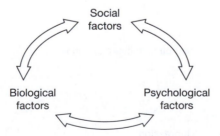

Figure 7.1   Feedback loops between social, psychological, and biological levels

Diathesis-stress model

As we have seen, therapies have tended to be concerned with the psychological level at the expense of the sociological and the biological. In Chapter 2, evidence was mentioned for an association between depression and low levels of the neurotransmitters serotonin and noradrenaline, and it has been hypothesized that low levels of these neurotransmitters might be a cause of depression. In Chapter 6, however, evidence was presented that stressful life-events cause depression. On the one hand it would seem that depression has a biological cause, and on the other that it has a social cause. However, perhaps these explanations are not mutually exclusive. Dinan (1994, 1998) has suggested that low levels of these neurotransmitters may be a proximal (i.e., closer in time) cause of depression, but that the low levels of these neurotransmitters are themselves caused by more distal (i.e., more distant in time) stressful life-events (see Figure 7.2). Approaches to counselling and psychotherapy based on such integrative approaches remain in their infancy. Specifying the relationships between the various causal pathways of the factors is problematic and calls for massive research interest.

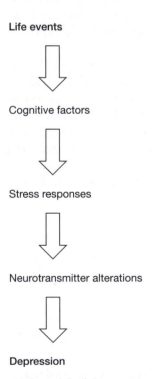

Life events

Cognitive factors

Stress responses

Neurotransmitter alterations

Depression

Figure 7.2   Biopsychosocial model of depression
After Dinan, 1998.

Much interest has focused on specifying diathesis-stress models of psychological problems. Diatheses refer to predisposing factors and stress refers to current environmental factors. This model has probably received the greatest attention with respect to the psychiatric diagnosis of schizophrenia. Meehl (1962), for example, suggested that, although only people with a genetic predisposition will develop schizophrenia, not all of those with a genetic predisposition will develop it. Only those who are also exposed to some form of detrimental learning environment and stressful life experience may go on to develop the condition. Here, the diathesis is a genetic predisposition and the stress is a stressful life experience. For other psychological problems the diathesis could be a particular personality disposition and the stress of an infection, for example. But what is important is that neither the diathesis, nor the stress, is sufficient on its own to produce psychological problems. When the stress is added to the diathesis, then problems occur. Certainly, research evidence would suggest that multiple factors are involved in the onset and maintenance of psychological problems.

However, although we might speculate on how a combination of genetic factors, childhood experience factors, patterns of thinking, personality, stressful life-events, and so on all interact to produce psychological problems, the difficulty is in conducting the research to test out such ideas. To illustrate, one study conducted by Card (1987) collected data from over 400 Vietnam veterans to see who had developed posttraumatic stress. These veterans were also people who had taken part in a large survey over 20 years previously when they were children, and at that time had completed various psychological measures of their personality. This earlier data enabled Card to investigate whether personality in childhood, in conjunction with later war experiences, was a determinant of posttraumatic stress. He found that those with lower self-esteem as children were more likely to develop posttraumatic stress as adults following the experience of combat compared with those who had higher self-esteem in childhood. Such research is, of course, not easy to carry out, is time-consuming, and expensive to fund.

For this reason, questions that might appear on the surface fairly simple to answer remain largely unanswered. For example, although we know that irrational thinking as discussed by Ellis and Beck is associated with depression, we are less certain of whether irrational thinking causes depression as opposed to irrational thinking being a result of depression. Often it has been assumed that causation operates in one direction only. However, the biopsychosocial model, with its emphasis on systems theory, leads us to understand causality as bi-directional. Changes in one level are accompanied by changes in another level. To address such questions usually calls for a massive research effort involving large samples of participants taking part in studies over lengthy periods of time.

Putting it into practice

Eclectic approaches

It is common for people setting off on their career as a counsellor or psychotherapist to initially specialize in one of the approaches. However, as they gain experience therapists often tend towards some form of eclecticism or integration, shaped by their own personality and their experience as practitioners, among other factors (O'Hara and Schofield, 2008). As we have seen in the biopsychosocial model, the different models are not necessarily competitive. Some aspects of human experience are better looked at from one perspective, other aspects from another. Providing specific treatments for specific problems is an *eclectic approach*. Eclecticism can be defined as

> Choosing what is best from diverse sources, styles, and systems; using techniques and rationales based on more than one orientation to meet the needs of the individual case; the systematic use of a variety of therapeutic interventions in the treatment of a single patient and the pragmatics of selecting a variety of procedures and wider interventions for specific problems. The common thread is that technical eclecticism is relatively atheoretical, pragmatic and empirical. (Norcross and Grencavage, 1990, p. 10)

The idea behind eclecticism is that no one therapeutic approach is adequate for all of the different psychological problems that a client may bring. Thinking about the biopsychosocial model, for example, the therapist could choose from a variety of biomedical, psychological, and social interventions depending on the particular client.

However, there is concern that many psychological therapists who describe themselves as working eclectically do so in an unstructured way, using a mix of approaches in a theoretically incoherent fashion. Technical eclecticism is relatively atheoretical and, although this might be appropriate in some contexts, working in this way with one client over a period of time could be extremely confusing for the client:

> Unless the counsellor is experienced and creative enough to meld different approaches and assumptions into a new and consistent synthesis, the result may be extremely confusing. Clients may pick up the message that life is confusing and that the counsellor does not really have a clue about which direction to follow. (van Deurzen-Smith, 1988, p. 3)

Technical eclectism at the level of the individual therapist may pose problems, but there is no reason why services should not offer different therapeutic approaches. In this way, the individual therapist is not faced with the complexities outlined above but can continue to offer what it is that he or she does best. Recognizing that people have different preferences for the sort of therapy they want, Gibbard and Baker (2008) offer a vision of a primary care mental health team that routinely offers both cognitive-behavioural (CBT) and person-centred therapy (PCT). Acknowledging the difficulties inherent in an integration of these two approaches if both therapies are offered, they write:

> Some people have no desire to explore their problems or revisit the past. They want a structured approach that focuses on strategies and techniques in the present. These people are referred for CBT … On the other hand some people see their problems in terms of present difficulties or past experiences … They often have a sense of these experiences being inadequately processed or unresolved, using phrases such as 'I realise I haven't dealt with it' or 'I just want to leave it behind and move on'. For these people a referral to PCT is considered. (Gibbard and Baker, 2008, pp. 16–17)

However, in answer to criticisms, it has been argued that those working in an eclectic way should use each approach discretely and in a planned sequence to avoid confusion (Messer, 1986). To do this requires a model with theoretical coherence. Working in this way has been referred to as theoretical eclecticism. Several such models have now been proposed which show how therapies can be incorporated into an eclectic way of working.

Egan's stages

One of the earliest attempts to develop a theoretically-based eclectic approach was that of Egan (1982), who suggested that therapy can be broken down into three stages: exploration, interpretation, and action. In the exploration stage a client-centred approach might be most useful, as the therapist builds up rapport with the client and gets to understand his experience and what has brought him to therapy. In the interpretation stage the therapist wishes to make a formulation of the problem, and psychodynamic and cognitive approaches might be useful. In the action stage behavioural strategies, such as homework assignments, are suggested as useful. Alex's therapist (see Box 3.1, p. 61) worked very much in an eclectic way, using the client-centred approach to establish rapport and trust with Alex and then using psychodynamic insights to explore the role of his early experiences in shaping his adult personality. Following this, Alex found motivational interviewing useful for helping him to deal with his alcohol problems.

Stages of change

Developing the idea of steps further, the stages of change model proposed by Prochaska and DiClemente (1983, 1984; Prochaska and Norcross, 1999) suggests that psychological change consists of a progression through five stages, from an initial stage in which the person has no intention of changing, through stages in which the person contemplates change, prepares for change, takes action towards making change, to finally maintaining that change. The five stages are:

- Precontemplation
- Contemplation
- Preparation
- Action
- Maintenance

At each stage, the client requires help with different processes. As Prochaska and Norcross write:

> The therapist's stance at different stages can be characterised as follows: with precontemplators, often the role is like a nurturing parent joining with a resistant and defensive youngster who is both drawn to and repelled by the prospects of becoming more independent. With contemplators, the role is akin to a Socratic teacher who encourages clients to achieve their own insights into their condition. With clients who are in the preparation stage, the stance is more like that of an experienced coach who has been through many crucial matches and can provide a fine game plan or can review the person's own plan. With clients who are progressing into action and maintenance, the psychotherapist becomes more of a consultant who is available to provide expert advice and support when action is not progressing as smoothly as expected. (Prochaska and Norcross, 1999, p. 510)

Thus, different therapeutic orientations might be useful at different stages. For example, a psychodynamic approach during the precontemplation stage might be useful in helping the client become more aware of the need to change. When the client has moved into the contemplation stage, a person-centred approach might be used to help her to think through the changes she wants to make. During the preparation stage a more cognitive approach might be employed to help the client think through how she might make changes. When the client has moved into the action stage a behavioural approach might be used to implement those changes. It would seem that by understanding the client's needs at each stage of the process, the therapist is able to provide an appropriate therapeutic intervention.

Assimilation of problematic experiences

Stiles and colleagues (1990) propose stages of emotional assimilation, ranging from stage 0, where problematic experiences are warded off and the client is unaware of emotional discomfort, through unwanted thoughts and feelings beginning to break into awareness (stage 1), acknowledgement of problematic experiences coupled with an inability to formulate the problem clearly (stage 2), making a clear statement of the problem (stage 3), understanding and insight (stage 4), working on the problem (stage 5), successful resolution of the problem (stage 6), and finally to generalization of the solution to other problem areas (stage 7). As with the stages of change model, and Egan's model, it has been suggested that psychodynamic and humanistic approaches might be more useful during the earlier stages, and cognitive and behavioural techniques in the later stages (Stiles et al., 1992).

Integrative approaches

We have already seen that the cognitive and the behavioural perspectives can be integrated. Another such development was *cognitive analytic therapy* (CAT) (Ryle, 1990) which attempted to integrate aspects of cognitive therapy with psychodynamic ideas, in particular those of the object relations school. CAT seems to possess much of the richness in thinking associated with the psychodynamic approach coupled with the clear scientifically testable methods of the cognitive-behavioural approach to produce a brief therapeutic approach.

Another development is *dialectical behaviour therapy* (DBT) (Linehan, 1987, 1993). DBT is a cognitive-behavioural technique developed for the treatment of people diagnosed with borderline personality disorder which attempts to integrate ideas from Zen Buddhism and client-centred therapy. More recently, meditation has become integrated with cognitive-behavioural therapy to produce a new therapy called *mindfulness-based cognitive therapy* (MBCT). In contrast to CBT, which is about changing thoughts, MBCT is about accepting non-judgementally our patterns of thinking and relating to them differently (Williams et al., 2006). Both of these therapies, along with a third new therapy, *acceptance and commitment therapy* (ACT), are concerned with experiencing the present moment and being aware of thoughts and feelings (Hayes, 2007). They all combine ideas traditionally associated with humanistic approaches with cognitive behavioural psychology.

A problem is that such circumscribed integration, rather than tidying up the field of therapy, has led to a greater proliferation of therapies, and even more confusion. Ivan Ellingham (2002) has offered the hopeful perspective that the current state of affairs with its multitude of approaches is a phase prior to a final integration and the creation of a unitary theory.

Construction of meaning

In his review of the role of emotional expression, Pennebaker (1993) concluded that what is important is that the person is not only able to express their negative emotions, but that they are also able to construct a coherent story. So, it is not just emotional expression per se which is important, but expression which involves some sort of cognitive working through. Brewin and Power write:

> all psychological therapies share a commitment to transforming the meanings that clients have attached to their symptoms, relationships and life problems. This common purpose has, we believe, been obscured by the use of different terminologies, by different conceptualisations of meaning, and by a tendency to focus on what divides therapies rather than on what unifies them. (Brewin and Power, 1997, p. 1)

By focusing on this common purpose, Brewin and Power are able to provide what seems to be an important step towards understanding how *integration* might take place. The recognition that counselling and psychotherapy involve a translation or transformation of meaning, whether it be changes in how we think about our relationships with others, and other more everyday concerns, or changes at a more profound and existential level, the modification of meaning is seen as the most important therapeutic activity by therapists from different approaches. Brewin and Power (1997) suggest that it is possible to integrate different psychotherapies at a theoretical level in terms of processes which involve translating and transforming meaning. One can see how different therapies help individuals to remodel their view of themselves and other people within the world. The creation of meaning as a common pathway has since received much attention in the therapy literature (Cole, 2002).

Narrative approaches

While the major theories previously considered in this book are concerned with trying to understand the objective reality of what it is to be human, the narrative approach in contrast is concerned with the stories we tell ourselves. The narrative approach takes the social constructionist view that each of the traditional theories is a way of looking at the world, but none can be said to be the truth. Clients are engaged in story telling, making sense of their lives, and in using metaphors to understand their experiences. The therapist's task is to help people re-author new stories. Building on the social constructionist view, narrative therapists invite their clients to see their stories from different points of view, search for new solutions, envision a new future, and develop new meanings (Freedman and Combs, 1996). Monk writes:

> In contrast to the normative, knowing stance, a narrative way of working invites the counsellor to take up the investigative, exploratory, archaeological position. She demonstrates to the client that being a counsellor does not imply any privileged access to the truth. The counsellor is consistently in the role of seeking understanding of the client's experience. (Monk, 1997, p. 25)

Pluralistic approaches

Similarly, Cooper and McLeod (2007) have argued for a pluralistic framework. Within their framework no therapeutic method is wrong, and all therapy can be structured around goals, tasks, and methods. This is a controversial position. If we take a social constructionist view that all theories are just fabrications, that is to say equally plausible but different ways of understanding, and all valid, then a pluralistic framework is possible. But if we adopt the position that these are scientific theories that attempt to approximate an objective reality, then it is simply not possible to integrate all theories, as they contain different versions of the truth.

Is a unified theory possible?

Although most commentators would agree that the translation and transformation of meaning is central to psychological change, it is difficult to see how some of the bedrock assumptions of all psychological therapies could come to be reconciled. The idea of integration is to blend different ideas into a co-operative whole. But as Arnold Lazarus (1989) argued, this may not always be possible as often these different ideas are irreconcilable.

Integrating ideas from different therapies in a theoretically consistent way is only therefore possible with those therapies which share similar basic assumptions about human nature, or at least between those theories which do not contain conflicting assumptions. What is important, therefore, is to look deeper into the theories – to understand the meta-theoretical position of each theory – that is to say the philosophical assumptions on which each is based (Joseph and Linley, 2006). As Worsley writes:

> Counselling theories are not just random accounts of how to do therapy. They start with a set of principles, a set of beliefs about:
>
> • What it is to be a human being;
> • What it is that leaves people distressed and in need of counselling;
> • What it is about therapy that is supposed to heal this distress;
> • And consequently, what the therapist actually does.
>
> It seems clear to me that if I cannot offer a principled set of answers to these very basic questions, then I literally do not know what I am doing. (Worsley, 2007, pp. 9–10)

Basic assumptions

Culley (1991), in her description of integrated counselling, makes the similar point that integrative counsellors must be able to be explicit about the basic theoretical assumptions. Some of the assumptions she makes are:

• Individuals are deserving of acceptance and understanding because they are human.
• Individuals are capable of change.
• Individuals create their own meaning.
• Individuals are experts on themselves.
• Individuals want to realize their potential.
• The behaviour of individuals is purposeful.
• Individuals will work harder to achieve goals which they have set for themselves.

Would you agree with each of the above assumptions? Are there some you agree with but others you disagree with? It is useful to discuss these basic assumptions with colleagues, particularly those from other therapeutic orientations, in order to begin to see where the fault lines are. There are fundamental differences between the basic assumptions of different approaches that simply cannot be reconciled (Wood and Joseph, 2007), and it is at this level that integration is difficult. For example, self-healing seems to be the most basic of assumptions, but not all therapists accept it.

Self-healing

O'Brien and Houston (2000) hold as a fundamental assumption the capacity for *self-healing*, and it is probably around this assumption that integration is most difficult. If we believe that people have an innate drive towards health, as the more humanistic approaches hold, then our task as therapists is to help promote this drive and to remove whatever blocks there exist to self-healing. However, other therapists do not share the belief that there are self-healing processes. Many behavioural and cognitive therapists, for example, will be directive over content as well as process in the belief that the client does not have an inner capacity for healing, and unless he or she is directed towards exploring material that the therapist views as important, no change will result. The assumption of whether or not there is a self-healing process is the foundation stone on which our choice of therapeutic style rests, and it is perhaps around this question that therapeutic style most diverges.

Where next?

It is clear that therapy is not just one thing. There are a many different brands of psychological therapy, and of coaching, each of which can be usefully grouped under one of the models as humanistic, cognitive-behavioural, or psychodynamic. At one level, each of the approaches simply observes the same thing but calls it by a different name, and thus there is much in common across the approaches. But, there are also mutually exclusive assumptions underpinning the approaches and at this level integration is simply not possible. In essence there is a tug of war between those approaches that view people's problems as just like any other medical disorder, and those approaches which adopt the view that therapy is a developmental process grounded in self-healing (Freeth, 2007).

Evidence-based therapy

Proponents of *evidence-based treatments* (EBT) assume that the practice of therapy is like the administration of a drug in so far as its effectiveness in alleviating a particular problem can best be evaluated using a randomized controlled trial (RCT) (see Dyer and Joseph, 2006). Thus, in the same way that we test for the effectiveness of drugs, we can test for the effectiveness of a therapy. Let us suppose that a person develops an illness and goes to the doctor, who says that there are two different drug treatments available. One of the treatments has been shown from scientific studies to cure 60 per cent of the people with this illness; the other has been shown to cure 20 per cent of the people with this illness. There is no difference in the possible side effects of the two treatments. Most people would choose the treatment with the best cure rate. Proponents of evidence-based treatments would argue that the practice of counselling and psychotherapy should be no different – the client should be offered the treatment that has been shown to be most effective for his or her problem. Do you agree with the idea of EBT?

Whether or not you agree with EBT will probably be related to which model of therapy you are most drawn to. While EBT is compatible with biomedical and medical model approaches, therapists from other approaches criticize EBT for its failure to tell us about the broader context of people's lives and their existential experiences (e.g., Bohart et al., 1998; Norcross et al., 2006; Schneider, 1998; Spence, 2004). Thus, the idea of *evidence-based practice* (EBP) takes a wider perspective on what research counts. Most counsellors and psychotherapists are probably more comfortable with the ideas of EBP than EBT. This tension between what types of evidence is most valuable was seen a few years ago in the letters page of *The Psychologist,* the house journal of the British Psychological Society. Bailey and Shevlin (1999) argued that therapists must be provided with quantitative research data using randomized controlled trials, for example, on the effectiveness of therapy. In response, Dorahy and Millar (2000) argued that the therapeutic process is not easily understood using such techniques of traditional scientific research. They concluded that, although randomized controlled trials have their uses, they also have limitations and must be coupled with other (often qualitative) research methods which can capture the individual's point of view.

Values-based therapy

While evidence-based practice may be important, how important is it in relation to our values? Ultimately, our choice of approach is an expression of moral and political ideology. It may not look like that – two people sitting in a room together talking, but what is being played out is something much bigger. Similarly, Totton (2004) has argued that there is a natural fault line running through the world of therapy, such that there are two different activities – the practice of psychological helping versus the practice of psychological truth. Both call themselves therapy, but they are different activities grounded in mutually incompatible epistemologies. The psychological truth therapies, that is, the more humanistic, existential, and transpersonal therapies, in contrast to the psychological helping therapies, that is, the more biomedical, behavioural, and cognitive therapies, are explicitly concerned with moral issues, and questions about the meaning and purpose of life (Bergin, 1980). As counsellors and psychotherapists we must be aware of our own value systems. In the context of this discussion on the future development of counselling and psychotherapy, we might also be aware that what we do is a moral and ethical endeavour. As van Deurzen writes:

> Those who take on this profession end up debating the big issues of life and the universe, often without any systematic training in the field of philosophy. Approaches to psychotherapy represent distinct value systems and belief systems although they remain non-explicit about their own philosophical and spiritual guidance role. The calibre of a lot of the thinking is therefore low. There is a risk that psychotherapists end up making interpretations from a background of unassimilated home-spun, popular philosophy ... Woven in with the personal and psychological problems that our clients bring are other deeper layers of difficulty which are to do with the perennial questions about the meaning of life and the moral issues about how a good human life should be lived. (van Deurzen, 1998, pp. 5–7)

How we decide what constitutes a good life is beyond the boundaries of scientific inquiry. Christopher (1996) has argued that we should give up pretensions to objectivity and value neutrality and acknowledge that psychological intervention is a morally imbued activity. Therapists, he argues, should:

(a) acknowledge our cultural embeddedness,
(b) seek to continually clarify and question the moral visions that motivate us,
(c) relentlessly attempt to discern how moral visions affect our work as counsellors, and
(d) regularly engage in public discourse on the nature and appropriateness of our moral visions. (Christopher, 1996, p. 23).

However, Christopher goes on to say that

> this does not necessarily thrust us into a debilitating relativism in the face of which we must conclude that every moral vision or way of life is equally 'good' and that there are no grounds for criticising values and practices that we deem oppressive, racist, sexist, or otherwise unworthy ... We need to define a middle ground or third way beyond objectivism and relativism based on a search for truth and

moral insight with full awareness that no final or certain formulations of them are possible (or even desirable) ... Our maturity as counsellors deepens when we recognise that our responsibility comes with uncertainty; we can never be certain that our theories, diagnoses, conceptualisations, and interventions are right ... When, as counsellors, we interact with clients or engage in research or theorising, we will be adopting a stance, presupposing a moral vision. Whether we admit it or not in our work with clients, we are engaging in a conversation about the good. Ultimately, counseling is part of a cultural discussion about ethos and world view, about the good life and the good person, and about moral visions. The only real choice becomes how honest we are with ourselves about our inescapable moral visions.

(Christopher, 1996, p. 24)

Conclusion

Although it would seem that all therapies are more or less equally effective, it has also been argued that some therapies are more suited for some problems than others. Since the original Smith and Glass (1977) study, as we have seen, there has been an increased emphasis on which type of therapy is most effective for which psychological problem (Roth and Fonagy, 2005). In both the UK and the USA there is currently an emphasis on evidence-based treatment and practice and the delivery of therapies which have been shown to be effective. However, the role of traditional scientific research in evaluating therapies remains contentious, with some claiming that it can only provide us with limited knowledge of what works for whom. More recently, researchers and clinicians have been interested in developing ways of understanding psychological problems which incorporate the different models. The biopsychosocial model emphasizes the interplay between biological, psychological, and social forces acting upon the person. Researchers have attempted to specify models of the interactions between various factors. Based on such ideas, therapists have begun to adopt eclectic and integrative ways of working with clients, rather than confining themselves to particular models. Researchers have attempted to understand the common factors that lead to therapeutic change. For example, recent theorists have emphasized that psychological therapies all involve, in some way, the transformation of meaning. At a practical level it has been suggested that different therapeutic approaches might be more or less appropriate depending on the person's stage of readiness to change. The question is whether it is possible to develop a unitary framework or whether there are irreconcilable differences between models.

Summary points

- The biopsychosocial model adopts a holistic view, conceptualizing biological, psychological, and social factors not as competitive, but as providing explanations at different but related levels of analysis.
- Modern psychological research often adopts a diathesis-stress model to investigate the interaction between different factors and how they cause psychological problems.
- Evidence-based treatment is based on the idea that there are specific treatments for specific problems. Therapists working in such a way describe themselves as eclectic.
- Integrative therapists attempt to meld the ideas from two or more models or approaches to therapy.
- Factors common to all therapies have been identified. The therapeutic relationship is one such factor and is believed to play an important part in the healing process in all therapies.
- Psychological therapy is also a morally imbued activity which raises questions for us about how a good human life should be lived.

Topics for reflection

1. If you were to seek therapy, what sort of therapy do you think you would prefer? If you were to suggest therapy for a friend, would you suggest the same for him or her? What are the reasons for your choices?
2. Do you agree with Christopher that therapy is ultimately a conversation about moral visions?
3. Are the different theories of therapy equal ways of understanding, or do some of them provide a better approximation of reality than others?

References

Ackerman, S.J., Benjamin, L.S., Beutler, L.E. , Gelso, C.J., Goldfried, M.R., Hill, C. et al. (2001) Empirically supported therapy relationships: conclusions and recommendations of the Division 29 Task Force, *Psychotherapy* 38: 495–7.

Adler, A. (1931) Compulsion neurosis, *International Journal of Individual Psychology* 9: 1–16.

Adler, A. (1964) *Social Interest: A challenge to mankind*, New York: Capricorn.

Agnew-Davies, R., Stiles, W.B., Hardy, G.E., Barkham, M. and Shapiro, D.A. (1998) Alliance structure assessed by the Agnew Relationship Measure (ARM), *British Journal of Clinical Psychology* 37: 155–72.

Ahn, H. and Wampold, B.E. (2001) Where oh where are the specific ingredients? A meta-analysis of component studies in counseling and psychotherapy, *Journal of Counseling Psychology* 48: 251–7.

Ainsworth, M.D.S., Blehar, M.C., Waters, E. and Wall, S. (1978) *Patterns of Attachment: A psychological study of the strange situation*, Hillsdale, NJ: Erlbaum.

Albee, G.W. (2000) The boulder model's fatal flaw, *American Psychologist* 55: 247–8.

Allyon, T. and Azrin, N. (1968) *The Token Economy: A motivational system for therapy and rehabilitation*, New York: Appleton Century Crofts.

American Psychiatric Association (1952) *Diagnostic and Statistical Manual of Mental Disorders* (1st edn), Washington, DC: American Psychiatric Association.

American Psychiatric Association (1968) *Diagnostic and Statistical Manual of Mental Disorders* (2nd edn), Washington, DC: American Psychiatric Association.

American Psychiatric Association (1980) *Diagnostic and Statistical Manual of Mental Disorders* (3rd edn), Washington, DC: American Psychiatric Association.

American Psychiatric Association (1987) *Diagnostic and Statistical Manual of Mental Disorders* (rev. 3rd edn), Washington, DC: American Psychiatric Association.

American Psychiatric Association (1994) *Diagnostic and Statistical Manual of Mental Disorders* (4th edn), Washington, DC: American Psychiatric Association.

American Psychiatric Association (2000) *Diagnostic and Statistical Manual of Mental Disorders* (4th edn, text revision), Washington, DC: American Psychiatric Association.

Anderson, E.M. and Lambert, M.J. (1995) Short-term dynamically orientated psychotherapy: a review and meta-analysis, *Clinical Psychology Review* 15: 503–14.

Argyle, M. (1994) *The Psychology of Social Class*, London: Routledge.

Arnkoff, D.B. and Glass, C.R. (1982) Clinical cognitive constructs: examination, evaluation, and elaboration, in P.C. Kendall (ed.) *Advances in Cognitive-behavioral Research and Therapy*, Vol 1, New York: Academic Press.

Bailey, F. and Shevlin, M. (1999) Letter, *The Psychologist*, December.

Bandura, A. (1969) *Principles of Behavior Modification*, New York: Holt, Rinehart & Winston.

Bandura, A. and Walters, R.H. (1963) *Social Learning and Personality Development*, New York: Ronald Press.

Banyard, P.E. (1996) *Applying Psychology to Health*, London: Hodder & Stoughton.

Barker, C., Pistrang, N., Shapiro D.A., and Shaw, I. (1990) Coping and help seeking in the UK adult population, *British Journal of Clinical Psychology* 29: 271–85.

Barlow, D.H. (1988) *Anxiety and its Disorders*, New York: Guilford.

Barnes, D., Hall, J. and Evans, R. (2008) *Survey of the current provision of psychological therapy services in primary care in the UK*, Chichester: Artemis Trust. Available from BACP website: http://www.bacp.co.uk/admin/structure/files/pdf/2440_pl_438_artemis_report_web_small.pdf.

Bateson, G., Jackson, D., Haley, J. and Weakland, J. (1956) Toward a theory of schizophrenia, *Behavioural Science* 1: 251–64.

Beck, A.T. (1963) *Depression: Clinical, experimental and theoretical aspects*, New York: Harper & Row.

Beck, A.T. (1967) *Depression, Causes and Treatment*, Philadelphia: University of Philadelphia Press.

Beck, A.T. (1974) The development of depression: A cognitive model, in R.J. Friedman and M. Katz (eds) *The Psychology of Depression: Contemporary theory and research*, New York: Wiley.

Beck, A.T. and Weishaar, M. (1989) Cognitive therapy, in A. Freeman, K.M. Simon, L.E. Beutler and H. Arkowitz (eds) *Comprehensive Handbook of Cognitive Therapy*, New York: Plenum Press.

Berger, P. and Luckmann, T. (1966) *The social construction of reality: A treatise in the sociology of knowledge*, London: Allen Lane.

Bergin, A.E. (1980) Psychotherapy and religious values, *Journal of Consulting and Clinical Psychology*, **48**: 95–105.

Berne, E. (1964) *Games People Play*, New York: Grove Press.

Berne, E. (1966) *Principles of Group Treatment*, New York: Oxford University Press.

Berne, E. (1971) Away from a theory of the impact of interpersonal interaction on non-verbal participation, *Transactional Analysis Journal* 1: 6–13.

Berne, E. (1972) *What Do You Say After You Say Hello?*, New York: Grove Press.

Bhaskar, R. (1975) *A Realist Theory of Science* (2nd edn), London: Verso.

Blaxter, M. (1990) *Health and Lifestyle*, London: Routledge.

Bohart, A.C., O'Hara, M. and Leitner, L.M. (1998) Empirically violated treatments: disenfranchisement of humanistic and other psychotherapies, *Psychotherapy Research* 8: 141–57.

Bohm, D. (1980) *Wholeness and the Implicate Order*, London: Routledge & Kegan Paul.

Boorstein, S. (ed.) (1980) *Transpersonal Psychotherapy*, Palo Alto, CA: Science and Behavior.

Bowen, M. (1978) *Family Therapy in Clinical Practice*, New York: Jason Aronson.

Bowlby, J. (1969) *Attachment and Loss: Volume 1: Attachment*, London: Hogarth Press.

Bowlby, J. (1973) *Attachment and Loss: Volume 2: Separation: Anxiety and Anger*, London: Hogarth Press.

Bowlby, J. (1980) *Attachment and Loss: Volume 3: Loss, Sadness and Depression*, London: Hogarth Press.

Boyle, M (1993) *Schizophrenia – A Scientific Delusion*, London: Routledge.

Bozarth, J. (1998) *Person-centred Therapy: A revolutionary paradigm*, Ross-on-Wye: PCCS Books.

Brazier, D. (1995) *Zen Therapy*, London: Constable.

Brettle, A., Hill, A. and Jenkins, P. (2008) Counselling in primary care: a systematic review of the evidence, *Counselling and Psychotherapy Research* 8: 207–14.

Brewin, C.R. and Power, M.J. (1997) Meaning and psychological therapy: Overview and introduction, in M. Power and C.R. Brewin (eds) *The Transformation of Meaning in Psychological Therapies: Integrating theory and practice*, Chichester: Wiley.

British Association for Counselling (1996) *Code of Ethics and Practice*, Rugby: British Association for Counselling.

Brown, G.W. and Harris, T. (1978) *The Social Origins of Depression*, London: Tavistock Press.

Bucher, B. and Lovaas, O.I. (1967) Use of aversive stimulation in behavior modification, in M.R. Jones (ed.) *Miami Symposium on the Prediction of Behavior 1967: Aversive stimulation* (pp. 77–145), Coral Gables, FL: University of Miami Press.

Cacioppo, J.T. and Bernston, G.G. (1992) Social psychological contributions to the decade of the brain: doctrine of multilevel analysis, *American Psychologist* 47: 1019–28.

Cameron, C.L. (2007) Single session and walk-in psychotherapy: a descriptive account of the literature, *Counselling and Psychotherapy Research* 7: 245–9.

Card, J.J. (1987) Epidemiology of PTSD in a national cohort of Vietnam veterans, *Journal of Clinical Psychology* 43: 6–17.

Cash, T.F. and Henry, P.E. (1995) Women's body images: the results of a national survey in the USA, *Sex Roles* 33: 19–28.

Chadwick, P.K. (1997) Recovery from schizophrenia: the problem of poetic patients and scientific clinicians, *Clinical Psychology Forum* 103: 39–43.

Chambless, D.L., Baker, M.J., Baucom, D.H., Beutler, L.E., Calhoun, K.S., Crits-Christoph, P., Daiuto, A., DeRubeis, R., Detweiler, J., Haaga, D.A.F., Bennett Johnson, S., McCurry, S., Mueser, K.T., Pope, K.S., Sanderson, W.C., Shoham, V., Stickle, T., Williams, D.A. and Woody, S.R. (1998) Update on empirically validated therapies, II, *The Clinical Psychologist* 51: 3–16.

Chemtob, C.M., Tolin, D.F., Van der Kolk, B.A. and Pitman, R.K. (2000) Eye movement desensitization and reprocessing, in E.A. Foa, T.M. Keane and M.J. Friedman (eds) *Effective Treatments for PTSD: Practice guidelines from the International Society for Traumatic Stress Studies* (pp. 139–55), New York: Guilford.

Christopher, J.C. (1996) Counseling's inescapable moral visions, *Journal of Counseling and Development* **75**: 17–25.

Clarkson, P. (1989) *Gestalt Counselling in Action*, London: Sage.

Cohen, S. and Wills, T.A. (1985) Stress, social support, and the buffering hypothesis, *Psychological Bulletin* **98**: 310–57.

Cole, S. (2002) The creation of meaning in the moment, *Counselling and Psychotherapy Journal* **13**(3): 10–13.

Comer, R.J. (1998) *Abnormal Psychology*, 3rd edn, New York: Freeman.

Cooper, D. (1967) *Psychiatry and Antipsychiatry*, London: Paladin.

Cooper, M. (2008) *Essential Research Findings in Counselling and Psychotherapy: The facts are friendly*, London: Sage.

Cooper, M. and McLeod, J. (2007) A pluralistic framework for counselling and psychotherapy: implications for research, *Counselling and Psychotherapy Research* **7**: 135–43.

Cornelius-White, J.H. (2002) The phoenix of empirically supported therapy relationships: the overlooked person-centered basis, *Psychotherapy: Theory Research/Practice/Training* **39**(3): 219–22.

Culley, S. (1991) *Integrative Counselling Skills in Action*, London: Sage.

Dakof, G.A. and Taylor, S.E. (1990) Victims' perceptions of social support: What is helpful from whom?, *Journal of Personality and Social Psychology* **58**: 80–9.

Dale, A.J.D. (1980) Organic mental disorders associated with infections, in H.I. Kaplan, A.M. Freedman and B.J. Sadock (eds) *Comprehensive Textbook of Psychiatry*, Vol 2 (3rd edn), Baltimore: Williams & Wilkins.

Dalgleish, T., Joseph, S., Thrasher, S., Tranah, T. and Yule, W. (1996) Crisis support following the Herald of Free Enterprise disaster: a longitudinal perspective, *Journal of Traumatic Stress* **9**: 833–45.

Davey, G. (1992) Classical conditioning and the acquisition of human fears and phobias: a review and synthesis of the literature, *Advances in Behaviour Research and Therapy* **14**: 29–66.

Davey, G. (2008) *Psychopathology: Research, assessment and treatment in clinical psychology*, Chichester: Wiley-Blackwell.

Davidson, P.R. and Parker, K.C.H. (2001) Eye movement desensitization and reprocessing (EMDR): a meta-analysis, *Journal of Consulting and Clinical Psychology* **69**: 305–16.

Dinan, T.G. (1994) The role of steroids in the genesis of depression: a psychobiological perspective, *British Journal of Psychiatry* **164**: 365–72.

Dinan, T.G. (1998) Physical treatments for depression, in G. O'Mahony and J.V. Lucey (eds) *Understanding Psychiatric Treatment: Therapy for serious mental health disorder in adults* (pp. 59–75), Chichester: Wiley.

Dorahy, M.J. and Millar, R. (2000) Letter, *The Psychologist* **13**: 121.

Duggan, C.E., Marks, I. and Richards, D. (1993) Clinical audit of behavior therapy training in nurses, *Health Trends* **25**: 25–30.

Duncan, B. and Miller, S. (2000) *The Heroic Client: Doing client-directed, outcome-informed therapy*, San Francisco: Jossey-Bass Wiley.

Durkheim, E. (1897) *Le Suicide*, Paris: Alcan.

Dyer, C. and Joseph, S. (2006) What is an RCT?, *Counselling and Psychotherapy Research* **6**: 264–5.

Egan, G. (1982) *The Skilled Helper* (2nd edn), Monterey, CA: Brooks/Cole.

Ellenberger, H. (1970) *The Discovery of the Unconscious: The history and evolution of dynamic psychiatry*, New York: Basic.

Ellingham, I. (2002) The need not to need 'the unconscious', *Counselling and Psychotherapy Journal* **13**: 20–3.

Ellis, A. (1959) Requisite conditions for basic personality change, *Journal of Consulting Psychology* **23**: 538–40.

Ellis, A. (1962) *Reason and Emotion in Psychotherapy*, New York: Stuart.

Ellis, A. (1973) Rational-emotive therapy, in R. Corsini (ed.) *Current Psychotherapies*, Itasca, IL: Peacock.

Erikson, E.H. (1959) *Identity and the Life Cycle*, New York: Norton.

Erikson, E.H. (1963) *Childhood and Society* (2nd edn), New York: Norton.

Erikson, E.H. (1968) *Identity, Youth and Crisis*, New York: Norton.

Evans, R. (1969) *Dialogue with Erik Erikson*, New York: Dutton.

Eysenck, H.J. (1952) The effects of psychotherapy: an evaluation, *Journal of Consulting Psychology* **16**: 319–24.

Eysenck, H.J. (1965) The effects of psychotherapy, *International Journal of Psychiatry* **1**: 97–142.

Eysenck, H.J. (1986) A critique of contemporary classification and diagnosis, in T. Millon and G.L. Klerman (eds) *Contemporary Directions in Psychopathology: Towards the DSM-IV*, New York: Guilford.

Eysenck, H.J. and Wilson, G.D. (1973) *The Experimental Study of Freudian Theories*, London: Methuen.

Fairbairn, W. (1952) *An Object-relations Theory of the Personality*, New York: Basic.

Falloon, I.R.H., Laporta, M., Fadden, G. and Graham-Hole, V. (1993) *Managing Stress in Families*, London: Routledge.

Fisher, S. and Greenberg, R.P. (1996) *Freud Scientifically Reappraised: Testing the theories and therapy*, New York: Wiley.

Foa, E.B., Rothbaum, B.O., Riggs, D.S. and Murdock, T.B. (1991) Treatment of posttraumatic stress disorder in rape victims: a comparison between cognitive-behavioral procedures and counselling, *Journal of Consulting and Clinical Psychology* **59**: 715–23.

Ford, C., Oliver, J. and Whitehead, B. (2006) Treating drug users: a collaborative method, *Therapy Today* **17**: 17–20.

Francis, M.E. and Pennebaker, J.W. (1992) Putting stress into words: the impact of writing on physiological, absentee, and self-reported emotional well-being measures, *American Journal of Health Promotion* **6**: 280–7.

Frank, J. (1961) *Persuasion and Healing: A comparative study of psychotherapy*, New York: Schocken.

Frank, J. (1971) Therapeutic factors in psychotherapy, *American Journal of Psychotherapy* 25: 350.

Frankl, V. (1963) *Man's Search for Meaning*, New York: Washington Square.

Frankl, V. (1967) *Psychotherapy and Existentialism: Selected papers on logotherapy*, New York: Washington Square.

Freedman, J. and Combs, G. (1996) *Narrative Therapy: The social construction of preferred realities*, New York: Norton.

Freeth, R. (2007) Working within the medical model, *Therapy Today* 18(9) 31–4.

Freud, S. (1900) *The Interpretation of Dreams, Standard Edition of the Complete Psychological Works of Sigmund Freud*, Vols 4 and 5, edited and translated by J Strachey (1953), London: Hogarth Press and the Institute of Psychoanalysis.

Freud, S. (1901) *The Psychopathology of Everyday Life, Standard Edition of the Complete Psychological Works of Sigmund Freud*, Vol. 6, edited and translated by J Strachey (1960), London: Hogarth Press and the Institute of Psychoanalysis.

Freud, S. (1917) *Mourning and Melancholia*, London: Hogarth Press.

Freud, S. (1933, [1964]) *New Introductory Lectures on Psychoanalysis, Standard Edition of the Complete Psychological Works of Sigmund Freud*, Vol. 22, edited and translated by J. Strachey (1964), London: Hogarth Press and the Institute of Psychoanalysis.

Freud, S. (1940/1969) *An Outline of Psycho-analysis*, New York: Norton.

Fromm-Reichman, F. (1948) Notes on the development of treatment of schizophrenics by psychoanalytic psychotherapy, *Psychiatry* 11: 263–73.

Garfield, S.L. (1992) Eclectic psychotherapy: a common factors approach, in J.C. Norcross and M.R. Goldfried (eds) *Handbook of Psychotherapy Integration*, New York: Basic.

Gewirtz, J.L. and Pelaez-Nogueras, M. (1992) B.F. Skinner's legacy to human infant behavior and development, *American Psychologist* 47: 1411–22.

Gibbard, I. and Baker, N. (2008) Person-centred therapy in primary care, *Therapy Today* 19(8): 14–17.

Gibbard, I. and Hanley, T. (2008) A five-year evaluation of the effectiveness of person-centred counselling in routine clinical practice in primary care, *Counselling and Psychotherapy Research* 8: 215–22.

Gilbert, P. and Leahy, R. (eds) (2007) *The Therapeutic Relationship in the Cognitive Behavioural Psychotherapies*, London: Routledge.

Gottesman, I.I. (1991) *Schizophrenia Genesis: The origins of madness*, New York: Freeman.

Gottesman, I.I. and Shields, J. (1972) *Schizophrenia and Genetics: A twin study vantage point*, New York: Academic Press.

Gray, P. (2005a) Letters, *Therapy Today* 16: 27.

Gray, P. (2005b) Beyond the medical model, *Therapy Today* 16: 33–6.

Greenberg, D. and Marks, I. (1982) Behavioural psychotherapy of uncommon referrals, *British Journal of Psychiatry* 141: 148–53.

Greenberg, L.S., Rice, L.N. and Elliot, R. (1993) *Facilitating Emotional Change: The moment-by-moment process*, New York: Guilford.

Greenberg, L.S. and Watson, J. (1998) Experiential therapy of depression: differential effects of client-centred relationship conditions with and without process experiential interventions, *Psychotherapy Research* 8: 210–24.

Grencavage, L.M. and Norcross, J.C. (1990) Where are the commonalities among the therapeutic common factors?, *Professional Psychology: Research and Practice* 21: 372–8.

Grof, S. and Bennett, H.Z. (1990) *The Holotropic Mind: The three levels of human consciousness and how they shape our lives*, San Francisco: HarperCollins.

Gusella, J.F., Wexler, N.S., Conneally, P.M., Naylor, S.L., Anderson, M.A., Tanzi, R.E., Watkins, P.C., Ottina, K., Wallace, M.R., Sakaguchi, A.Y., Young, A.B., Shoulson, I., Bonilla, E. and Martin, J.B. (1983) A polymorphic DNA marker genetically linked to Huntington's disease, *Nature* 306: 234–8.

Hagan, T. and Smail, D. (1997a) Power mapping – I. Background and basic methodology, *Journal of Community and Applied Social Psychology* 7: 257–67.

Hagan, T. and Smail, D. (1997b) Power mapping – II. Practical application: The example of sexual abuse, *Journal of Community and Applied Social Psychology* 7: 269–84.

Hansen, J.T. (2007) Should counselling be considered a healthcare profession?, *Therapy Today* 18(8): 4–11.

Harlow, J.M. (1868) Recovery from the passage of an iron bar through the head, *Publication of the Massachussetts Medical Society* 2: 327 ff.

Hartmann, H. (1958) *Ego Psychology and the Problem of Adaptation*, New York: International Universities Press.

Haugh, S. and Paul, S. (2008) Is the relationship the therapy?, *Therapy Today* 19(10): 34–7.

Hayes, S.C. (2007) Hello darkness, *Therapy Today* 18(8): 14–18.

Heston, L.L. (1992) *Mending Minds: A guide to the new psychiatry of depression, anxiety, and other serious mental disorders*, New York: Freeman.

Hollingshead, A.B. and Redlich, F.C. (1958) *Social Class and Mental Illness: A community study*, New York: John Wiley & Sons.

Hollon, S.D. and Beck, A.T. (1994) Cognitive and cognitive-behavioural therapies, in A.E. Bergin and S.L. Garfield (eds) *Handbook of Psychotherapy and Behavior Change* (4th edn), New York: Wiley.

Horvath, A.O. and Luborsky, L. (1993) The role of the therapeutic alliance in psychotherapy, *Journal of Consulting and Clinical Psychology* 61: 561–73.

Horvath, A.O. and Symonds, B.D. (1991) Relationship between working alliance and outcome in psychotherapy: a meta-analysis, *Journal of Counseling Psychology* 38: 139–49.

Hyer, L. and Brandsma, J.M. (1997) EMDR minus eye movements equals good psychotherapy, *Journal of Traumatic Stress*, 10: 515–22.

Jacobson, B. (2007) *Invitation to Existential Psychology: A psychology for the unique human being and its applications in therapy*, Chichester: Wiley.

Jones, M.C. (1925) A laboratory study of fear: the case of Peter, *Pedagogical Seminary* 31: 308–15.

Joseph, S. (2002) Emperor's new clothes, *The Psychologist* 15: 242–3.

Joseph, S. (2007) Agents of social control, *The Psychologist* 20: 429–31.

Joseph, S. and Linley, P.A. (2002) EMDR: what's the evidence?, *Counselling and Psychotherapy Journal* 13(3): 18–19.

Joseph, S. and Linley, P.A. (2006) *Positive Therapy: A meta-theory for positive psychological practice*, London: Routledge.

Joseph, S. and Worsley, R. (eds) (2005) *Person-centred Psychopathology: A positive psychology of mental health*, Ross-on-Wye: PCCS Books.

Joseph, S., Andrews, B., Williams, R. and Yule, W. (1992) Crisis support and psychiatric symptomatology in adult survivors of the Jupiter cruise ship disaster, *British Journal of Clinical Psychology* 31: 63–73.

Joseph, S., Yule, W., Williams, R. and Andrews, B. (1993) Crisis support in the aftermath of disaster: a longitudinal perspective, *British Journal of Clinical Psychology* 32: 177–85.

Kantorovich, F. (1930) An attempt at associative reflex therapy in alcoholism, *Psychological Abstracts* 4282.

Kazdin, A.E. and Wilcoxin, L.A. (1976) Systematic desensitization and nonspecific treatment effects: a methodological evaluation, *Psychological Bulletin* 83: 729–58.

Kendler, K.S., MacLean, C., Neale, M., Kessler, R., Heath, A. and Eaves, L. (1991) The genetic epidemiology of bulimia nervosa, *American Journal of Psychiatry* 148: 1631.

Kernberg, O.F. (1976) *Object-relations Theory and Clinical Psychoanalysis*, New York: Jason Aronson.

Khele, S. (2008) NICE guidelines for mental health, *Therapy Today* 19(10): 40–1.

King, J.L. and Mallinckrodt, B. (2000) Family environment and alexithymia in clients and non-clients, *Psychotherapy Research* 10: 78–86.

King, M., Sibbald, B., Ward, E., Bower, P., Lloyd, M., Gabbay, M. and Byford, S. (2000) Randomised controlled trail of non-directive counselling, cognitive behaviour therapy, and usual general practitioner care in the management of depression as well as mixed anxiety and depression in primary care, *British Medical Journal* 321: 1383–8.

Klein, M. (1932) *The Psychoanalysis of Children*, London: Hogarth.

Kleinman, J.E., Karson, C.N., Weinberger, D.R., Freed, W.J., Berman, K.F. and Wyatt, R.J. (1984) Eye-blinking and cerebral ventricular size in chronic schizophrenic patients, *American Journal of Psychiatry* 141: 1430–2.

Kohut, H. (1971) *The Analysis of the Self*, New York: International Universities Press.

Krupnick, I.J., Sotsky, S.M., Simmens, S., Moyer, J., Elkin, I., Watkins, J. and Pilkonis, P.A. (1996) The role of the therapeutic alliance in psychotherapy and pharmacology outcome: findings in the National Institute of Mental Health Treatment of Depression Collaborative Research Programme, *Journal of Consulting and Clinical Psychology* 64: 532–9.

Laing, R.D. (1966) *Self and Others*, Harmondsworth: Penguin.

Laing, R.D. (1970) *Knots*, Harmondsworth: Penguin.

Laing, R.D. (1976) *The Politics of the Family and Other Essays*, Harmondsworth: Penguin.

Lambers, E. (1994a) Borderline personality disorder, in D. Mearns (ed.) *Developing Person-centred Counselling*, London: Sage

Lambers, E. (1994b) Psychosis, in D. Mearns (ed.) *Developing Person-centred Counselling*, London: Sage.

Lambers, E. (1994c) Personality disorder, in D. Mearns (ed.) *Developing Person-centred Counselling*, London: Sage.

Lambert, M.J. (1992) Psychotherapy outcome research: implications for integrative and eclectic therapists, in J.C. Norcross and M.R. Goldfried (eds) *Handbook of Psychotherapy Integration*, New York: Basic.

Lambert, M.J. and Bergin, A.E. (1994) The effectiveness of psychotherapy, in A.E. Bergin and S.L. Garfield (eds) *Handbook of Psychotherapy and Behavior Change*, New York: Wiley.

Lang, P. and Melamed, B. (1969) Case report: avoidance conditioning therapy of an infant with chronic ruminative vomiting, *Journal of Abnormal Psychology* 74: 1–8.

Lazarus, A.A. (1989) Why I am an eclectic (not an integrationist), *British Journal of Guidance and Counselling* 17: 248–58.

Levin, P., Lazrove, S. and Van der Kolk, B. (1999) What psychological testing and neuroimaging tell us about the treatment of post-traumatic stress disorder by eye movement desensitization and reprocessing, *Journal of Anxiety Disorders* 13: 159–72.

Lieberman, J.A., Kinon, B.J. and Loebel, A.D. (1990) Dopaminergic mechanisms in idiopathic and drug-induced psychosis, *Schizophrenia Bulletin* 16: 97–110.

Linehan, M.H. (1987) Dialectical behavior therapy for borderline personality disorder, *Bulletin of the Menninger Clinic* 51: 261–76.

Linehan, M.H. (1993) *Cognitive-behavioral Treatment for Borderline Personality Disorder*, New York: Guilford.

Littlewood, R. and Lipsedge, M. (1993) *Aliens and Alienists: Ethnic minorities and psychiatry* (3rd edn), London: Routledge.

Lynch, T. (2004) *Beyond Prozac: Healing mental distress*, Ross-on-Wye: PCCS Books.

Maddux, J.E., Gosselin, J.T. and Winstead, B.A. (2005) Conceptions of psychopathology: a social constructionist perspective, in J.E. Maddux and B.A. Winstead (eds) *Psychopathology: Foundations for a contemporary understanding* (pp. 3–18). Mahwah, NJ: Lawrence Erlbaum Associates.

Mahrer, A.P. (1998) Embarrassing problems for the field of psychotherapy, *Psychotherapy Section Newsletter of the British Psychological Society* 23: 19–29.

Makari, G. (2008) *Revolution in Mind: The creation of psychoanalysis*, London: Duckworth.

Margraf, J., Barlow, D.H., Clark, D.M. and Telch, M.J. (1993) Psychological treatment of panic: work in progress on outcome, active ingredients, and follow up, *Behaviour Research and Therapy* 31: 1–8.

Marks, I.M. (1990) Behavioral therapy of anxiety states, in N. Sartorius, V. Andreoli, G. Cassano, L. Eisenberg, P. Kielholz, P. Pancheri and G. Racagni (eds) *Anxiety: Psychological and clinical perspectives*, New York: Hemisphere.

Marks, I.M. and O'Sullivan, G. (1988) Drugs and psychological treatments for agoraphobia/panic and obsessive-compulsive disorders: a review, *British Journal of Psychiatry* **153**: 650–8.

Marks, I.M., Gelder, M.G. and Bancroft, J. (1970) Sexual deviants two years after electrical aversion, *British Journal of Psychiatry* **117**: 73–85.

Maslow, A. (1968) *Toward a Psychology of Being* (2nd edn), New York: Harper & Row.

Maslow, A.H. (1970) *Motivation and Personality* (2nd edn), New York: Harper & Row.

Maslow, A.H. (1993) *The Farther Reaches of Human Nature*, London: Penguin Arkana.

Mattick, R.P., Andrews, G., Hadzi-Pavlovic, D. and Christensen, H. (1990) Treatment of panic and agoraphobia: an integrative review, *Journal of Nervous and Mental Disease* **178**: 567–76.

McGuffin, P. and Katz, R. (1989) The genetics of depression and manic-depressive disorder, *British Journal of Psychiatry* **155**: 294–304.

McLeod, J.D. and Kessler, R.C. (1990) Socioeconomic status differences in vulnerability to undesirable life events, *Journal of Health and Social Behavior* **31**: 162–72.

McNally, R. (1999) On eye movements and animal magnetism: A reply to Greenwald's defense of EMDR, *Journal of Anxiety Disorders*, **13**: 617–20.

Mearns, D. (ed.) (1994) *Developing Person-centred Counselling*, London: Sage.

Mearns, D. and Cooper, M. (2005) *Working at Relational Depth in Counselling and Psychotherapy*, London: Sage.

Mearns, D. and Thorne, B. (1999) *Person Centred Counselling in Action*, London: Sage.

Meehl, P.E. (1962) Schizotaxia, schizotypy, schizophrenia, *American Psychologist* **17**: 827–38.

Meichenbaum, D.H. (1977) *Cognitive-behavior Modification*, New York: Plenum.

Menzies, R. and Clarke, J. (1993) A comparison of in vivo and vicarious exposure in the treatment of childhood water phobia, *Behaviour Research and Therapy* **31**: 9–15.

Messer, S.B. (1986) Eclectism in psychotherapy: underlying assumptions, problems and trade-offs, in J.C. Norcross (ed.) *Handbook of Eclectic Psychotherapy*, New York: Brunner/Mazel.

Middleton, H. (2007) Critical psychiatry, *Mental Health Review* **12**: 40–3.

Miller, W.R., Zweben, A., DiClemente, C.C. and Rychtarik, R.G. (1992) *Motivational Enhancement Therapy Manual: A clinical research guide for therapists treating individuals with alcohol abuse and dependence*, Rockville, MD: National Institute on Alcohol Abuse and Alcoholism.

Moncrieff, J. (2009) *A straight talking introduction to psychiatric drugs*, Ross-on-Wye: PCCS Books.

Monk, G. (1997) How narrative therapy works, in G. Monk, J. Winslade, K. Crocket and D. Epston (eds) *Narrative Therapy in Practice: The archaeology of hope* (pp. 3–31), San Francisco: Jossey-Bass.

Morgan, S. (2006) EMDR comes of age, *Therapy Today* 17: 35–7.

Morrall, P. (2008) *The Trouble with Therapy: Sociology and psychotherapy*, Maidenhead: Open University Press.

Mosher, L.R. (1999) Soteria and other alternatives to acute psychiatric hospitalization: a personal and professional review, *Journal of Nervous and Mental Disease* 187: 142–9.

Mowrer, O. (1947) On the dual nature of learning, *Harvard Educational Review* 17: 102–48.

Mowrer, O. and Mowrer, W. (1938) Enuresis: a method for its study and treatment, *American Journal of Orthopsychiatry* 8: 436–9.

Neill, D. (2006) Reconnecting families, *Therapy Today*, 17: 19–22.

Nelson-Jones, R. (1984) *Personal Responsibility Counselling and Therapy: An integrative approach*, London: Harper & Row.

Newnes, C. (1996) The development of clinical psychology and its values, *Clinical Psychology Forum* 95: 29–34.

Norcross, J.C. (1990) An eclectic definition of psychotherapy, in J.K. Zeig and W.M. Munion (eds) *What is Psychotherapy?*, San Francisco: Jossey-Bass.

Norcross, J.C. and Grencavage, L.M. (1990) Eclecticism and integration in counselling and psychotherapy: major themes and obstacles, in W. Dryden and J.C. Norcross (eds) *Eclecticism and Integration in Counselling and Psychotherapy* (pp. 1–33), Loughton: Gale Centre.

Norcross, J.C., Beutler, L.E. and Levant, R.F. (2006) *Evidence-based Practices in Mental Health. Debate and dialogue on the fundamental questions*, Washington, DC: American Psychology Association.

O'Brien, M. and Houston, G. (2000) *Integrative Therapy: A practitioner's guide*, London: Sage.

O'Callaghan, E., Sham, P.C., Takei, N., Murray, G.K., Hare, E.H. and Murray, R.M. (1991) Schizophrenia following prenatal exposure to influenza epidemics between 1939 and 1960, *British Journal of Psychiatry* 160: 461–6.

O'Callaghan, E., Sham, P.C. and Takei, N. (1993) Schizophrenia after prenatal exposure to 1957 A2 influenza epidemic, *The Lancet* 337: 1248–50.

O'Carroll, L. (2002) Do we make a difference?, *Counselling and Psychotherapy Journal* 13: 10–12.

Ogden, J. (2003) *The Psychology of Eating: From healthy to disordered behavior*, Oxford: Blackwell.

O'Hara, D. and Schofield, M.J. (2008) Personal approaches to psychotherapy integration, *Counselling and Psychotherapy Research* 8: 53–62.

O'Sullivan, G. and Marks, I. (1991) Follow-up studies of behavioral treatment of phobic and obsessive compulsive neuroses, *Psychiatric Annals* 21: 368–73.

Pakenham, K.I., Dadds, M.R. and Terry, D.J. (1994) Relationships between adjustment to HIV and both social support and coping, *Journal of Consulting and Clinical Psychology* 62: 1194–203.

Paley, G. and Lawton, D. (2001) Evidence-based practice: accounting for the importance of the therapeutic relationship in UK National Health Service therapy provision, *Counselling and Psychotherapy Research* 1: 12–17.

Palmer, S. and Szymanska, K. (2007) Cognitive behavioural coaching: an integrative approach, in S. Palmer and A. Whybrow (eds) *Handbook of Coaching Psychology: A guide for practitioners* (pp. 86–117), London: Routledge.

Passmore, J. (2007) Behavioural coaching, in S. Palmer and A. Whybrow (eds) *Handbook of Coaching Psychology: A guide for practitioners* (pp. 73–85), London: Routledge.

Passmore, J. and Whybrow, A. (2007) Motivational interviewing: a specific approach for coaching psychologists, in S. Palmer and A. Whybrow (eds) *Handbook of Coaching Psychology: A guide for practitioners* (pp. 160–73), London: Routledge.

Pavlov, I.P. (1928) *Lectures on Conditioned Reflexes*, New York: Liveright.

Payne, L.R., Bergin, A.E. and Loftus, P.E. (1992) A review of attempts to integrate spiritual and standard psychotherapy techniques, *Journal of Psychotherapy Integration* 2: 171–92.

Pennebaker, J.W. (1993) Putting stress into words: health, linguistic, and therapeutic implications, *Behaviour Research and Therapy* 31: 539–48.

Pennebaker, J.W. (1997) *Opening up: The healing power of expressing emotion*, New York: Guilford Press.

Pennebaker, J.W. (2004) *Writing to Heal: A guided journal for recovering from trauma and emotional upheaval*, Oakland, CA: New Harbinger Press.

Pennebaker, J.W. and Beall, S. (1986) Confronting a traumatic event: toward an understanding of inhibition and disease, *Journal of Abnormal Psychology* 95: 271–81.

Pennebaker, J.W. and O'Heeron, R.C. (1984) Confiding in others and illness rates among spouses of suicide and accidental death victims, *Journal of Abnormal Psychology* 93: 473–6.

Pennebaker, J.W., Kiecolt-Glaser, J.K. and Glaser, R. (1988) Disclosures of traumas and immune functioning: health implications for psychotherapy, *Journal of Consulting and Clinical Psychology* 56: 239–45.

Persaud, R. (1998) *Staying Sane: How to make your mind work for you*, London: Metro.

Pilgrim, D. (1997) *Psychotherapy and Society*, London: Sage.

Pointon, C. (2004) Counselling and psychotherapy: is there a difference?, *Counselling and Psychotherapy Journal* 15(2): 5–9.

Pointon, C. (2008) Debt despair, *Therapy Today* 19(8): 4–7.

Popper, K.R. (1959) *The Logic of Scientific Discovery*, New York: Basic.

Prioleau, L., Murdock, M. and Brody, N. (1983) An analysis of psychotherapy versus placebo studies, *Behavioural and Brain Sciences* 2: 275–85.

Prochaska, J.O. and DiClemente, C.C. (1983) Stages and processes of self-change of smoking: towards an integrative model of change, *Journal of Consulting and Clinical Psychology* 51: 390–5.

Prochaska, J.O. and DiClemente, C.C. (1984) *The Transtheoretical Approach: Crossing the traditional boundaries of therapy*, Homewood, IL: Dow Jones-Irwin.

Prochaska, J.O. and Norcross, J.C. (1999) *Systems of Psychotherapy: A transtheoretical analysis* (4th edn), Monterey, CA: Brooks/Cole.

Proctor, G. (2005) Clinical psychology and the person-centred approach: an un-comfortable fit?, in S. Joseph and R. Worsley (eds), *Person-centred Psychopa-thology: A positive psychology of mental health* (pp. 276–92), Ross-on-Wye: PCCS Books.

Proctor, G., Cooper, M., Sanders, P. and Malcolm, B. (2006) *Politicising the Person-centred Approach: An agenda for social change*, Ross-on-Wye: PCCS Books.

Prouty, G.F. (1976) Pre-therapy, a method of treating pre-expressive psychot-ic and retarded patients, *Psychotherapy: Theory, Research and Practice* 13: 290–5.

Prouty, G.F. (1990) A theoretical evolution in the person-centered/experiential psychotherapy of schizophrenia and retardation, in G. Lietaer, J. Rombauts and R. Van Balen (eds) *Client-centered and Experiential Psychotherapy in the Nineties* (pp. 645–85), Leuven: Leuven University Press.

Prouty, G.F. and Kubiak, M.A. (1988) The development of communicative con-tact with a catatonic schizophrenic, *Journal of Communication Therapy* 4: 13–20.

Purton, C. (1998) Unconditional positive regard and its spiritual implications, in B. Thorne and E. Lambers (eds) *Person-centred Therapy: A European per-spective*, London: Sage.

Rapaport, D. (1958) The theory of ego autonomy: a generalization, *Bulletin of the Menninger Clinic* 22: 13–35.

Reeves, A. (2009) The limits of training, *Therapy Today* 20(8): 7.

Rennie, D.L. (1998) *Person-centred Counselling: An experiential approach*, London: Sage.

Roberts, A.H., Kewman, D.G., Mercier, L. and Hovell, M. (1993) The power of non-specific effects in healing. Implications for psychosocial and biological treatments, *Clinical Psychology Review* 13: 375–91.

Roberts, V. Z. and Brunning, H. (2007) Psychodynamic and systems-psychody-namics coaching, in S. Palmer and A. Whybrow (eds) *Handbook of Coaching Psychology: A guide for practitioners* (pp. 253–77), London: Routledge.

Rogers, C.R. (1942) *Counseling and Psychotherapy*, Boston: Houghton Mifflin.

Rogers, C.R. (1951) *Client-centred Therapy*, London: Constable.

Rogers, C.R. (1957) The necessary and sufficient conditions of therapeutic per-sonality change, *Journal of Consulting Psychology* 21: 95–103.

Rogers, C.R. (1959) A theory of therapy, personality, and interpersonal relation-ships as developed in the client-centered framework, in S. Koch (ed.) *Psychol-ogy, the Study of a Science, Vol. 3: Formulations of the Person and the Social Context* (pp. 184–256), New York: McGraw Hill.

Rogers, C.R. (1961) *On Becoming a Person: A therapist's view of psychothera-py*, Boston: Houghton Mifflin.

Rogers, C.R. (1973) My philosophy of interpersonal relationships and how it grew, *Journal of Humanistic Psychology* 13: 3–15.

Rogers, C.R. (1980) *A Way of Being*, Boston: Houghton Mifflin.

Rollnick, S. and Miller, W.R. (1995) What is motivational interviewing?, *Behav-ioral and Cognitive Psychotherapy* 23: 325–34.

Rosen, J. (2004) Letter, *Counselling and Psychotherapy Journal* 15: 5.

Rosenhan, D.L. (1973) On being sane in insane places, *Science* 179: 250–8.

Rosenhan, D.L. (1975) The contextual nature of psychiatric diagnosis, *Journal of Abnormal Psychology* 84: 442–52.

Roth, A. and Fonagy, P. (2005) *What Works for Whom? A critical review of psychotherapy research* (2d edn), New York: Guilford.

Rowan, J. (1993) *The Transpersonal: Psychotherapy and counselling*, London: Routledge.

Rowan, J. (2005) *The Transpersonal: Spirituality in psychotherapy and counselling* (2nd edn), London: Routledge.

Rowe, D. (2001) The story of depression, *Counselling and Psychotherapy Journal*, 12: 4–5.

Rowe, D. (2009) One to one with Dorothy Rowe, *The Psychologist* 22: 560.

Russell, R. (1995) What works in psychotherapy when it does work?, *Changes* 13: 213–18.

Russo, D.C., Carr, E.G. and Lovaas, O.I. (1980) Self-injury in pediatric populations, in J. Ferguson and C.R. Taylor (eds) *Comprehensive Handbook of Behavioral Medicine, Vol. 3: Extended Applications and Issues*, Holliswood, NY: Spectrum.

Ryle, A. (1990) *Cognitive Analytic Therapy: Active participation in change*, Chichester: Wiley.

Samelson, F. (1980) J.B. Watson's Little Albert, Cyril Burt's twins, and the need for a critical science, *American Psychologist* 35: 619–25.

Sanders, P. (2005) Principled and strategic opposition to the medicalisation of distress and all of its apparatus, in S. Joseph and R. Worsley (eds) *Person-centered Psychopathology: A positive psychology of mental health*, Ross-on-Wye: PCCS Books.

Sanders, P. (ed.) (2007a) *The Contact Work Primer: A concise, accessible, comprehensive introduction to pre-therapy and the work of Garry Prouty*, Ross-on-Wye: PCCS Books.

Sanders, P (2007b) Decoupling psychological therapies from the medical model. Therapy Today, 18 (9), 35-38.

Sanders, P. (2007c) Series introduction, in R. Worsley (ed.) *The Integrative Counselling Primer: A concise, accessible and comprehensive introduction to integrative counselling with a person-centred foundation* (pp. 1–5), Ross-on-Wye: PCCS Books.

Sanders, P. (2007d) In place of the medical model: person-centred alternatives to the medicalisation of distress, in R. Worsley and S. Joseph (eds) *Person-centred Practice: Case studies in positive psychology* (pp. 184–99), Ross-on-Wye: PCCS Books.

Satir, V. (1964) *Conjoint Family Therapy*, Palo Alto, CA: Science and Behavior.

Schaap, C., Bennun, I., Schinder, L. and Hoogduin, K. (1993) *The Therapeutic Relationship in Behavioural Psychotherapy*, Chichester: Wiley.

Schmid, P. (2005) Facilitative responsiveness: non-directiveness from anthropological, epistemological and ethical perspectives, in B.E. Levitt (ed.) Embracing Nondirectivity: *Reassessing person-centred theory and practice in the 21st century* (pp. 75–95), Ross-on-Wye: PCCS Books.

Schneider, K.J. (1998) Toward a science of the heart: romanticism and the revival of psychology, *American Psychologist* 53: 277–89.

Seligman, M.E.P. (1995) The effectiveness of psychotherapy, *American Psychologist* 50: 965–74.

Shaikh, A. (1985) Cross-cultural comparison: psychiatric admission of Asian and indigenous patients in Leicestershire, *International Journal of Social Psychiatry* 31: 3–11.

Shapiro, D.A. and Shapiro, D. (1982) Meta-analysis of comparative therapy outcome studies. A replication and refinement, *Psychological Bulletin* 92: 581–604.

Shapiro, F. (1989a) Efficacy of the eye movement desensitization procedure in the treatment of traumatic memories, *Journal of Traumatic Stress* 2: 199–223.

Shapiro, F. (1989b) Eye movement desensitization: a new treatment for posttraumatic stress disorder, *Journal of Behaviour Therapy and Experimental Psychiatry* 20: 211–17.

Shapiro, F. (1995) *Eye Movement Desensitization and Reprocessing: Basic principles, protocols and procedures*, New York: Guilford.

Sheldrake, R. (1981) *A New Science of Life*, Los Angeles: J.P. Tarcher.

Skinner, B.F. (1953) *Science and Human Behavior*, New York: Macmillan.

Skinner, B.F. (1971) *Beyond Freedom and Dignity*, New York: Vintage.

Skinner, B.F. (1990) Can psychology be a science of the mind?, *American Psychologist* 45: 1206–10.

Smail, D. (1996) *How to Survive without Psychotherapy*, London: Constable.

Smail, D. (2005) *Power Interest and Psychology: Elements of a social materialist understanding of stress*, Ross-on-Wye: PCCS Books.

Smith, M.L. and Glass, G.V. (1977) The meta-analysis of psychotherapy outcome studies, *American Psychologist* 32: 752–60.

Snaith, R.P. (1994) Psychosurgery: controversy and enquiry, *British Journal of Psychotherapy* 161: 582–4.

Spence, S. (2004) Letter, *Counselling and Psychotherapy Journal* 15: 5.

Spinelli, E. (2001) Letter, *Counselling and Psychotherapy Journal* 12: 20.

Spurling, L. (2002) One model is enough, *Counselling and Psychotherapy Journal* 13: 14–16.

Starr, P. (1982) *The Social Transformation of American Medicine*, New York: Basic.

Stewart, I. (1989) *Transactional Analysis Counselling in Action*, London: Sage.

Stiles, W.B., Barkham, M., Shapiro, D.A. and Firth-Cozens, J. (1992) Treatment order and thematic continuity between contrasting psychotherapies: exploring an implication of the assimilation model, *Psychotherapy Research* 2: 112–24.

Stiles, W.B., Elliot, R., Llewelyn, S.P., Firth-Cozens, J.A., Margison, F.R., Shapiro, D.A. and Hardy, G. (1990) Assimilation of problematic experiences by clients in psychotherapy, *Psychotherapy* 27: 411–20.

Stiles, W.B., Shapiro, D.A. and Elliott, R.K. (1986) Are all psychotherapies equivalent?, *American Psychologist* 41: 165–80.

Stiles, W.B. et al. (2006) Effectiveness of cognitive-behavioural, person-centred and psychodynamic therapies as practised in UK National Health Service settings, *Psychological Medicine* 36: 555–66.

Stravynski, A., Marks, I. and Yule, W. (1982) Social skills problems in neurotic outpatients: social skills training with and without cognitive modification, *Archives of General Psychiatry* 39: 1378–85.

Sutherland, S. (1992) *Irrationality: The enemy within*, Harmondsworth: Penguin.

Sutherland, S. (1998) *Breakdown: A personal crisis and a medical dilemma* (2nd edn), Oxford: Oxford University Press.

Szasz, T.S. (1961) *The Myth of Mental Illness*, New York: Hoeber.

Szasz, T.S. (1971) The sane slave: an historical note on the use of medical diagnosis as justificatory rhetoric, *American Journal of Psychotherapy* 25: 228–39.

Szasz, T.S. (1974) *The Second Sin*, London: Routledge & Kegan Paul.

Tansella, M. and Williams, P. (1987) The Italian experience and its implications, *Psychological Medicine* 17: 283–9.

Tart, C.T. (1975) *States of Consciousness*, New York: E.P. Dutton.

Therapy Today (2006) A selection of theories, *Therapy Today* 17: 29–30.

Thorndike, E L (1898) Animal intelligence: an experimental study of the associative processes in animals, *Psychological Monographs* 2 (No. 8).

Thorne, B. (1991) *Person-centred Counselling: Therapeutic and spiritual aspects*, London: Whurr.

Thorne, B. (1992) *Carl Rogers*, London: Sage.

Thorne, B. (1994) Developing a spiritual discipline, in D. Mearns (ed.) *Developing Person-centred Counselling*, London: Sage.

Thorne, B. and Lambers, E. (1998) (eds) *Person-centred Therapy: A European perspective*, London: Sage.

Totton, N. (2003a) Psychotherapy and politics, *Counselling and Psychotherapy Journal* 14: 4–6.

Totton, N. (2003b) Turning to the body, *Counselling and Psychotherapy Journal* 14(4): 8–12.

Totton, N. (2004) Two ways of being helpful, *Counselling and Psychotherapy Journal* 15(10): 5–8.

van Deurzen, E. (1988) *Existential Counselling in Practice*, London: Sage.

van Deurzen-Smith, E. (1998) Beyond psychotherapy, *Psychotherapy Section Newsletter of the British Psychological Society* 23: 4–18.

Van Etten, M.L. and Taylor, S. (1998) Comparative efficacy of treatments for posttraumatic stress disorder: a meta-analysis, *Clinical Psychology and Psychotherapy* 5: 126 –44.

Vaughan, K., Wiese, M., Gold, R. and Tarrier, N. (1994) Eye-movement desensitization: symptom change in post-traumatic stress disorder, *British Journal of Psychiatry* 164: 533–41.

Walker, A. (1993) *Warrior Marks: Female genital mutilation and the sexual blinding of women*, New York: Harcourt Brace.

Waller, G. (2009) Evidence-based treatment and therapist drift, *Behaviour Research and Therapy* 47: 119–27.

Wampold, D.E. (2001) *The Great Psychotherapy Debate: Models, methods and findings*, Mahwah, NJ: Erlbaum.

Warren, R. and Zgourides, G.D. (1991) *Anxiety Disorders: A rational-emotive perspective*, New York: Pergamon Press.

Watson, J.B. (1913) Psychology as the behaviourist views it, *Psychological Review* 20: 158–77.

Watson, J.B. (1930) *Behaviorism*, Chicago: University of Chicago Press.

Watson, J.B. and Rayner, R. (1920) Conditioned emotional reactions, *Journal of Experimental Psychology* 3: 1–14.

Weiner, R.D. and Krystal, A.D. (1994) The present use of electroconvulsive therapy, *Annual Review of Medicine* 45: 273–81.

White, J. (2000) Cognitive therapy – what is left when you remove the hype?, *Proceedings of the British Psychological Society* 8: 16.

Wilber, K. (1998) *The Essential Ken Wilber: An introductory reader*, Boston: Shambha.

Williams, D.R. (1990) Socioeconomic differentials in health: a review and redirection, *Social Psychology Quarterly* 53: 81–99.

Williams, J.B.W., Gibbon, M., First, M.B., Spitzer, R.L., Davies, M. et al. (1992) The Structured Clinical Interview for DSM-III-R (SLID): 2. Multisite test-retest reliability, *Archives of General Psychiatry* 49: 6306.

Williams, J.M.G., Teasdale, D., Segal, Z.V., and Kabat-Zinn, L. (2006) *Mindfulness and the Transformation of Emotion*, New York: Guilford.

Wolpe, J. (1958) *Psychotherapy and Reciprocal Inhibition*, Stanford, CA: Stanford University Press.

Wolpe, J. (1990) *The Practice of Behavior Therapy* (4th edn), New York: Pergamon.

Wolpe, J. and Rachman, S. (1960) Psychoanalytic evidence: a critique based on Freud's case of Little Hans, *Journal of Nervous and Mental Disease* 131: 135–45.

Wood, A. and Joseph, S. (2007) Grand theories of psychology can not be reconciled: a comment on McAdams and Pals, *American Psychologist* 62: 57–8.

World Health Organization (WHO) (1992) *Tenth Revision of the International Classification of Diseases*, Geneva: WHO.

Worsley, R. (2007) *The Integrative Counselling Primer: A concise, accessible and comprehensive introduction to integrative counselling with a person-centred foundation*, Ross-on-Wye: PCCS Books.

Wynne, L.C., Singer, M.T., Bartko, J.J. and Toohey, M.L. (1977) Schizophrenics and their families: recent research on parental communication, in J.M. Tanner (ed.) *Developments in Psychiatric Research*, London: Hodder & Stoughton.

Yalom, I.D. (1980) *Existential Psychotherapy*, New York: Basic.

Zeig, J.K. (1987) *The Evolution of Psychotherapy*, New York: Brunner/Mazel.

Zigler, E. and Phillips, L. (1961) Psychiatric diagnosis and symptomatology, *Journal of Abnormal Psychology* 63: 69–75.

Zilboorg, G. and Henry, G.W. (1941) *A History of Medical Psychology*, New York: Norton.

Index